THE MAKING OF
MODERN MALAYSIA
AND SINGAPORE

8/18/81

To Will —

Just because

- it's still vacation-time
- you shouldn't forget to read English
- it's good to dream!

Love,
A

THE MAKING OF
MODERN MALAYSIA
AND SINGAPORE

A HISTORY FROM EARLIEST TIMES
TO 1966

N. J. RYAN, o.b.e., p.m.p.
formerly Malayan Education Service

KUALA LUMPUR   SINGAPORE
OXFORD UNIVERSITY PRESS: 1969

Oxford University Press, Ely House, London W.1

GLASGOW NEW YORK TORONTO MELBOURNE WELLINGTON
CAPE TOWN SALISBURY IBADAN NAIROBI LUSAKA ADDIS ABABA
BOMBAY CALCUTTA MADRAS KARACHI LAHORE DACCA
KUALA LUMPUR SINGAPORE HONG KONG TOKYO

Tanglin Halt Close, Singapore

© *Oxford University Press 1963, 1967 and 1969*
First published 1963 with the title
'The Making of Modern Malaya'
Fourth edition (revised) 1969

PRINTED IN SINGAPORE BY PRINTERS AND CONVERTERS (PTE) LTD

PREFACE

The formation of the state of Malaysia in 1963 has necessitated the reshaping of the existing histories of Malaya. Malaysia is a much larger entity than the former Federation of Malaya for it includes the territories of Sabah and Sarawak in north-western Borneo. This has meant that the history of Malaysia must be presented with a much wider coverage than a history of Malaya. It must include not only the events in Sabah, Brunei and Sarawak leading up to the formation of Malaysia but also the earlier history of these states from the fifteenth to the nineteenth century.

A considerable part of this book is based upon the author's *The Making of Modern Malaya* but many sections have been recast and much new material has been added. This new material relates particularly to the history of Sabah and Sarawak in the nineteenth century and also to events in South-East Asia between 1957 and 1966. There are also many more illustrations and maps and it is hoped that these will enhance the usefulness of the book.

Nevertheless the general layout of the contents of the book is based on the experience gained in teaching in the upper forms of Malaysian secondary schools. The book is primarily intended for teachers and pupils but it should also meet the needs of the general reader who requires a short, up-to-date history of Malaysia. It has been the intention of the author to present the history of Malaysia in a South-East Asian context rather than as an adjunct to European politics; for it is now realized, for example, that the Malay Peninsula in the seventeenth and eighteenth centuries was affected more by the Achinese and the Bugis than by the Dutch. In recent years a new approach to Malaysian history has been developed; this is an approach which places less reliance on uncritical acceptance of the works of earlier writers. In following this fresh outlook the author would like to acknowledge his indebtedness to the work of Dr. C.D. Cowan, Dr. D.K. Bassett and Dr. A. Lamb.

Since the publication of the last edition of this book Singapore's attainment of independence in 1965 and its subsequent activities as an independent nation have required a fresh approach to its history. Accordingly, in this new edition an attempt has been made to provide a proper perspective for an understanding of its history by examining comprehensively Singapore's growth in the last one hundred and fifty years. The picture supplements have been adapted to provide an adequate visual parallel to the historical record. In order to tailor the book more closely to student requirements exercises have been added and a consolidated bibliography provided to encourage further reading.

Hong Kong, 1969   N. J. R.

CONTENTS

ILLUSTRATIONS

MAPS

TABLE OF EVENTS

Malaysia's Earliest History

c. 2500 B.C.   Proto-Malays reach Malay Peninsula
c. 300 B.C.   Deutero-Malays arrive in Malay Peninsula
c. A.D. 100   Indian trading contact with north-west Malaya
c. A.D. 350   Indianized settlements in Kedah
c. A.D. 700-1000 Srivijaya
1292   Marco Polo's voyage through Straits of Malacca

The Malacca Sultanate

1398/1400 Foundation of Malacca by Parameswara
1405   Chinese Admiral Yin Ching visits Malacca
1411   Parameswara visits China with Admiral Cheng Ho
1414   Parameswara converted to Islam
1445   Islam becomes Malacca's state religion
1470   Malacca strongest state in South-East Asia
1498   Death of Tun Perak
1509   First arrival of the Portuguese (de Sequeira)
1511   The fall of Malacca to d'Albuquerque

The Sixteenth Century

1520's   Brunei at the height of its power—Sultan Bulkeiah
1526   Johore capital of Bintang destroyed by Portuguese
1539   Johore and allies defeat Achinese
1547   St. Francis Xavier in Malacca—Achinese attack
1564   Johore Lama attacked by Achinese
1575   Achinese conquest of Perak
1577   Spanish attack on Brunei
1587   Portuguese destruction of Johore Lama
1595-6   Dutch arrival in South-East Asia

The Seventeenth Century

1606   Dutch defeat of Portuguese fleet off Johore
1606   Combined Johore-Dutch attack on Malacca
1629   Achinese attack on Malacca—Mahkota Alam
1639   Dutch Treaty with Johore
1641   Dutch capture Malacca
1670   Dutch build fort on Pulau Pangkor
1673   Johore capital Batu Sawar destroyed by Jambi. Capital transferred to Riau
1680   Bugis settlement in Selangor begins

1699   Assassination of Sultan Mahmud ends Johore direct succession from Malacca

The Eighteenth Century

1717-8 Fall of the Johore Empire to Raja Kechil from Siak
1721-2 Bugis mercenaries used to defeat Raja Kechil
1722   Daeng Merewah becomes first Bugis under-King in Johore
1742   Establishment of Bugis Sultanate in Selangor
1771   British offered a trading post in Kedah
1773-5 British settlement at Balambangan in Borneo
1777   Raja Haji becomes under-King in Johore
1784   Bugis attack on Malacca (Raja Haji)
1786   The British acquisition of Penang (Capt. Francis Light)
1791   Sultan of Kedah's attempt to invade Penang
1799   British capture of Malacca from the Dutch
1800   Acquisition of Province Wellesley by Penang

The Nineteenth Century

1811   British invasion and capture of Johore
1817   Raffles becomes Lieutenant-Governor of Bencoolen
1819   Founding of Singapore by Raffles
1821   Siamese invasion of Kedah
1824   The Anglo-Dutch Treaty of London
1826   Anglo-Siamese Treaty of Bangkok
1826   Low's treaty with Perak
1831-2 Naning War in Malacca
1842   James Brooke becomes Raja of Sarawak
1842   Siamese detach Perlis from Kedah
1847   Brunei cedes Labuan to Britain
1850   Tin discovered in Larut (Long Ja'afar)
1858   Beginning of tin mining round Kuala Lumpur
1862   British bombard Kuala Trengganu
1862   Outbreak of Larut Wars in Perak
1866   Beginning of Selangor civil war
1867   Supervision of Straits Settlements transferred from the India to the Colonial Office
1874   The Pangkor Engagement—British intervention in the Malay States
1875   British Residents appointed to Perak and Selangor
1876   First cultivated rubber seedlings in Singapore
1881   Formation of British North Borneo Company
1885   First railway—Taiping to Port Weld

The Twentieth Century

ACKNOWLEDGEMENTS

The author and publishers would like to acknowledge with thanks the generous assistance they received from Arkib Negara, Malaysia; Muzium Negara, Malaysia; the Universities of Malaya and Singapore; The University of Malaya Press; The National Library, Singapore; The National Archives and Records Centre, Singapore; The Ministry of Culture, Singapore; and the Sarawak Museum in their search for illustrations.

Acknowledgement of the source of each illustration is made against the illustration itself.

Every effort has been made to contact the holders of copyright to the reproductions, but in some cases without success. To these, the author and publishers offer their apologies.

INTRODUCTION:
MALAYSIA IN HISTORY

THROUGHOUT history Malaysia has been influenced by both India and China, the two ancient centres of civilization lying to the west and to the east. This influence has in some periods been very strong, especially from India, from where Malaysia received much of her early culture and her religions. Chinese influence was always less direct but at certain times, as we shall see, the Chinese Empire took a very keen interest in the events of South-East Asia.

Thus Malaysia's importance in early history was governed by her geographical position. Not only did it so happen that on the earth's surface Malaysia was placed between India and China, but other geographical factors helped to increase the importance of this position. There were many other places which were half-way between India and China, but few of them had Malaysia's special advantages.

West Malaysia is part of a peninsula pointing southward from the Asian land mass; it is almost entirely surrounded by the sea. If people wanted to sail from China to India they had to sail close to both East and West Malaysia, and even if they did not want to sail all the way, the Peninsula being narrow in the north offered the easiest place for the transhipment of goods from the China Sea to the Indian Ocean. But whether men sailed all the way or only did half the journey, the Malay Peninsula and the North-Western coast of Borneo played an important part in their plans. This was because of another important geographical and climatic factor, the monsoons. It is now commonplace to say that Malaysia is a place where the monsoons meet; in the days of sailing this geographical factor was vital. The monsoons are winds which blow from two directions at different times of the year. There is the south-west monsoon, blowing across the Indian Ocean from the Equator between the months of May and August. Then there is the north-east monsoon blowing down the China coast and across the China Sea from November to April. They could be said to meet at the Malay Peninsula or more generally in the region of the Malaysian Archipelago. Ships sailing from China would travel southward on the north-east monsoon while from India ships would come east with the south-west winds. When the monsoon changed, the ships would then be able to make the return journey. Thus the Malay Peninsula and the north-west coast of Borneo were in advantageous positions to provide landing places for those who were either making the complete journey from India to China and who were waiting for the monsoon to change, or those who were only doing half the journey but were meeting fellow traders at this 'half-way house'. Chinese traders, for example, could come south between November and April, complete their business, and return home between May and August.

In this way, because of the geographical advantages which she possessed, Malaysia was drawn into world history; in fact, Malaysia's geographical position is the most important factor to take into account if one is to understand her past and even her present and future. Geography introduced Malaysia to the stage of world history; so also did geography keep her there. Because of her open position, because she is not landlocked but is wide open to the out-side world, Malaysia has come into contact with many civilizations and many peoples. In her early history these peoples brought her the beginnings of culture and civilization, they brought her trade and commerce, and they brought her many different religions and political systems. Later came settlers from the lands of India and China, at first in small numbers, but very much later in the nine-teenth century, when Malaysia's mineral and agricultural resources were properly exploited, they came in large numbers. Malaysia's geographical position also brought her into early contact with nine-teenth-century technology and applied science, and these have enabled her to attain today one of the highest standards of living in Asia. Malaysia's position near the East-West trade routes meant that she was quickly introduced to the inventions of nineteenth-century Europe. Thus geography has brought Malaysia into history, has brought her a cosmopolitan population, and has brought her one of the most developed economies in Asia.

We shall see later how important have been the geographical and economic factors in influencing the cycle of Malaysian history. The stress that has been placed on geography in this introductory section merely illustrates what can be seen by glancing at any map. It is the results of this geographical position which are important; when we discuss Malaysian political and economic history we shall see how trade routes and voyages of exploration have influenced her position in the world. We shall see how Malaya and Brunei were prosperous and important during the days of the Malacca Sultanate when East-West trade was channelled through the Straits of Malacca, and Malacca itself was the entrepôt for this trade and for the whole Archipelago. Later when the commerce of the region was under the control of the Dutch, the main trade routes between East and West passed through the Sunda Straits, and Batavia (Djakarta) prospered and Malacca and Brunei declined. A further change was to come when Malaya again became involved in international politics, when the British renewed their interest in Malaysia at the end of the eighteenth century. The establishment of settlements in Penang and Singapore brought much trade back to the Straits of Malacca and led eventually to the development of modern Malaysia's mineral wealth. And at about the same time British subjects began to take an interest in Sarawak and Sabah leading to the establishment of British influence there. Malaysia's place in history therefore has fluctuated with the interest the rest of the world has shown in the area and what she has been able to offer to the economic intercourse of Asia and to the world generally.

Political events in Malaysia have also been affected by the interest which other countries have shown in the region—whether it be the introduction of Islam leading to the establishment of sultanates, or the industrial revolution in England leading to the establishment of the Straits Settlements and British protection over the Malay States. Thus Malaysia in many ways has a cosmopolitan history. Although this book will naturally concentrate on the internal history of the country, it will also attempt to relate Malaysian events to their wider setting in Asian and world history.

MALAYSIA'S EARLIEST HISTORY

WE have said that Malaysia owes her historical importance to her geographical position. Because of this position she has long had contact with India and China, contact both political and cultural, which has continued into the present century. It would have been natural in any case for Malaysia to have been in touch with these countries, but the immigration of large numbers of people from China and India who have become part of Malaysia's permanent population has established definite ties.

Chinese influence on Malaysia had been fairly slight in comparison with that of India, at least until the nineteenth century. And although Malaysia does lie half-way between China and India, during the centuries before the nineteenth it was India much more than China that affected the Peninsula and the Malaysian Archipelago as a whole.

Why was this so? In part, the answer lies in the self-sufficiency of the Chinese Empire. The Chinese were disinclined to undertake long sea voyages of exploration except on certain rare occasions. There were occasional exceptions to this general practice: the voyages during the Sung dynasty (A.D. 960-1127), the voyages of the Ming dynasty in the early 1400's, and the earlier travels of individual Chinese like Fah Hsien in the early fifth century and I Tsing in the seventh century. There is no doubt that from the time of the Han dynasty in China (206 B.C. to A.D. 221) Chinese traders were looking for a sea route to India, and in the course of their search they sailed to the Malay Peninsula and the north-west coast of Borneo. They made use of the facilities which they found but unlike the Indians who also used these facilities, Chinese culture seems to have had little permanent effect on the population in general. China was politically a powerful state—more powerful than any in India—but it was India which provided Malaysia with her first contacts with civilization during the first century, and Indian civilization was to have a great effect on the Peninsula's early history.

The earliest Malaysians

The earliest evidence of human habitation in Malaysia has been found in Borneo, which itself is a European misspelling of Brunei, the most powerful state on the island at the time of the first European contacts. Archaeological excavations in the Niah caves in Sarawak have uncovered a human skull which is estimated to be 35,000 years old. This evidence is much older than that found in the Malay Peninsula where the material which has been excavated is about 10,000 years old; so that we can say that the earliest humans in Malaysia lived in Borneo.

The inhabitants of the Peninsula whom the early Indian traders and voyagers encountered had originally entered Malaya from the north—it is thought about 2500 B.C. These people were Proto-Malays, who, spreading south from Yünnan in a long drawn-out series of migrations, forced the original Negrito inhabitants (today known as Semang and Jakun) back into the hills and jungles. The latter now live mainly in the northern part of the Peninsula. But many thousands of years ago their ancestors were probably the only inhabitants. They lived in the period known as the Middle Stone Age (about 8000-2000 B.C.) inhabiting rock shelters and caves in the limestone hills of Malaya. They used some stone implements for cutting and grinding, and they were able to hunt and kill wild animals. These Negritos may possibly be descendants of the same people as the aborigines of Australia, for during the Ice Age (about 200,000 B.C.) Australia may have been joined to South-East Asia. The newly-arrived Proto-Malays had their origin in southern China and between 2500 and 1500 B.C. forced their way southward through the Peninsula and on to the islands beyond. It is from these Proto-Malays that the Dyaks in Borneo are descended. Much later in history these peoples spread north-eastwards from the Kapuas river area of Borneo so that to-day the Dyaks are the most numerous group in Sarawak. The Proto-Malays were also a stone-age people, that is, they had not learnt the use of metals, and they used stones for their implements and tools; but because their stone implements were better made than those of the Negritos, this period is called the Neolithic or New Stone Age.

Evidence of their habitation, which has been found in Malaysia in places like Gua Cha, Kelantan, shows that they could make pottery and ornaments quite skilfully. They were not only hunters but also cultivators and sailors. As they were able to use better-made stone axes, they built wooden houses and boats and their culture was as far developed as stone implements would allow. Their culture was therefore of a higher standard than that of their predecessors and largely because of their better skills they could live a more settled existence. They could cultivate the land, and they could begin farming by means of shifting cultivation.

But these people were in their turn to be dispossessed in the Malay Peninsula by others with superior material techniques, just as they themselves had dispossessed the Negritos. From about 300 B.C., new immigrants from the Yünnan area of China entered the Peninsula. Known as Deutero-Malays they over-came the Proto-Malays and pushed them inland where they remained mainly in southern Malaya, and are known today as Jakuns.

The Deutero-Malays were basically Mongoloid, the same race as the first immigrants from Yünnan, but they had acquired the knowledge of metals, using iron weapons and tools. They used other metals also; bronze drums and bells found in Klang, Selangor, are evidences from this period. Like the earlier settlers, these metal-age people spread out to the islands of the Archipelago. Thus the final wave of immigrants, who together with the Deutero-Malays later formed the Malay population of Malaysia, came to the Peninsula and Borneo from the islands of Java and Sumatra in the centuries that followed, especially when the area was part of the island-Empire of Srivijaya.

Deutero-Malay settlers, the ancestors of the Malays today, had a reasonably high standard of material culture; they were not nomadic but lived in villages which were the main units of society. Controlled by a headman and elders and situated on the banks of rivers or on coasts these village units were generally self-sufficient in food and other necessities. But by the end of the last century B.C. trade started to develop between the coastal villages. Social customs were based on communal ownership, that is, the land belonged to the village, and the produce was shared among the inhabitants of the village. Such a system continued until quite modern times in Indonesia.

In religion these original inhabitants were animists; that is, they believed in the widespread existence of spirits which dwelt in trees, stones, animals and other objects. These spirits affected their every-day lives, and the people believed they had to ensure that the spirits were not displeased or disturbed. Thus the spirit of the forests would be placated before a hunter set off on his trapping, or the spirit of the sea would be pacified before the fisherman sailed away on a fishing expedition.

Trade and the influence of India

But the early Malaysians were very soon to be brought into touch with older and stronger civilizations. The beginnings and importance of trade with India have been mentioned. However, although Indian influences were to predominate at this time in western Malaysia, Chinese trading contacts still continued, and many fragments of Chinese pottery have been found in Malaysia, some of which have been dated from the Han dynasty, indicating that Chinese trade had begun very early. There is quite a lot of evidence of early Chinese contact with north-west Borneo; for example, coins earlier than the first century A.D. have been found at the mouth of the Sarawak river and there are probable references to Brunei in the Chinese Annals of the seventh century. At this time the Chinese were trading with Kota Batu in Brunei and there is evidence of a trading settlement at Santubong at the mouth of the river near Kuching. However these contacts were probably not connected with east-west trade but were rather a means by which the Chinese obtained specialized produce, like birds' nests, which they wanted from Borneo.

The Peninsula's geographical position meant that Indian traders on their way further east soon discovered the advantages of a central landing point between the seasons of the north-east and south-west monsoons. Crossing the Bay of Bengal from the Coromandel coast of south India the traders would make first landfall on the Peninsula somewhere between Trang and Kedah. Here they waited for the monsoon to change before proceeding on their journey. They also discovered later that goods could be transferred and carried across the isthmus to be picked up by other ships on the eastern side; to do this would mean avoiding the pirate-infested Malacca Straits. During the early centuries A.D., Indian contact with the Peninsula was largely confined to trade visits, but it soon became obvious that certain areas were suitable for permanent trading settlements. One of them was Kedah. It was in this way that fourth-century north Malaya was drawn into the complex of 'Indian-type' kingdoms established in South-East Asia.

Kedah had certain important advantages and distinctions which made it a most suitable place to select for such settlements. As has been said it was in the area of first landfall for the voyagers, but it also has a distinctive high mountain, Kedah Peak (3,987 feet), which can be seen thirty miles out to sea. To the Indians it was both a landmark and a home of the gods whom they believed dwelt in such heights. But Kedah had further attractions: a good anchorage in the Sungei Merbok estuary which was larger than it is today; sufficient flat land suitable for growing food to support the traders; relatively easy access to the east coast at Patani following the present railway routes. Thus we know from archaeological evidence that the area to the south of Kedah Peak, especially on the banks of the Sungei Bujang supported Indian settlements from the fourth to the twelfth centuries. There is no doubt that it was the area of a prosperous town-port, which traded between East and West having its own temples and settled government. It was a town (or towns) which was considerably influenced by south Indian connexions, but there was probably no great migration of Indians themselves. As Braddell states, it was probably 'an Indo-Malay kingdom and town ruled by kings (racially of early Malay type) with a basic population also racially of early Malay type. The royal customs were Indian, but the customs of the people were a blend of their own with Indian, the latter becoming progressively stronger.' Previously it was thought that the Indian-influenced area of Malaysia may well have been composed of settlements of Indian colonizers—that South-East Asia was 'further India'. However this is now thought to be unlikely. There was no large immigration of Indian settlers; rather there was the influence of traders and missionaries. These people, rather like the Europeans in later centuries, were responsible for popularizing their way of life and religion. Many inhabitants—Malaysians by race—became Hindus or Buddhists, and they built the temples whose remains have been found in Kedah. Thus the population of Kedah, for example, did not change, and Chinese reports affirm that the native societies had adopted Indian culture but had not become Indian colonies.

Therefore by the middle of the eighth century there were Indianized states established in many parts of South-East Asia, and Chinese chronicles do testify to the dominance of Indian culture in the region. I Tsing visiting Srivijaya (Palembang) in the seventh century remarked that 'Buddhist priests there number more than a thousand who investigate and study all the subjects that exist, just as in India'. Sanskrit was a common language; Indian names for the months and an Indian system of measurement were used. Extremely important also was the introduction of Indian religion, art, and literature. In fact, until the contacts with Srivijaya and Majapahit in the later centuries brought Sumatran and Javanese influences, the Malay Peninsula was indebted from about A.D. 300 onwards to what was derived more directly from the Coromandel coast of India; a civilization that was basically Hindu but which included both Brahmin-istic and Buddhistic elements.

It is probable that there were three main periods of Indian in-fluence which affected western Malaysia and more especially Kedah. The first from A.D. 300 to 550 was largely Buddhist; remains of Buddhist temples have been found in Kedah, and Gupta-style images have been recovered from the Kinta Valley. The second period was from about the seventh to the eleventh century coinci-ding with the Empire of Srivijaya though the Kedah region was still more important as an agricultural area than as a trading centre. Its greatest importance as an entrepôt probably came during the third period, from the late eleventh to the late fourteenth century. This was after the decline of Takuapa (a trading centre further north near the Kra Isthmus) when the trade route changed from the isthmus to the Malacca Straits.

Thus South-East Asia, and Malaysia as part of it, was brought into contact with Indian culture. This changed architectural methods and tastes and also introduced the region to the glories of ancient Indian literature; and especially in Java, the literature which grew up owed a great deal to Indian epics and poems.

As we have said, the settlements which existed in Malaysia in the early centuries A.D. were small ones, usually near the coasts or by the sides of rivers. The inhabitants, who lived by farming, fishing, and by certain limited types of trade, were easily influenced by visitors who came to Malaysia from older and more advanced centres of civilization. In most cases what was imported was more efficient or more convincing than the home product. Thus Hinduism and Buddhism were more convincing than animism, and using iron and bronze was much more efficient than using stone.

CENTRES OF POWER: FIRST TO FOURTEENTH CENTURIES

However these Malaysian settlements were seldom the centres of important kingdoms or empires. Malaysia was usually an outlying region of an empire which had its capital elsewhere, perhaps in the Archipelago or to the north in what is now Thailand. Archaeology, however, has uncovered numerous sites in the region of present-day Kedah which may one day reveal the existence of an important centre of civilization in northern Malaysia and southern Thailand.

Fu-nan

The first important 'Indianized' kingdom in South-East Asia was probably Fu-nan which had its centre at the delta of the Mekong

River. Its period of strength was from the first to the seventh century
A.D., and it probably exercised influence as far south as the Peninsula.
Here the earliest state whose name is known today is Langkasuka,
a first-century east-coast state stretching from Singgora northwards
with its capital perhaps at Patani. Its importance probably lay in its
control of the trans-isthmian trade route between the Indian Ocean
and the South China Sea. In A.D. 568 it was important enough to
send its own embassy to China.

The most important area of settlement on the west coast was
undoubtedly that which has already been described in the region of
Kedah, and this may also have come under the indirect influence
of Fu-nan which, because of its sea power, was able to dominate the
trade routes between India and China. But at the beginning of the
seventh century, Fu-nan had lost so much of its territory and power
to other states which had developed in Indo-China that in 627 it
was finally absorbed by a state named Chen-la.

Srivijaya and the Sailendras

Fu-nan's successor as the dominant state of South-East Asia was
not Chen-la, however, which was primarily a land-based power, but
a new kingdom which had its capital at Palembang in Sumatra.
This was Srivijaya which as early as 670-3 had sent ambassadors to
China. In the 670's the Sumatran state had become a centre of
Buddhist influence in the region and had been visited by the Chinese
traveller, I Tsing, who was on his way to India. By the end of the
seventh century, Srivijaya had gained control of the southern part
of the Malacca Straits. Later came the extension of her influence
to the Malaysian side even as far north as Ligor, and by the end of
the eighth century, this Sumatran kingdom controlled both sides
of the Straits of Malacca and also the west coast of Borneo. In this
way she was able to suppress piracy, and as a result the trade route
through the Straits flourished. Srivijaya was to be the dominant
power in the Malaysian region for the next three hundred years.
However the most important trading centre during this period was
not Kedah but Takuapa situated further north on the western side
of the Kra Isthmus. From the seventh to the eleventh century Takuapa was an entrepôt port; and archaeological research has shown
evidence of Chinese and Arab trade.

Later the strength of Srivijaya received an additional boost with
the development of another strong state in central Java. The rulers
of this state were the Sailendras; they lived in the area near Djokja-
karta and were responsible for the building of the huge Buddhist

shrine of Borobudur which served as the tomb of the Sailendra kings.

This dynasty became important in the eighth century, and it is conceivable that these people were descendants of those who had been dispossessed from Fu-nan in 627. 'Sailendra' is an old Fu-nan title, meaning 'the kings of the mountain'. In the middle of the ninth century there was a dynastic marriage between the Sailendras and Srivijaya, and the two kingdoms eventually became one, with the Sailendras moving to Sumatra, and Palembang remaining the capital of the greatly enlarged state. Srivijaya continued to grow in wealth and influence, and by the eleventh century was at the height of her power, controlling the east coast of Sumatra, western Java, the Malay Peninsula and the south-western part of Borneo. In Malaya, Kedah itself was of growing importance as a trading centre, visited by Arab merchants who came there to purchase goods from China. As she controlled the main sea routes, the Malacca Straits and the Sunda Straits, Srivijaya attempted to impose a trade policy aimed at restricting all competitors in the area of her influence and forcing those foreigners who wished to trade to pay heavy duties for the privilege. This monopolistic policy made her many enemies: in the eleventh century there had been attacks by the Cholas who had become rulers of the most powerful State in southern India; there had also arisen a rival power in eastern Java which by the middle of the twelfth century was considered by the Chinese to be even more important than Palembang. Parts of the Empire of Srivijaya in Sumatra—Kampar for example—had declared their independence and in the thirteenth century there were revolts in the Malay Peninsula. Srivijaya's days of supremacy were passing and her downfall was imminent.

The decline of Srivijaya

The downfall of Srivijaya was brought about by two states, one to the north and one to the south. The former was the Kingdom of Sukhotai, a state established in what is now Thailand by the Siamese (Thais) who had migrated southwards from Yünnan. They had been encouraged in their migration by the Mongol rulers of China (the Yuan dynasty: 1260-1368) who wished to have the Siamese as subordinates or vassals in the region of Indo-China. Kadiri, the state to the south which threatened Srivijaya, was in Java and had been growing hostile since the beginning of the thirteenth century.

This east-Javanese kingdom seems eventually in the thirteenth century to have absorbed most of Srivijaya's former possessions in the Indonesian Archipelago. By the 1290's Srivijaya had become too weak to put up much resistance, for she had already suffered the loss of her possessions in the Malay Peninsula. These had been conquered by the rulers of Sukhothai who took Ligor in 1292 and then began to spread further southwards. Pressed upon from both sides, Srivijaya had virtually ceased to exist. Her collapse is confirmed by the evidence of the Venetian merchant and traveller, Marco Polo. In 1292 he visited Sumatra, on his way home after seventeen years in China, and he made no mention of Srivijaya. He only noted eight small principalities, which must have been the successor states to the former empire.

Thai and Majapahit influence

In the fourteenth century the greater part of the Malay Peninsula was under the influence of the Siamese (Thais), while the most powerful state in Borneo and the Indonesian islands was the Javanese Kingdom of Majapahit. However, not all the Peninsula was subject to the Thais. The state of Tumasik on the island of Singapore, founded in 1299, had been able to defend itself against the Thais and had also begun to acquire a reputation for piracy. Until recently it had been thought that Majapahit in the fourteenth century had become an even more extensive state than Srivijaya, exercising control over most of the Indonesian islands as well as the Malay Peninsula. However Majapahit's claims to this supremacy are now considered to be exaggerated, and the territories which she ruled directly only included east Java, Madura and Bali; she also had some influence over vassal states in south-east Sumatra and western Borneo. The Malay Peninsula itself however was probably not part of the Majapahit Empire.

There is evidence that Brunei paid tribute to Majapahit at this time and according to Javanese sources an army from Java expelled Sulu invaders from Brunei in 1368. These same records also say that the last king of Majapahit conquered Brunei not long before the final decline of his kingdom.

While Majapahit's political influence in the Malay Peninsula in the fourteenth century had been negligible, that of the Thais had continued to grow. By the latter part of the century even Tumasik had to acknowledge the overlordship of the powerful Thai kingdom with its capital at Ayuthia. We will see in the following chapter that it was a Siamese expedition sent to punish the ruler of Tumasik which led indirectly to the establishment of the town of Malacca. However, although it is probable that the dominant political power in the Peninsula was that of the Thais, it is nevertheless true that the permanent culture pattern remained Hindu rather than Thai Buddhist, suggesting that indirectly Majapahit, which was a Hindu state did have some cultural influence.

Before turning to the history of the Malay Sultanates let us first summarize the main points of Malaysian history before the fifteenth century. The first fact of importance is that Malaysia lay between the two dominant centres of civilization at that time: India and China. Malaysia was affected by both, though in different ways. As far as trade was concerned the Malay Peninsula was a useful 'half-way-house', and traders not only from India and China, but also from distant lands like Arabia, used its geographical facilities. A second factor of importance is the different effect which China and India had on this region. We have seen how relations between the Peninsula and these two civilizations were constant throughout the centuries. Yet it is important to note that China's influence was almost entirely political, while India's was largely cultural. China was the dominant political power because she was generally a united empire while India was a collection of small states. It was to the Chinese Emperor that embassies and gifts were sent; it was to China that almost all the states of South-East Asia, at one time or another, looked for protection. China was the overlord rather than India. She did not directly interfere very much in South-East Asian affairs but she was always there in the background.

India, however, was the main cultural influence. Chinese culture and customs, including Confucianism and Taoism, were peculiar to China and were not exported; in fact it was from India that China herself accepted Buddhism. So also did the Indians convey their religions of Hinduism and Buddhism to Malaysia and the islands. This Indian influence was strong enough to have a permanent effect on the culture and literature of this part of the world. Thus, although the states of South-East Asia were usually careful to recognize the strength of the Chinese Empire, the latter had almost no effect on the early way of life of the peoples of the region.

EXERCISES

1. Write a brief account of the early influence of India and China on Malaya.
2. What do you understand by the phrase, 'Indianized kingdoms'? Write brief notes on two of them.
3. Write short notes on the following: Fah Hsien, Neolithic culture, Indian influence in Kedah, Borobudur.

2

THE MALACCA AND BRUNEI SULTANATES

ORIGINS AND EARLY HISTORY

LIKE most population centres situated on the sea coast and at the mouth of a river, Malacca began its existence as a small fishing village. This village grew in size and importance because it attracted the attention of a Hindu prince who had been forced to leave Tumasik (now Singapore). Before this prince—whose name was Parameswara—arrived in Malacca there were probably about twenty or thirty families in the settlement. It was very small and certainly not large enough to be mentioned by Marco Polo when he passed through the Straits of Malacca in 1292 on his way back to Europe from China. It was not mentioned either by the Arab traveller, Ibn Battuta, in 1343, but in the fourteenth century it must have become known for the name is found in a Javanese poem of 1324 and in a list of Siamese dependencies in 1360.

The original population was composed of those whom today we would call *orang asli* and *orang laut*[1]; the influx of Malay inhabitants came later with Parameswara's arrival. He was a Sumatran prince, a Hindu, who had been forced to flee from Palembang where

[1] Coastal Proto-Malay tribes.

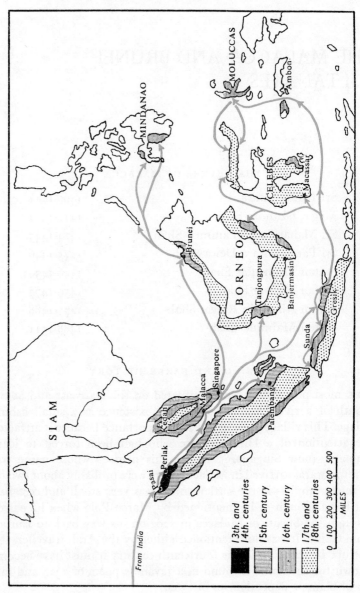

THE SPREAD OF ISLAM IN SOUTH-EAST ASIA

MILES

0   100   200   300   400   500

13th. and
14th. centuries

15th. century

16th. century

17th. and
18th. centuries

From India

SIAM

Pasai
Perlak
Kedah
Malacca
Singapore
Palembang
Sunda

BORNEO
Brunei
Tanjongpura
Banjermasin
Gresik

CELEBES
Macassar

MINDANAO

MOLUCCAS
Ambon

he was no longer acceptable to the ruling group. He made his way to Tumasik, where he was well received and, as a refugee, allowed to stay. However apparently he was a treacherous man for he soon decided to kill his host who had received him so well, and thus Parameswara established himself as the new ruler of the island.

Once established, Parameswara and his followers quickly turned Tumasik into a pirate base from where they were able to prey on the ships passing round the point of the Peninsula. This menace to trading was to last about five years. But it eventually became too much of a menace to the Siamese who in 1398 or 1400 sent an armed force (probably from their vassal states of Patani and Pahang) to suppress the pirates who were causing so much trouble. The Siamese in any case claimed the allegiance of Tumasik and would obviously have been annoyed by Parameswara's overthrow of the previous ruler. Parameswara and his followers were ejected from Tumasik and, once again fugitives, were forced to make their way northwards. They probably stopped first in the region of present-day Muar and later went further north to Malacca. Parameswara was extremely resourceful. We have seen how he had set himself up as the ruler of Tumasik. He now did the same in the small fishing settlement where he found himself, and we shall see how under his rule this fishing settlement became a thriving port.

These new immigrants who arrived in Malacca at the beginning of the fifteenth century were of a higher culture than the inhabitants, and they introduced the planting of new crops like sugar cane, spices, and bananas and also discovered the inland deposits of tin. The staple food, rice, could be grown but not in sufficient quantities to feed the growing population which in ten years increased to about two thousand. There were probably not enough skilled cultivators, as the majority of the people lived by trade. Rice was imported from Sumatra, and trade was begun in a small way with the produce of the Peninsula. Gradually as the settlement grew the passing ships made a point of stopping at Malacca for revictualling, and in this way the first trading ventures were begun. It was in these circumstances that Malacca became a port of call—a port of call which was in a very advantageous position. The geographical advantages which Malacca enjoyed helped considerably with the rapidity of its development.

However, to begin with, Malacca was a small settlement struggling to expand and to acquire some of the trade of its neighbours. It was likely to arouse the jealousy of established states and therefore was in need of the protection of a strong power. There were two powers strong enough to provide this protection, Siam and China. However, as we have seen, Parameswara was no friend of the Siamese authorities, for they had driven him out of Tumasik. Moreover, though the Siamese had recognized his administration, they were near enough to Malacca to be tempted to interfere too often.

CHINESE INFLUENCE

China was much farther away and so less likely to be interested in direct interference; and China was of course much the more powerful state of the two. If Parameswara could obtain China's protection it would be a useful counter-weight to hold against the Siamese if they became aggressive. Probably because of these considerations Parameswara sent envoys to China almost as soon as he had established himself in Malacca. This was the time of the Ming dynasty (1368-1644) in China. The first Ming Emperor, who had died in 1398, had concentrated on the internal reorganization of the state, but the third Emperor, Chu Ti (1403-24), was interested in the world outside China, and his reign was a time of most unusual Chinese maritime activity. The Chinese because of their self-sufficiency have throughout history been little interested in other countries, but this reign is one of the few exceptions. It is difficult to explain the sudden change of attitude, but it is probable that the Chinese wished to investigate the use of sea routes as an alternative to the overland route to the West, especially for the importing of luxuries. There also seems to have been a desire to extend Chinese prestige in other parts of Asia by offering protection and enforcing Chinese suzerainty or overlordship.

Thus during the early Ming dynasty a series of missions visited Tibet, Java, Siam, Bengal, the Malay Peninsula, and even the Persian Gulf within the space of twenty-eight years. The Chinese Government was not averse, therefore, to accepting Parameswara's request for protection. In 1403 a Chinese fleet led by an admiral named Yin Ching arrived in Malacca from China bringing presents and also confirming Parameswara as the ruler of the settlement. In return further envoys were sent to China in the same year and again in 1407.

There was now to follow a series of visits from the Chinese admiral, Cheng Ho, who made seven voyages to the West between 1408 and 1431. His main purpose seems to have been to enforce Chinese suzerainty and to collect tribute. Some of his expeditions were very large; on his first voyage he had with him sixty-three ships; others were punitive, for on one occasion he captured a Palembang prince and on another a king from Ceylon, probably because they would not agree to acknowledge the suzerainty of the Chinese Emperor. And of course Cheng Ho was also collecting information for the Chinese court. In 1411 he took Parameswara with him to China so that the ruler of Malacca could hand over his tribute in person. Parameswara was accompanied by five hundred and forty followers, and it was on this voyage that Cheng Ho was returning with the captured Ceylonese king mentioned above. This visit in effect confirmed Parameswara's new status as an independent king owing suzerainty to China alone.

In 1413 Cheng Ho was accompanied on his visit to Malacca by a Chinese Muslim called Ma Huan. Ma Huan later wrote a book describing the voyage, and of Malacca he said 'the soil of Malacca was very barren, the crops poor and agriculture was not in favour'. It was therefore necessary to import food, and the inhabitants used their trading profits to pay for this.

Trade had become the main enterprise of Malacca; Parameswara had by this time established a secure enough settlement to attract traders to the port. He had long given up the idea of piracy and had settled down to providing the amenities required of a trade centre: food and water, a stable government and the ability to offer protection to merchants using the port. As we have seen Parameswara depended considerably on the goodwill of China which he was at pains to preserve. Until the new settlement was firmly established he could not afford to ignore the possibility of a Siamese attack. During this period the trade of Malacca benefited greatly from the overseas ventures and voyages of the Chinese who used Parameswara's settlement as a port of call.

One of the places with which Malacca traded was Sumatra, particularly the northern states of Pasai and Perlak. The connexion that was established with these states was to be extremely important later for it was from northern Sumatra that the religion of Islam was introduced to Malacca.

THE INFLUENCE OF ISLAM

Islam came to South-East Asia from India and became established in northern Sumatra sometime towards the end of the thirteenth century. At this time Islam had not been long established in India itself, and it had only been accepted by people in certain regions of the sub-continent. However it was from these Muslim regions that merchants and traders visited South-East Asia. North Sumatra had long-standing connexions with both the merchants from Gujerat in north-west India and also those from the Coromandel coast in the east, and these were the areas where Islam had been accepted. There is little doubt that Islam was brought to Malaysia by traders from India (rather than by Arabs from Arabia) and the general opinion has been that the Gujerati merchants were responsible. However quite a convincing case has been presented by Marrison that Islam was brought in the first instance by merchants from the Coromandel coast. It is pointed out in this interpretation that Gujerat itself did not become a Muslim state until 1297 whereas the east-Sumatran state of Melayu was using traders with Muslim names as envoys to China in 1281.[1] Also Marco Polo passing through the Straits of Malacca in 1292 called in at Pasai and Perlak and found that these states had Muslim rulers. Finally in Pasai there is the tombstone of a ruler with the Muslim name of Malek-al-Salleh stating that he died in 1297. The *Hikayat Raja2 Pasai* also states that Islam came from south India.

But while there may be argument over which part of India Islam came from, there is little doubt that it came from India and that it came some time towards the end of the thirteenth century. The fact that Islam came from India rather than Arabia is important for it helps to explain the continued presence of Indian cultural influences in South-East Asia. Though the missionaries of Islam did eliminate the material and concrete examples of Hinduism, for example temples and idols, they did not change, or perhaps did not want to change, customs and traditions which were part of Indian cultural life.

The Islam that came to South-East Asia was thus not the completely orthodox Islam of Arabia, for this would probably have demanded the abolition of many traditional customs connected with Hinduism and animism. The Indians who brought the new religion wanted it to be accepted by the people of South-East Asia and therefore did not demand the alteration of all old customs which conflicted with Islam. If the missionaries of Islam had been the more orthodox Arabs then it is possible that the new religion would not have been accepted so readily. But, as we know today, many of the old traditions were absorbed into Islam: for example the Hindu ceremonies connected with royal coronations and with marriage; the animism which is involved in *keramat*;[2] and the high station awarded to women, higher than in the Arab lands, for example.

[1] However Muslims had been living round Gujerat since the 1230's.
[2] A place or object inhabited by spirits.

Another point to remember is that the people of South-East Asia were well acquainted with these Indian traders; because of the long contact between India and this part of the world they were not strangers. Thus when the new religion was brought by such long-standing acquaintances, themselves newly converted, Islam was not thought of as something completely alien. As a result Islam was introduced relatively easily, by peaceful means rather than by conquest.

As has been said, the states of northern Sumatra accepted Islam some time towards the end of the thirteenth century. During the fourteenth century the new religion does not seem to have expanded particularly quickly to other areas, and it was not until the conversion of the rapidly growing state of Malacca that progress became spectacular.

By the time Parameswara died in 1414 there was a fairly numerous Muslim trading community in the city. Malacca itself was now firmly established with the support and protection of the Ming emperors and there is little doubt that Parameswara had been successful in this his last venture.

The Muslim merchant community became increasingly influential during the region of Parameswara's son and successor, Megat Iskandar Shah. The latter continued the policy of gaining the protection of China, paying an immediate visit there in 1414-15. He went there again in 1419 to report the threat of an attack on Malacca by the Siamese. He was successful in persuading the Chinese to put pressure on Siam and in this way the attack on Malacca was prevented.

Iskandar Shah's reign was a relatively short one and when he died in 1424 he was succeeded by Sri Maharaja Mohammed Shah. It was this ruler the third in Malacca's history, who according to the Sejarah Melayu (the Malay Annals) was converted to Islam after marrying the daughter of the ruler of Pasai. During this reign the influence of the Muslim-Tamil group of merchants continued to grow and this growth was naturally helped by the ruler's own conversion to Islam. But at the same time conflict developed between this Muslim trading community and the essentially Hindu-Malay ruling class.

Sri Maharaja visited China in 1424 for confirmation of his position as ruler, and he went there again in 1433. Admiral Cheng Ho made one more visit to Malacca during this reign, but soon after his death the Chinese interest in overseas voyages stopped, and China withdrew again into her policy of seclusion. By this time, however, Malacca was probably strong enough to stand on her own feet and no longer required continued Chinese protection. With the ending of these official voyages from China, Chinese influence in Malaysia declined although a small number of traders had established a settlement for themselves in Malacca. When he died in 1444 Sri Maharaja left two sons. The younger, Sri Parameswara Dewa Shah, was a Hindu and was supported by most of the Malay chiefs, for he was born of a royal mother. Though he was the younger son, he succeeded his father to the throne. This was because the mother of his elder half-brother was a Muslim-Tamil commoner and was not accepted by the Malay chiefs. This elder brother, following his mother's family, appears to have become a Muslim and had taken the name of Raja Kassim. He was supported by the Muslim-Tamil faction led by Tun Ali, his uncle, and it was this group which eventually placed him on the throne.

After only seventeen months as ruler, the young king, Sri Parameswara Dewa Shah, was overthrown and killed in a *coup d'état* led by Tun Ali. Raja Kassim was made ruler by the victorious Muslim faction, and during his reign Islam replaced Hinduism as the accepted religion of Malacca. He took the name of Sultan Mudzaffar Shah and ruled from 1445 to 1458/9. During these years Malacca became the centre of Muslim influence in South-East Asia, and of course this in itself helped his kingdom to grow in importance. The Muslim-Tamil merchants who had previously used northern Sumatra as the base for their trade now used Malacca which was much more advantageously situated. The reign of Sultan Mudzaffar Shah was to have a three-fold importance in Malacca's history.

In the first place, as we have seen, Islam became the state religion, for the general population soon accepted the religion of the ruler. There was a natural tendency for this to happen for the ruler was not only the political and religious head of the state, but the most influential group at his court were also Muslims. Again Islam was not forced on the population; traditional customs were not abolished; as a result, what opposition there was soon died out, especially when Islam was accepted by the leading Malay families. They had, as we have seen, opposed and been defeated by the Muslim-Tamil faction, one of whom, Tun Ali, had taken over from the Malay chiefs the position of *Bendahara* or Chief Minister. But in 1456 the Sultan realized the unpopularity of his uncle, Tun Ali, persuaded him to resign, and appointed in his place Tun Perak, the son of a former Bendahara and a member of the Malay ruling class.

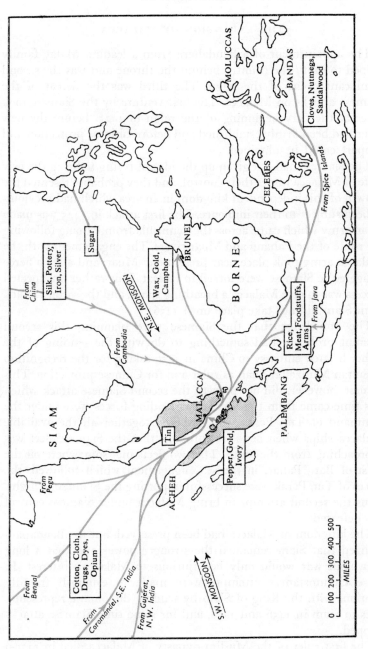

MALACCA'S TRADE IN THE FIFTEENTH CENTURY

Silk, Pottery, Iron, Silver

Sugar

From China

From Cambodia

From Pegu

SIAM

Tin

ACHEH

Cotton, Cloth, Drugs, Dyes, Opium

From Bengal

From Coromandel, S.E. India

From Gujerat, N.W. India

Pepper, Gold, Ivory

N.E. MONSOON

S.W. MONSOON

MALACCA

PALEMBANG

Wax, Gold, Camphor

BRUNEI

BORNEO

CELEBES

MOLUCCAS

BANDAS

Cloves, Nutmegs, Sandalwood

From Spice Islands

Rice, Meat, Foodstuffs, Arms

From Java

MILES

0   100   200   300   400   500

THE EXPANSION OF MALACCA

The appointment of a Bendahara from a leading Malay family helped to unify the country behind the throne and was the second significant event of the reign. The third was the defeat of the Siamese attacks on Malacca. The first venture by the Siamese took place at the very beginning of the reign in 1445, before the new ruler had been firmly established and before Chinese protection and support could be obtained.

The Siamese had not given up the idea of trying to bring the new state of Malacca under their control, and they probably resented the growth of this independent kingdom in an area which had previously been subject to their influence. The first attack in 1445 was made by an army which came across the Peninsula from Pahang following the route of the Pahang and Muar rivers. The engagement with the Malacca army took place near present-day Muar, and after a fierce struggle the Siamese were forced to retreat. This rather unexpected success was to give Malacca a breathing space, and the second attack from Siam did not take place until 1456.

The knowledge that the Siamese were planning this second attempt probably had something to do with the sending of the rather belated embassy to China in 1456 asking for the recognition of Sultan Mudzaffar Shah as ruler and for Chinese protection. This request, however, did not prevent the second Siamese attack which this time came from the sea. The defending forces were under the command of Tun Perak who gathered together all the available Malacca ships when news was brought that the Siamese fleet was approaching from the south. The two fleets met somewhere off the coast of Batu Pahat; in the sea engagement which followed, the forces of Tun Perak were successful in putting the Siamese to flight. Thus the second attempt to bring Malacca under Siamese control was defeated.

The kingdom of Malacca had been preserved, but the Bendahara realized that Siam remained the stronger power and that a long drawn-out war would only be injurious to Malacca's interest. In these circumstances attempts were made to establish friendly relations with the King of Siam by sending diplomatic representatives to Siam in 1456 and 1458, and for some time Siamese attacks stopped.

The first ruler of the Muslim dynasty of Malacca died in 1458-9 leaving a kingdom that was firmly established and ably administered by his Bendahara, Tun Perak. The foundations of Malacca's future success had now been laid, and its great expansion was to come during the reign of his successor.

The next ruler, Sultan Mansur Shah (1459-77), was the son of the previous king and a cousin of Tun Perak, whose sister he later married. He began his reign by sending an embassy to China in 1459 to secure recognition of his succession to the throne. This recognition he obtained, and the potential threat from Siam was thereby lessened.

Wilkinson calls the reign of Mansur Shah perhaps the most glorious period in Malay history, and there is little doubt that Malacca flowered and flourished during these years. However it is also true that in this judgement he gave little credit to the ruler himself; rather he credits the success to the energy of the Bendahara. Tun Perak appears to have been the brains behind the policy of expansion. Malacca was now the strongest state in the Peninsula and was in a position to try to exert her control over other states which had formerly owed allegiance to Siam.

The first attack was made on Pahang, a vassal state of Siam. It was perhaps a way of showing the Siamese that Malacca, too, was capable of taking the offensive. The expedition to Pahang was strikingly successful; the Governor and his daughter were captured and, together with loot, brought to Malacca. There the Governor was made the keeper of the royal elephants, while his daughter became one of the Sultan's wives.

The success of this first offensive venture encouraged Tun Perak to continue the policy of expansion. Soon the whole of the southern part of the Peninsula, Johore and the islands to the south, were brought under Malacca's control. The next step was to gain ascendancy over the states on the east coast of Sumatra so that Malacca could control both sides of the Straits. Expeditions were sent first to Kampar and Siak, both states were conquered, and Kampar became a dependency ruled by a viceroy from Malacca. Two other states, Jambi and Indragiri, were also forced to acknowledge Malacca's supremacy and pay tribute to her Sultan. Thus in a short time the river states on the opposite side of the Straits came under Malacca's control. However, expeditions which were sent against Acheh and Pasai in north Sumatra were not as successful, and Malacca's control did not extend to the far north of Sumatra.

By 1470 Malacca had risen to become a power of the first rank and had become the strongest state in South-East Asia. Equally important, Malacca had also become the diffusion centre for the spread of Islam. As she asserted her political dominance and brought other states into her trading system so also her religion was spread to her dependencies. The political dominance which Malacca exercised encouraged the rulers of the subsidiary states to embrace Islam, and their subjects soon followed their lead. This trend was also encouraged by royal marriages between the Malacca royal house and other rulers. As has been said, the moving force behind the policy of expansion was Tun Perak, the Bendahara who held that office from 1456 to 1498, a long period. The sultan, Mansur Shah, was not a very forceful character; perhaps he was too much under the control of his Bendahara. He was mainly interested in the affairs of his own city and court. He encouraged the development of the cultural life of Malacca and his capital became the showpiece of the empire.

He himself was interested in religion and literature, and he attracted to his court religious teachers and wise men whose patron he became. Many of these religious teachers were 'Sufis' and were mystics rather than theologians. As a result they were not rigidly orthodox. Therefore they did not meet with much opposition when they became the missionaries of Islam to other parts of the Archipelago. It was these teachers who were responsible for converting the people of the peninsula and the islands to Islam. The wealth of Malacca and its court financed the patronage that was essential for the encouragement of literature, literature which was not only indigenous but was also influenced by the cultures of India and Java.

The city had probably now developed a population of about 40,000 and the Sultan had built himself a large palace, beautifully decorated and said to be nearly a hundred yards long. The city and court had become wealthy, and this period saw the full development of what today we call classical Malay culture. This was the age which developed court ceremonials, the age of Hang Tuah (the famous *Laksamana* or admiral) and the *Budak Raja*[1] and the stories which are associated with their names. The expansionist policies of Tun Perak gave plenty of scope for the dashing Malay warriors to demonstrate their prowess, and Hang Tuah became the most famous of these as well as a successful Laksamana.

The Sultan himself, as has been said, seems to have been little interested in affairs of state, for the initiative in matters of policy lay with Tun Perak. It is probable that the Bendahara was so forceful a person that he did not allow the ruler much influence, making sure that he kept power in his own hands. His control over Sultan

[1] Young warriors at court.

Mansur Shah is well illustrated by the incident when the heir to the throne, Raja Mohamed, killed Tun Perak's son after the latter had knocked off Raja Mohamed's head-dress when they were playing *sepak raga*.[1] Tun Perak was powerful enough to force the Sultan to banish his son to Pahang, where he was later to become Sultan. The Sultan was also unfortunate in that another of his sons was killed by a man who ran amok, so that when he himself died in 1477 he was succeeded by a much younger son, who was in fact the nephew of Tun Perak.

TUN PERAK AND TUN MUTAHIR

Alauddin Riayat Shah, the third Sultan of Malacca, ruled from 1477 to 1488 and was only about fifteen years old when he came to the throne. Naturally he was at first very much under the influence of his uncle who was thus able to continue his control over Malacca's government.

But gradually Sultan Alauddin began to resent his inferior position, and as he grew older he began to take more and more interest in the affairs of his kingdom. He was obviously an energetic man, and he disliked the fact that his ministers had more power than himself. He was interested in improving the internal administration of Malacca and was not content to delegate his authority to others. The story is told of how he himself assisted in the capture of some robbers much to the discomfort of the *Temenggong* (chief of police). As described by Wilkinson it seems that the Sultan had learnt that the police were not being as efficient as they should be, and he decided that he would personally investigate their conduct. One night disguised as an ordinary citizen and accompanied by two body-guards, Sultan Alauddin was making his rounds when he and his companions suddenly came upon five men carrying a box. Startled at being challenged, the five robbers, for that was what they were, dropped the box and ran. The Sultan gave chase with one companion, leaving the other to guard the valuables. In the pursuit three of the robbers were killed and two managed to escape. The next morning at the court the Sultan asked Tun Mutahir, the Temenggong, whether his police had caught three robbers during the night. The Temenggong of course had to plead ignorance of the whole affair, and was suitably embarrassed when he discovered that the robbery had been prevented by the Sultan himself and not by the police.

[1] A game played with a ball made of *rattan*.

To return however to the political events of the reign: following the usual custom, envoys were sent to China in 1481, the occasion this time being a suspected attack from Annam which was in fact restrained by the Chinese Emperor. Secure with this long-distance protection, Malacca continued to extend her own influence in South-East Asia especially through the progressive expansion of Islam. One way in which Islam spread was through the army because Malacca employed many Javanese mercenary soldiers. In many cases while serving in Malacca these men were converted to Islam, and when they returned home they took their new religion with them. Islam was taken to Java not only by soldiers but also by merchants trading with Malacca. Merchants were also largely responsible for the further spread of Islam to Banda, the Moluccas, Brunei and the outlying parts of Sumatra. Thus Malacca remained very much at the centre of affairs in South-East Asia and continued to grow in size and prosperity.

As has been said, Sultan Alauddin was an energetic ruler and was probably the most competent of all the Malacca sultans. However the fact that he was so energetic was bound to bring him many enemies, especially amongst those whose influence seemed to be threatened by his initiative. Tun Perak and the other ministers had probably thought that they were getting another puppet ruler when Alauddin came to the throne, but as we have seen the Sultan was not content to remain a figurehead. This independence of outlook may in fact have been responsible for Alauddin's mysterious death in 1488 at the early age of twenty-six. As he was preparing to go to Mecca he died so suddenly and with such mystery that poison was immediately suspected. At the time the Sultan's eldest son was across the Straits in Kampar, Sumatra, where he had been appointed Sultan so that he could represent his father and be brought up to learn something about government. The suspicion that Alauddin was removed by ministers fearful of their own position may be supported by the fact that Alauddin's eldest son (in Kampar) was passed over in the succession in favour of a younger brother Mahmud, who was also—and perhaps this is more important—related to both Tun Perak and Tun Mutahir (the son of Tun Ali).

Sultan Mahmud Shah (1488-1511), the fourth and last Sultan of Malacca, was also only a young boy when he ascended the throne. Therefore he too was very much under the influence of Tun Perak during the early years of his reign. But the Bendahara himself was now becoming an old man, and the period of his great influence in Malacca was coming to an end. During his lifetime of service to the state he had watched over the development of Malacca as it grew from a trading port to become the centre of an expanding empire—the foremost state in South-East Asia. Tun Perak was not entirely unselfish in his administration, for beside nurturing the growth of Malacca's strength he also watched over the increase in influence of his own family. We have seen how he manipulated the succession to the throne by ensuring that the rulers of Malacca were not only related to him but also under his control. He was the power behind the throne for many years. and he realized that by remaining out of the limelight he could exercise greater influence.

Malacca had grown strong and during its growth had remained internally peaceful. Although Tun Perak retained power within his own family he also made sure that rivalries within Malacca were not allowed to disrupt the state. There were rival groups in Malacca, for Malacca itself was not a very homogeneous city. Tun Perak, himself the leader of the Malay element, had become Bendahara after the period of office of Tun Ali, who was a Muslim Tamil. This Tamil faction, mainly composed of wealthy merchants, still remained a powerful group, despite the fact that political power lay with the Malays. The latter were the ruling class but were probably only a minority of the population. The majority were traders of alien or mixed descent and even the armed forces were largely composed of Javanese mercenaries. The greater part of the population therefore owed little loyalty to the ruling class and to the state itself. They owed it only to themselves. This unreliability was to be exposed in the crisis that arose at the time of the Portuguese attack in 1511.

During his lifetime Tun Perak had made sure that internal rivalry was played down. When he died in 1498, he was succeeded as Bendahara by his brother Tun Puteh, who was himself an old man. The rising influence in Malacca was now Tun Mutahir, the leader of the Muslim-Tamil group, who was related to both Tun Perak and to the Sultan who was his nephew. For a number of years he had held the position of Temenggong and had built up a considerable following in the city.

Tun Puteh did not long survive his brother and died in 1500. The decision had now to be made about the appointment of a new Bendahara. This was a most crucial decision, for not only was the office itself most important—it was made doubly so by the character of the ruler. Sultan Mahmud, brought up to kingship under the dominant influence of Tun Perak, was not a strong character and was moreover not much interested in affairs of state. Rather, like

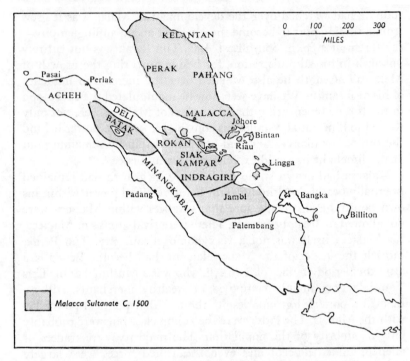

EXTENT OF THE MALACCA SULTANATE

Sultan Mansur Shah, his interests lay in the direction of literature and religion (and, according to the Portuguese, opium, but perhaps they were biased). Nevertheless he did not concern himself much with the administration of the state and therefore the appointment of the new Bendahara was of vital importance for the future of Malacca.

The two rival factions were the Malays and the Muslim Tamils. Sultan Mahmud was prevailed upon by his mother to appoint Tun Mutahir, who was her step-brother, to the position of Bendahara. As a result the Muslim Tamils were once again in control of the government. As things turned out this was to be an unfortunate choice, but in the circumstances it was probably inevitable.

Tun Mutahir was Bendahara from 1500 to 1510, and during those years, although the prestige and influence of Malacca continued to grow, he himself became more and more unpopular. Unlike Tun Perak, he was not content to remain in the background in order to control the state. He wanted to be known as a powerful man; in carrying out this ambition, he not only antagonized almost the whole population but he also alienated the Sultan.

The extension of Malacca's influence continued throughout the Peninsula so that by the beginning of the sixteenth century her empire included most of Malaya as far north as Kedah and Patani. She was strong enough to protect Pahang from an attack by Ligor, a vassal state of Siam, while another attack by the Siamese themselves was beaten off. Nevertheless, for the sake of insurance, a further embassy was sent to China in 1508; for although Malacca had now succeeded to the predominant position of a 'modern Srivijaya', it was never known when powerful protection would be required. But although Malacca had the appearance of strength, internally all was not so well, for the policies of Tun Mutahir tended to emphasize division rather than unity. He himself grew in unpopularity for he seemed to be mainly interested in advancing his own position. He used his political powers to further his own trading ventures by eliminating competition. He could also be bribed in matters concerning trading concessions and even in the administration of justice. In a word, Tun Mutahir was corrupt.

The downfall of the Bendahara was to be hastened, however, by two fatal mistakes. In the first place he had become arrogant and too sure of himself, so much so that he antagonized the Sultan and this opened the way for an opposition group to develop, an opposition group which had the Sultan's support. The second mistake concerned his reception of the Portuguese ships whose unexpected arrival in Malacca occurred in 1509. These ships, under the command of de Sequeira, were supposedly coming to Malacca to trade and at first had been welcomed by the Malacca authorities.

But the Indian-Muslim merchants in Malacca had no wish to see their rivals established in the port, for they had had experience in India of the competition that would be likely to arise with the Portuguese, who had already set themselves up in Goa. They therefore prevailed upon the Bendahara to change his policy of friendliness, hoping this would discourage further Portuguese voyages. The Bendahara decided to attempt the capture of the Portuguese fleet, but the Portuguese were warned of the plot against them and the greater part of the fleet was able to escape from the harbour before the attack could be launched. Nevertheless in their haste the Portuguese were forced to leave behind about twenty of their number as prisoners. The result of this unsuccessful attack was that the Portuguese now considered the authorities in Malacca untrustworthy, and they were given an opportunity to return to

Malacca to rescue the captives. We shall read about the consequences of these events of 1509 in the next chapter.

Tun Mutahir's policy of antagonism towards the Portuguese, at the prompting of the Indian-Muslim merchants, was not popular with the Malay faction in the city. As has been said, the Bendahara's biggest mistake was to arouse the opposition of Sultan Mahmud, for the opposition group now had reason to merge their grievances with those of the Sultan. The ruler resented the independent attitude of his chief minister. This resentment was increased by the fact that Tun Mutahir had allowed his very beautiful younger daughter to marry his own nephew rather than the Sultan, who was at that time without a consort. The Bendahara made a further mistake by making an enemy of a powerful Malacca merchant who, wishing to gain revenge, persuaded the Laksamana to tell the Sultan that Tun Mutahir was planning to seize the throne. This information gave Sultan Mahmud the necessary excuse to support openly the opposition group. The next step was for him to order that the Bendahara and his family be killed. This was duly done in 1510, and with the elimination of the leader of the Tamil faction the post of Bendahara reverted to the rather elderly son of Tun Perak.

Unfortunately for the state of Malacca, however, the Bendahara's removal came too late. Too much damage had been done, and in the following year, 1511, a second Portuguese fleet arrived outside the port of Malacca. This time the newcomers had not only come to trade but to try to capture the city of Malacca itself.

BRUNEI

However, while Malacca held the centre of the stage in South-East Asia, another important sultanate had developed in Brunei and the influence of this state came gradually to extend over the area of present day Sabah and Sarawak. The present dynasty of Brunei was established in the early part of the fifteenth century and it soon came into contact with the expanding power of Malacca from where it received the new religion of Islam in about the year 1440. Traditionally the first Muslim ruler of Brunei was Awang Alak ber Tabar who took the name of Mohammed and married a Muslim princess from Johore. Trading relations were soon begun between Malacca and Brunei, the latter exporting camphor, wax, sago, rice and gold and receiving Indian piece-goods in exchange. The first Sultan, whose daughter is thought to have married a Chinese, Ong

Sum Ping, who had gone to Borneo with Cheng Ho, was succeeded by his brother Ahmad. The latter's daughter married an Arab from Taif, Sheriff Ali, who became Sultan Berkat and who ruled vigorously, building mosques and converting the people to Islam. Islam therefore came quite early to the territory of Brunei and the present day Muslim population is composed of indigenous peoples and not migrants. However Islam spread slowly within Borneo itself because of the difficulty of communications.

Throughout the fifteenth century Brunei was overshadowed by the more powerful Malacca but after 1511 its wealth increased as many Muslims fled there from Malacca to escape from the Portuguese. By this time Brunei had a well developed system of administration; under the Sultan there were officers of state holding the titles of Bendahara, Temenggong, Laksamana and Shahbandar, and the Portuguese were to remark on the splendour of the court in the sixteenth century.

EXERCISES

1 Write a brief account of the establishment of a settlement at Malacca by Parameswara.

2 Describe the spread of Islam to South-East Asia.

3 Why did Malacca flourish as a trading centre in the fifteenth century?

4 Why was the reign of Sultan Mansur Shah particulary important in the history of Malacca?

5 Assess the importance of the role of Tun Perak in the administration of Malacca.

6 Write short notes on the following:
Cheng Ho, Hang Tuah, Sultan Allauddin, Tun Mutahir, the Trengganu stone.

3
THE PORTUGUESE IN SOUTH-EAST ASIA

PORTUGAL, a small country situated at the extreme south-west of Europe and a part of the Iberian Peninsula, in the late fifteenth century had a population of only about one and a half-million. Though so small in numbers, she was to play a most decisive part in the history of the world, for Portugal's activities in the sixteenth century were to have results out of all proportion to her size. She was to be the country primarily responsible for bringing about direct links between Asia and Europe.

THE ARAB TRADING MONOPOLY

Asia and Europe had long had trading contacts which had used the region of the Middle East as the place of exchange for the goods which they sold to each other. As a result of this East-West commerce, prosperous trading cities such as Baghdad, Alexandria, Aleppo, and Constantinople had developed. Thus from the fifth to the eleventh century the Middle East was huge and prosperous entrepôt market, the essential link between East and West.

However, after the tenth century there was a radical change in the Middle-Eastern balance of power, with the decline of the Roman Empire and the increasing strength of the Muslim powers: the Arabs and later the Turks. As the power of the Turkish Ottoman Empire grew, it gradually brought the whole of the Middle-Eastern region under its control and with it control over the prosperous trade between Europe and Asia. The Ottomans were determined that the wealth from this commerce should remain in the Middle East. The years between the late eighth and fifteenth centuries were the years during which the Muslim Arabs extended their influence along the North African coast into Spain and then later into south-eastern Europe. They thus came to control a very large part of the trade of the Mediterranean and monopolized trade between Europe and Asia after their capture of Constantinople in 1453. Venice and Genoa were the only European states allowed to participate in this lucrative trade and then only on the terms laid down by the rulers of the Ottoman Empire. We tend to think that the basis of this trade was in luxury goods, things that were not essential and therefore goods which Europe could perhaps have done without if it had so wished. But while items like silk, ivory and precious stones may be considered luxuries, the most important single element in the exchange between Europe and Asia was the spice trade. Spices were important for the preservation and flavouring of meat that had to be salted and spiced in order to preserve it for the winter. Spices had very nearly become a necessity in Europe, and Europe disliked being dependent for these necessities on the Ottoman Empire whose prosperity moreover was increased by the monopoly prices it was able to charge for the spices. These spices could only be obtained from Asia: pepper from India and the East Indies, cinnamon from Ceylon, and cloves from the Moluccas. Throughout Asia by the end of the fifteenth century this trade was largely in Muslim hands. Collected in Malacca, the spices from the East Indies were taken by Muslim merchants to the spice ports of Malabar and Gujerat. From there Arab merchants transhipped the goods to the Red Sea and Persian Gulf, to the centres of Alexandria and Baghdad. It was from these cities that Venetian merchants took the spices to Europe.

The Europeans resented the fact that the middleman was making large profits; they resented these profits all the more because they were being obtained by Muslims. As has been said, the centuries after A.D. 1000 had seen the rapid expansion of Arab power to south-west and south-east Europe as well as throughout the Middle East itself. The 'crusades', which were wars between Christians and Muslims, had been fought in Palestine for possession of the 'holy' places—places connected with the life of Christ and with ancient prophets like Abraham and Solomon. These wars were essentially religious wars in which the Christians tried, with little success, to prevent the expansion of Islam. Similar crusades were fought in the Iberian Peninsula between the inhabitants there and the Muslims or Moors[1] from North Africa; and though they had left most of the Peninsula by about 1250 it was not until 1492 with the surrender of Granada that the Moors were finally forced out of Spain and Portugal. The inhabitants of the Iberian Peninsula had therefore developed very strong reasons for disliking the Moors. Firstly they

[1] This was the term used by the Spanish and Portuguese for all Muslims, even those whom they met in Asia.

had been trying to free themselves of Muslim control for five centuries, and secondly they knew that trade with Asia was controlled by people of the same religion as the Moors and that there were large profits to be gained from this trade. By the fifteenth century the inhabitants of the Iberian Peninsula had begun to take the offensive; they successfully defeated the Moors in Portugal and were now eager to consolidate their position by weakening their rivals elsewhere. The desire to win trade from the Muslims was coupled with the hope of extending Christianity in competition with Islam. The Portuguese allied a missionary zeal with their commercial enterprise. The signal for this change to the offensive was the successful Portuguese capture of Ceuta in North Africa in 1415. The Portuguese knew that Muslims controlled trade with Asia and that the prosperity of the Middle East depended to a considerable extent on the monopoly of this trade. Herein lies the first clue to Portuguese intentions.

THE VOYAGES OF DISCOVERY

The Portuguese voyages to the East were part of the movement known in history as the 'voyages of discovery'—voyages through which the East and the West discovered each other by direct contacts and by which the earlier trading relationship, which had been interrupted by the Ottoman Empire, was restored, though this time on a different basis. These voyages were begun by Spain and Portugal, in the first instance as a result of the teaching that the world was round; the ideas of the Greek philosopher, Aristotle, were translated into Latin in the twelfth century and scientists in the fifteenth century suggested that the earth was a sphere. This 'new' idea meant that it was possible to find another route to China and the East—a route that was not controlled by the Ottoman Empire. The Spaniards set about trying to find this route by sailing westwards. This was the purpose of the voyage of Christopher Columbus in 1492, when he discovered the West Indies. The Portuguese set out to try to find a sea route eastwards by sailing south round Africa. To begin with, the Portuguese were the more successful, reaching China in 1514. However, the Spaniards also reached East Asia by way of America later in the sixteenth century when they established themselves on the islands which are now called the Philippines. In so doing the expedition commanded by Magellan and del Cano accomplished the first circumnavigation of the earth in 1519-22.

But in discussing the history of Asia and more especially Malaysia, the Portuguese rather than the Spanish are our main concern. The extraordinary activity of the Portuguese in the late fifteenth and sixteenth centuries owed much to the foresight and determination of the Portuguese prince, Prince Henry the Navigator. His name may be slightly misleading for he never led any famous voyages of navigation himself. However it was largely because of his activity that Portugal was able to take the lead in the expeditions of discovery which occurred after his death.

Prince Henry was born in 1394, the fourth son of the King of Portugal and an English mother, who was a sister of Henry IV of England. He won his knighthood in 1415 at Ceuta fighting against the Moors, but thereafter he took almost no part in public affairs, living a most secluded life until his death in 1460.

However he did not live without a purpose, for he aimed at not only increasing geographical knowledge but also extending Portuguese trade at the expense of the Muslims. In achieving these aims he revolutionized maritime practice and encouraged his captains to sail longer distances than anyone in Europe had ever sailed before. His sailors were trained in new navigational techniques and encouraged to strike out to sea, whereas earlier sailors had been afraid to leave the sight of land. In this way Prince Henry's methods discovered the path to the East by sailing south round the tip of Africa. The expeditions gradually pushed further and further south from Portugal until in 1434 one captain did actually sail as far as Cape Bajador and, more important, he also returned to Portugal. But Portugal did not have unlimited resources to spend on exploration, and Prince Henry himself had died before the actual rounding of the Cape of Good Hope was achieved. In 1488 Bartolomeus Dias sailed round the Cape and ten years later Vasco da Gama reached India. The stage was now set for the sixteenth-century Portuguese expansion and the establishment of bases all over Asia. The sailors from Portugal had now found the direct route to Asia.

The new way to Asia had been shown by Portuguese sailors, but the consolidation of Portuguese power in Asia was left to generals and administrators. On his famous first voyage to India in 1498 Vasco da Gama knew that he was nearing India because a Portuguese traveller named Pero de Covilha had already visited the Malabar Coast. Covilha had travelled through the Middle East to Aden and from there had continued by sea. A report of his travels had probably reached Portugal in 1495. Da Gama sailing up the coast of east Africa had taken on board a Muslim pilot named Ibn Majid in the region of Zanzibar and had been guided across the

Indian Ocean to the port of Calicut. Despite the fact that Calicut had a Hindu ruler, da Gama found that trade in this part of India was controlled by Arabs. Naturally enough these Arabs strongly opposed the granting of trade facilities to the Portuguese.

PORTUGUESE SETTLEMENTS IN ASIA

Vasco da Gama's reports of the trading opportunities available in India resulted in further trading expeditions being dispatched from Lisbon, and this was followed by the establishment in 1500 of a trading port in Cochin, a town a little to the south of Calicut. This was a landmark in the history of Asia just as had been the voyage of da Gama in 1498, for it was the first European settlement in Asia. A further important event took place in 1509 when the Portuguese viceroy, Almeida, defeated a combined Egyptian and Gujerati fleet outside the port of Diu. The success of the Portuguese in this battle illustrated the effectiveness of the armament and manoeuverability of their ships. They were now in a position to gain control of the sea, a vital step towards winning control of the trade routes.

However it was to the next viceroy, Afonso d'Albuquerque, that the Portuguese owed the rapid expansion of their influence in the East. He became viceroy in 1509, the year of Almeida's victory and the year of the first Portuguese voyage to Malacca. D'Albuquerque realized that in the spice trade the Portuguese could not compete with the Muslims in open competition. The voyage round the Cape of Good Hope was very long and expensive and trade through the Middle East would always be the cheaper and more competitive route. He saw that the Arab monopoly could only be broken by forcibly driving away competitors, and he also realized that this policy could not be carried out by periodic fleets being sent out from Lisbon. It was essential to have Portuguese fortresses placed in strategic positions so that they would be able to control the trade routes; also there was a vital need for a permanent naval base somewhere on the Indian coast which could be used for the refitting and revictualling of the fleets. The first fortress was established at Socotra in 1507 and the next at Ormuz in 1515. These would control the entrances to the Red Sea and Persian Gulf. Then, most important of all, in 1510 Goa was captured so that it could become the Portuguese headquarters and naval base. The Portuguese were now established in the centre of the trading chain that led from the

The next logical step was to gain control of the actual collecting Indonesian Archipelago to Alexandria and Baghdad.

centre itself in the East Indies, Malacca. The capture of Malacca would be a worthwhile prize, for it would give the Portuguese not only the collecting centre of the spice trade but also control of the main sea route to China. Thus it was no accident that the 'investigating fleet' led by de Sequeira arrived at Malacca in 1509. The capture of some of his members by the authorities in Malacca gave the Portuguese an excuse to return in force. However it was unlikely that the Portuguese needed any excuse, for the capture of Malacca was a logical extension of their plans, and there is little doubt that they would eventually have attacked Malacca, excuse or no excuse. Malacca was the next link in the chain.

To summarize, then we can see that the main reasons for the Portuguese voyages to Asia were:

(a) to discover an alternative route to Asia from which Europe obtained spices;

(b) to wrest control of this spice trade from the Muslims and impose their own monopoly;

(c) to spread Christianity and weaken Islam.

By gaining control of this trade, the Portuguese would enrich themselves as well as weaken Muslim strength in the Middle East. They believed that anything which helped to weaken the Muslim powers in the Middle East would mean fewer obstacles to the spread of Christianity. The Portuguese were missionaries as well as traders, and they looked upon the voyages of discovery and the establishment of settlements as suitable opportunities to bring about the extension of Christian teaching.

THE PORTUGUESE TAKE MALACCA

We have seen how the rather unexpected reception received by the first Portuguese visitors gave d'Albuquerque an excuse, if one was needed, to pay a return visit to the city. We have also seen how Tun Mutahir had been urged to this policy by the Muslim merchants in Malacca who knew of Portuguese competition in India. However by the time d'Albuquerque arrived in 1511, Tun Mutahir had been overthrown and the Sultan had new advisers.

D'Albuquerque had received a letter from one of the Portuguese captives in the city describing the wealth and importance of Malacca. The letter also stressed the necessity of bringing a strong force if the city was to be captured. Thus when he did set out from Goa in April 1511, d'Albuquerque had with him eighteen ships and approximately fourteen hundred men, about half of whom were

Portuguese, the remainder being Indian auxiliaries. As will be seen, this force was not sufficiently large to impress the Malacca authorities when it arrived in July, but it eventually proved large enough to capture the city. At first d'Albuquerque tried to achieve his aims by negotiation—namely the return of the prisoners and later, permission to build a fortress. The Sultan thought that he was in a strong position and at first he gave rather non-committal answers. There is little doubt that the Malacca authorities consider-ed themselves too strong for the Portuguese. However although this strength seemed sufficient to the Sultan, when it came to the test, much of it was illusory. For example, the Sultan anticipated popular support in the city, especially from the merchant community. The Sultan might naturally have expected this, for he had been urged on by some merchants to prevent the establishment of a Portuguese foothold. He also wanted to keep the merchants, his source of wealth, in Malacca. But although there were many merchants, mainly Muslims, who supported the Sultan, there were many others, among these the non-Muslim Chinese and Indians, who did not. These people resented the privileged position given to the Muslim merchants and the impositions placed upon them by the Malacca authorities. These Indian and Chinese merchants hoped for, but, when they saw the size of d'Albuquerque's force, did not expect, a Portuguese victory. Thus a large proportion of merchants were either actively or passively hostile to the government.

The second illusion of strength lay in the support expected from the armed forces. A great part of the army was composed of Javanese mercenaries, for Malacca, like many other empires, had come to depend on foreigners for its defence. There was little love lost between Java and Malacca; like most mercenaries fighting for money, rather than loyalty, the Javanese had no intention of being killed fighting to the death for a state which was about to be defeated. Thus when during the battle it appeared that the Portuguese were gaining the upper hand, the Javanese retreated. This was enough to ensure a more rapid Portuguese victory. The very cosmopolitan nature of Malacca's population increased its weaknesses, for the majority of the people did not like the privileged position of the Malay ruling class. Popular support for the Sultan was therefore very meagre.

These two influences undermined the confidence that had been built up by an underestimation of Portuguese strength. Although the Portuguese force appeared small in numbers and ill-equipped for assaulting a city, d'Albuquerque did have a considerable advantage in artillery. His guns were more accurate and had a longer range than the artillery possessed by Malacca.

Negotiations with Sultan Mahmud continued for some time as d'Albuquerque attempted to achieve his aims without fighting. The Sultan, however, was confident of his strength, and, following his decision not to return the prisoners nor give permission for a fortress to be built, he continued to gather together his own armed forces. Seeing that the defending forces were growing in size, d'Albuquerque decided that an attack would be made on the city on the feast day of St. James, July 25th, 1511.

It can be seen from Plate 8 that the strategic centre of Malacca was the bridge across the river. If the Portuguese could capture this bridge, the Malacca armed forces would be divided and could then be dealt with separately. The first Portuguese attack was therefore made against both ends of this bridge, and after fierce resistance these objectives were taken. However the Portuguese were so exhausted by their success that they were not strong enough to consolidate their position before nightfall. Therefore, after they had set fire to the houses along the banks of the river, d'Albuquerque gave orders to withdraw. The first Portuguese attack was something of a failure for they had had to retire to their ships.

There now followed a lull during which the Sultan and his forces carried on strengthening the city's defences while the Portuguese prepared plans for a second assault. This came on August 10th when the attackers were again successful in capturing the bridge, and this time were also successful in holding it. The capture of the bridge had been carried out by means of a ship which had been floated up the river on the high tide. From this position the Portuguese had swarmed on to the bridge and set up previously prepared barricades. While all this was going on, the Portuguese ships were bombarding the city from the harbour.

The third phase of the battle took place almost two weeks after the Portuguese had established themselves ashore. This pause benefited no one except the Portuguese, for while d'Albuquerque was able to build up his strength, that of the Sultan was being weakened by desertions from his side. Many of the foreign merchants were trying to come to terms with the Portuguese, while the Sultan's forces did not gain anything in strength by waiting for the next Portuguese attack. Perhaps it would have been far better for the defenders' morale if they had taken the offensive and tried to drive the Portuguese back to their ships.

The final attack, when it came on August 24th, was therefore very quickly successful, for the morale of the defenders had wasted away. By the same evening the city of Malacca was captured and given over to organized looting by d'Albuquerque's men. The foreign inhabitants of Malacca quickly came to terms with the Portuguese in return for permission to continue trading. Those from Java and the Indians who were Hindus were among the first to do so, for from the outset they had not been enthusiastic supporters of the Malacca government. There was in fact little resistance in the city itself once it was learnt that the Sultan had escaped southwards with his close followers. It had taken the Portuguese just about a month to capture the city; the fighting had been long drawn out because of the smallness of the Portuguese attacking force in relation to the size of the city. The attackers had been finally successful because throughout the fighting they had retained the initiative while the Malacca government had been on the defensive. One gains the impression that, despite the warnings of the Gujerati merchants, the Malacca authorities always underestimated the seriousness of the Portuguese threat. They seemed to take refuge in the belief that if they prevented the Portuguese from capturing Malacca, they would eventually go away. Thus many opportunities for offensive action were lost. Finally once it became apparent that even the policy of defence was not being successful, the disaffected elements in the population soon deserted the Malacca government.

EXERCISES

1 Why did the Portuguese sail from Europe to Asia in the early fifteenth century?

2 Explain why the Portuguese came to Malacca and why they were successful in capturing it.

3 What advantages and disadvantages did both sides have in the battle for Malacca in 1511?

4 Write short notes on:
Prince Henry the Navigator, Albuquerque, Vasco da Gama.

4
MALAYSIA IN THE SIXTEENTH CENTURY

THE capture of Malacca by the Portuguese in 1511 was to bring about many changes in the balance of power in South-East Asia. In the first place the loss of its capital was to be a fatal blow to the Malacca Empire which virtually ceased to exist as such after 1511. It was to have successor states in the Peninsula—for example, the Johore Empire and Perak—but Malayan control over large parts of the Archipelago, especially the east coast of Sumatra was gone forever. In fact, although the Johore Empire continued to have pretensions to succeed to the former position of Malacca it did not have the vigour to rival that of Acheh for it was this state in northern Sumatra that was the most dynamic in the sixteenth century.

A glance at a map will illustrate the historical geography of Malaysia during this period. The Johore Empire laid claim to the greater part of the Peninsula and the neighbouring islands. Off the coast of Johore lived the former Sultan of Malacca, Mahmud, and he had established his capital on the island of Bintan, south of Singapore. In the north-west of the Peninsula, there was to be established, by one of his sons, a new state, Perak, while the other son succeeded him in Johore. Brunei still remained in independent control of the north and western parts of Borneo but areas covering present-day Kedah, Kelantan and Trengganu were subject to Siamese suzerainty. Finally the city of Malacca was occupied by the Portuguese, a foreign element in an otherwise Malay world, with the nearest other Portuguese base at Goa in India. The Portuguese thus occupied a very limited area, though the occupation of this particular area had far-reaching effects.

However, the long-term effects of the Portuguese on the Malay world in general and on the Peninsula in particular must not be exaggerated. Although they had a considerable effect on the trade of the area by taking it out of one country's hands and putting it into their own, they nevertheless had little influence on the majority of the inhabitants of Malaysia. The Portuguese were confined almost entirely to Malacca and came into contact with very few of the inhabitants of the Peninsula with whom they were not on very friendly terms. The main contact between the Portuguese and the Malays was generally warlike, for the former were either trying to gain control of trade or spread Christianity. Neither of these activities was likely to cause them to win friends among Muslims who also wanted control of the area's trade. In fact, as the Portuguese never made up their minds whether having a trading monopoly was more important than fighting Muslims on behalf of Christianity, they were never able to do either successfully. Most of the rulers of the South-East Asian states seldom trusted the Portuguese, and friendly relations were never really established.

The main exception in this respect was Brunei which reached the height of its power and splendour in the sixteenth century. This was one state with which the Portuguese had almost no quarrel; rather the reverse, for the Portuguese were impressed by what they saw of Brunei, and friendly relations were established with the signing of a commercial treaty in 1526.

The first contemporary descriptions which we have of Brunei are those of an Italian, Pigafetta, who was a member of Magellan's Spanish expedition round the world. He visited Brunei in 1521 during the reign of Sultan Bulkeiah, perhaps the most famous of Brunei's rulers and also known as Nakoda Ragam. While he was Sultan, Brunei made many conquests and claimed sovereignty over the whole of Borneo, the Sulu Archipelago and the southern part of the Philippines; Manila was captured and paid tribute to Brunei. Pigafetta and his companions were impressed, just as the Portuguese were to be, by the highly civilized court of the fifth Brunei Sultan. The royal palace was surrounded by a brick wall on which were mounted fifty-six cannons while inside the building the visitors saw an abundance of silk brocade hangings and gold and silver tableware. The city was large, Pigafetta estimated 25,000 households, with all the houses on stilts above the water except those of the Sultan and the chiefs. There was a well-established system of government and a wealthy ruling class.

Brunei was better as a friend than as an enemy to the Portuguese for its port was useful as a stopping place between Malacca and the Moluccas, and between Malacca and Macau. By 1530 trade was re-established between Malacca and Brunei and a Portuguese trading factory had been set up. The Portuguese also found Brunei useful for the purchase of Chinese 'cash' or currency for there were a number of resident Chinese merchants in the city carrying on trade

FROM PREHISTORY TO THE STRAITS SETTLEMENTS

Diggers at work in the floor of the Great Cave at Niah. They have dug to a depth of nearly ten feet

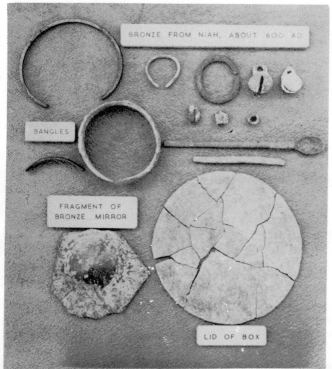

Bronze-age finds from Niah

MUZIUM NEGARA. MALA

The reconstructed Indian temple, the Chandi Bukit Batu Pahat at Merbok, Kedah, shows Indian contact during early centuries A.D. The pictures show the reconstructed temple and its model

MUZIUM NEGARA MALAYSIA

The Trengganu Stone which suggests that Islam may have been known on the east coast of Malaysia as early as the fourteenth century.

MANSELL COLLECTION

Henry the Navigator

Vasco da Gama

A Famosa

Afonso d'Albuquerque

St. Francis Xavier

Tomb and altar of St. Francis Xavier

MANSELL COLLECTION

ALAYAN BRANCH, ROYAL ASIATIC SOCIETY

Malacca, about 1665

ALAYAN BRANCH, ROYAL ASIATIC SOCIETY

Portuguese-Dutch battle off Malacca

Philip II

Batavia, *c.* 1665

Jan Pieterzoon Coen

THE CITTY OF BATAVIA

Dutch fort at Pangkor

A Bugis vessel and sword

MALAYAN HISTORICAL SOCIETY

Bunga Emas, the symbolic gift of flowers made of gold sent as tribute to the King of Siam by the Sultans of Kelantan, Trengganu, Pahang, Perak and Kedah

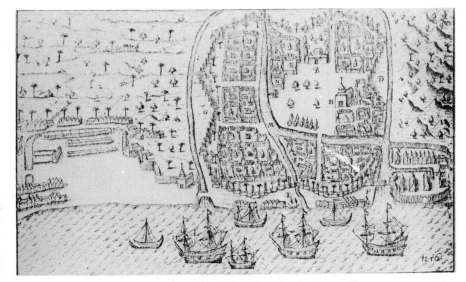

Bantam, where the British held a trading post until 1682

MALAYAN BRANCH. ROYAL ASIATIC SOCIETY

Founding of the British Settlement of Penang

Penang, from the sea, showing a Chinese junk and an East Indiaman

Sir Stamford Raffles

FABER AND FABER

NATIONAL MUSEUM. SINGAPORE

Treaty of 1819 between the Johore Sultanate and the British

Singapore in the 1830's

Singapore viewed from Fort Canning *c.* 1846

UNIVERSITY OF MALAYA PRESS

A view of the Court House built in the early 1930s. The growth of such institutions helped traders for their dealings could be regulated by law.

UNIVERSITY OF MALAYA PRESS

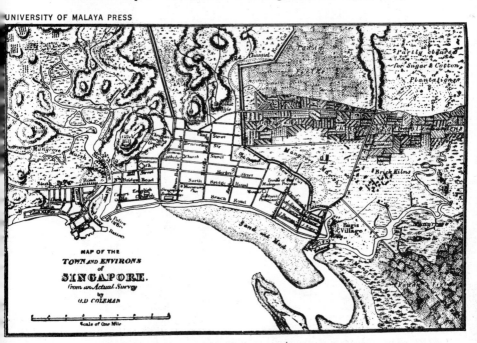

A map of Singapore of the 1830s. Note the extent of mangrove marshes and the existence of paddy fields and sugar and cotton plantations.

NATIONAL ARCHIVES. SINGAPORE

The Unknown Immigrants — seen here are representatives of the three major races. The Chinese girls are in traditional costumes, the Indians are shown as traders and the Malays are represented by a cultural group.

between Brunei and south China, and Brunei and Patani. Portuguese captains newly appointed to the Moluccas would pay a courtesy call on the Sultan on the way to their new post and the Portuguese were even able to build a centre for Catholic missionaries.

While Brunei maintained friendly relations with Portugal her contacts with Spain were not so amicable. During the sixteenth century the Spaniards spread their influence to the Philippines and were gradually pushing southwards. Spanish attempts to coerce Brunei were generally not successful, though a Spanish expedition was able to capture Brunei in 1577. But despite this and further expeditions in 1588 and 1645 the Spaniards were never able to exert a permanent influence over the sultan, though in the seventeenth century they would have dearly liked to have been able to do so, in order to suppress the piratical activities of some of his nominal subjects.

However, Brunei did not become involved in the long drawn out conflict between the Portuguese and the rest of the Malay world. Brunei was able to maintain her independence in the sixteenth century and was little affected by these newcomers to the Malaysian Archipelago.

Portuguese influence in Malaysia generally, apart from Malacca, has been negligible. Few of the Peninsula's inhabitants were converted to Christianity and few traded with the Portuguese if they could trade with someone else. It is also important to remember that Portugal's position and influence in Asia depended not upon the acquisition of territory but upon sea power. Trade was developed not by conquering lands but by conquering seas; it was sea power which forged the links between Portugal's chain of fortresses. It was only within those fortresses, like Goa, Malacca and Macao, that any sort of permanent Portuguese influence was established in the form of churches and a Christian element in the population.

MALACCA UNDER THE PORTUGUESE

The sixteenth-century history of west Malaysia can be described as a triangular contest for supremacy between Johore, Acheh and the Portuguese who were based on Malacca. The contest was mainly over the control of trade, for therein lay wealth; in fact to begin with none of the powers was particularly interested in the conquest of territory for conquest's sake, but all were interested in the possession of Malacca, the key to the region's trade. The fact that the Portuguese were able to keep possession of the city throughout the century was due to the strength of the fortress which they had built there and to the fact that Johore and Acheh were generally as jealous of each other as they were of the Portuguese. Nevertheless the Portuguese had to spend a great deal of their time defending their position against attacks from the other two.

The Portuguese had captured Malacca to gain control of the collecting centre of the spice trade and also in order to build a fortress. We have seen that in the eyes of d'Albuquerque, Portuguese trade depended upon the establishment of adequate bases along the routes of trade. Thus no sooner had the city been taken in 1511 than d'Albuquerque set to work building the fortress. It was built at the mouth of the Malacca River on the right bank, close enough to the sea and the river to be able to be kept supplied by ships. This was *A Famosa*, a fortress which was so strongly constructed that it was able to withstand all assaults until the Dutch attack of 1641. It was perhaps the first stone building to be constructed in the city. Later the fortifications were extended so that, as the century progressed, a fortified city grew up on the same side of the river as *A Famosa*. Inside the fortifications the Portuguese built a cathedral as well as three churches, two hospitals, and a school attached to one of the churches.

But the most important task facing d'Albuquerque was the re-establishment of Malacca as a trading centre, for unless he was successful in persuading the former merchants to return to the city, its future as a centre of trade was most uncertain. In this task he was at first partly successful; the merchants who had been opposed to the Sultanate, for example, the Chinese and the Hindus, quickly returned. Furthermore the former vassal states of Malacca, Kampar and Java, and also Brunei, soon established friendly relations with the Portuguese.

Expeditions were sent to discover the Molucca Islands, the actual source of the spice which was the mainstay of trade. The agreements made there enabled the Portuguese to obtain a monopoly and to close the spice trade to the merchants of the Middle East. D'Albuquerque himself did not stay in Malacca long after the fortress had been built for he considered that it was time that he returned to Goa. Before leaving he established the basis of Portuguese administration which during the following century gradually came to consist of the important offices which will be described below.

The most influential man in Malacca was the Captain or Governor, who was usually a nobleman appointed by the King of Portugal for a term of three years. He was paid a salary but the money thus obtained was small in relation to the profit to be made from commerce. The Captain was advised by a council consisting of the Chief Justice, the Mayor and the Bishop. Also important was the Captain-General who had command of all the armed forces in the city. He was appointed to his post by the Viceroy in Goa, who also appointed another leading member of the administration, the Chief Justice. The three Malay offices of Bendahara, Temenggong and Shahbandar were kept in existence and were filled by Malacca residents. The holder of the first office virtually controlled all the foreigners who came to Malacca, and he had both civil and criminal jurisdiction over them. The Temenggong dealt with all the Malays who came to Malacca to trade, while the Shahbandar received those who were envoys or visitors to the city. Also appointed were *capitans* who were leading men chosen to look after the interests of their own people and who were similar to headmen or community representatives. It is important to remember that the Portuguese in Malacca were servants of the king, in fact civil servants, rather than employees of a trading company like the Dutch who came later. However they certainly took part in trade and made their profits from this rather than from their salaries. There were never very many Portuguese in the city; in fact six hundred was probably the maximum at any one time.

As has been said the primary purpose of this administration was to ensure the smooth running of Malacca so that it would still continue to be the centre of trade in the Malaysian Archipelago. However trade does not depend upon providing facilities alone; it is very much a two-way transaction; there must be those who sell as well as those who buy. The Portuguese intended to try to gain complete control of the spice trade, and in so doing it was only natural that they should antagonize others who wanted to share in the profits of this trade. Furthermore the religious fervour of the Portuguese, their determined Christianity, brought them into constant conflict with the Muslim inhabitants of the surrounding countries.

The trade system which the Portuguese established in Asia was most lucrative. From Goa, Indian cloth, especially cotton goods, would be taken to Malacca and there exchanged for spices. This cargo could then either be sent on to China and exchanged for silk and good or brought back to Goa ready to be shipped to Europe. From Asia to Europe the Portuguese would take spices, silk, and porcelain, all of which fetched high prices. For example, an amount of pepper bought in the East for the equivalent of $45 could be sold in Portugal for the equivalent of $1,800. Such were the profits to be made that the Crown's share of the proceeds was four times Portugal's internal revenue.

Malacca itself was a collecting centre for local trade. From Sumatra came pepper, gold, ivory and rice; from Java came other foods, rice, camphor and cloth. Tin was collected from Perak, while gold was sometimes imported from Siam.

The monopoly of this trade depended on command of the sea and the enforcement of this command was very much dependent on the Portuguese position in Malacca. The Malacca Straits was the main highway of East-West trade and the Portuguese tried to keep strict control of all competitors. All ships trading in the area had to obtain passes from the Portuguese, and all ships using the Straits had to put in at Malacca and pay duties on their cargo. Such an attempt at monopoly was not at all popular especially when the duties levied in Malacca depended on the arbitrary decision of each individual governor. A monopoly policy was almost impossible to enforce and attempts to do so aroused even more anti-Portuguese feeling. These two factors alone caused fewer ships to use Malacca; they began to go elsewhere, for example to Johore and Acheh, and the trade revenue of Malacca declined rapidly. The introduction in 1544 of a flat rate of 6 per cent. duty on all goods rather than an arbitrary charge fixed by the governor did encourage more use of port, and its prosperity continued to increase to the end of the century. However, Portugal's isolated garrisons were never really able to control the region's trade and, after the opening of trade with Japan in 1543 and acquisition of Macau in 1557, Malacca became more important as a strategic point to guard the sea route to the Far East.

As has been said the policy of making conversions to Christianity was another factor which militated against successful trade. Many missionary priests went to Asia from Portugal, the most famous of them being St. Francis Xavier, who was living in Malacca at the time of the Achinese attack on the city in 1547. He soon moved further east in an attempt to enter China. He was unsuccessful, for after visiting Japan he died on the small island of Sancian off the Chinese coast in 1533. His body was eventually brought to Malacca where it lay for a short time before being taken to Goa where it still remains today. Like many other missionaries, St. Francis often clashed with the Portuguese civil authorities who were more interested in trading profits than in missionary activities. The traders' desire for large profits often conflicted with the more humanitarian goals of the priests, and it was generally the former which won.

JOHORE AGAINST PORTUGUESE MALACCA

It has been said that with the exception of Brunei the Portuguese did not establish particularly friendly relations with the states of the Malaysian Archipelago because of their restrictive trade policy and because of their determination to spread Christianity. The state which had the most reason to dislike the Portuguese was, of course, Johore. This, the successor state to the Malacca Empire, was ruled by the last Malacca Sultan, Mahmud, and his descendants; during the whole period that the Portuguese were in Malacca, Johore never gave up the idea of trying to force them out of the city. In fact as late as 1641 Johore provided some assistance to the Dutch when the Portuguese were finally defeated.

After his flight from Malacca in 1511 Sultan Mahmud went first to Pahang; it is thought to what is now Pekan. From there he sent messages to the Emperor of China, asking for assistance to recover his throne. The Chinese ruler, however, sent back a discouraging reply saying that he himself was engaged in fighting the Tartars. He did not provide any assistance later, for when the Chinese merchants who had been in Malacca at the time of the Portuguese attack returned to China, they took with them such praiseworthy accounts of the Portuguese that when the Portuguese reached China they received a friendly reception. Sultan Mahmud therefore received no Chinese assistance and was dependent on his own resources. He was still nominally the ruler of all the Malay Peninsula up to the territory of Siam but he needed a new capital. He left Pahang to be nearer the centre of the Malay world, making a short stop on a tributary of the Johore River at Sayong Pinang. However this site was too far up the river to attract any trade. Sometime later, early in 1513, he decided to move to Bintan, one of the islands south of Singapore. There he re-established the Malacca court and from there he attempted to regain possession of Malacca.

Attacks were made by both land and sea and would probably have been successful if the Portuguese had not built their fortress. These attacks were made in 1515, 1516, and again in 1519 and almost always brought the city to the verge of famine. Johore returned to the attack again in 1523 and 1524 when the blockade of Malacca caused great hardship to the Portuguese. As Malacca was dependent on imported food the Sultan hoped to starve the Portuguese into surrender, for it was impossible to capture *A Famosa*. He came so near to succeeding in 1524 that the Portuguese decided on a counter-attack, and in 1526 they sent a fleet to Bintan. The fleet attacked and destroyed the Sultan's capital, and he was forced to move to Kampar in Sumatra where he died in 1528. Sultan Mahmud had not succeeded in recapturing Malacca but he had done a considerable amount of damage to Malacca's trade.

After his death Sultan Mahmud was not succeeded by his eldest son, the Raja Muda, but by a younger son who had the support of the Bendahara and the chiefs. The Raja Muda was forced to leave Kampar in haste and according to the *Sejarah Melayu* made his way first to Siak and then to Klang. In Klang he met a merchant who told him of the possibilities of establishing his court on the banks of the Perak River. Following this advice the Raja Muda set out for Perak with those followers who had come with him from Kampar. He had little difficulty in setting up the capital of a new state in the middle reaches of the river, and it was in these circumstances that a distinct and separate dynasty was established in Perak about the year 1529. The first ruler—the eldest son of the last Sultan of Malacca—took the name of Sultan Mudzaffar Shah.

Apart from one break in the male line of descent during the period of Achinese conquest, the Perak dynasty can trace its ancestry to the Malacca Sultanate. This explains the many examples of Malacca court procedure and Malacca titles such as Bendahara Laksamana, Temenggong, which still persist in Perak today.

The younger son, whose mother was Tun Mutahir's daughter took the title of Sultan Alauddin, and sometime in the 1530's he moved the capital of his state back to the mainland. The site chosen was on the banks of the Johore River in the vicinity of the present town of Kota Tinggi. Later in the 1540's when conditions became a little more settled the Sultan moved the capital further downstream to Johore Lâma, a site about ten miles from the mouth of the Johore River. From here Alauddin attempted to carry on the fight against Malacca's trade and shipping. In 1533 Johore made another actual attack on Malacca itself but again without success, for the fortress was impossible to capture.

ACHEH AGAINST JOHORE AND PORTUGUESE MALACCA

The political situation in Malaysia was now to be complicated by the arrival of a third power, Acheh. A state in the north of Sumatra, Acheh had been growing in strength since the early years of the century and especially after the Portuguese had captured Malacca. The establishment of the Portuguese in Malacca resulted in many of the merchants from the Middle East, especially the Muslims, using Acheh as their port of call in South-East Asia. In fact many Muslims had fled from Malacca to Acheh as well as to Brunei in 1511. This trade caused the inhabitants of Acheh to become richer and more powerful, so much so that they began to think of expansion. To this end Acheh made an attack on Malacca in 1537 but without success, though one result was to make the Johore Empire and its allies, for example Perak and Pahang, suspicious of this new intruder. This suspicion increased to such active dislike when the expansionist policies of Acheh included the conquest of a vassal state of Johore in Sumatra, that Johore and her allies together defeated the Achinese in a sea battle in 1539. The development of this enmity between Johore and Acheh was to be of great benefit to the Portuguese for it prevented their enemies from combining against them; for example, in 1547 the Achinese made a further attack on Malacca while the combined forces of Johore and her allies stood by and watched. When they saw that the Portuguese were victorious they sailed away and made no attempt to assist the Achinese. On the other hand in 1551 an unsuccessful attack on the fortress came from Johore, this time without Achinese assistance. Rivalry and war characterized sixteenth-century Malaysia; sometimes the Portuguese were on the defensive against the other powers, sometimes it was Johore which was being attacked. Between 1555 and 1563 conditions in Malacca itself were relatively peaceful. Conflict erupted again, however, in 1564 when the Achinese made a sudden attack on the Johore capital, at Johore Lama, destroying the town and capturing Sultan Alauddin who later died mysteriously in Acheh.

The succeeding Johore ruler was Sultan Mudzaffar Shah (1564-70), and during his reign and that of the following Sultan, Ali Jalla Abdul Jalil, Johore was able to recover a little of her strength because the Achinese turned their attention once again to Malacca. The city was attacked in 1568 by a large fleet and an army of twenty thousand men, but the Portuguese continued to hold out. There were further assaults in 1574 and 1575, but the Achinese could not take the fortress. However, alternative Achinese plans of territorial acquisition were soon to be tried against Johore rather than the Portuguese. Earlier the Achinese had built a fort in Perlis hoping to close the northern end of the Straits, and in 1575 they conquered the state of Perak, Johore's ally.

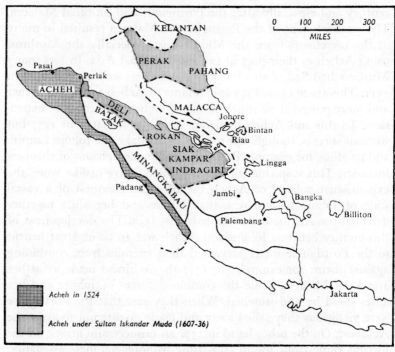

EXTENT OF ACHINESE CONQUESTS

The Achinese retained control over Perak for very nearly the next hundred years. The sultans were appointed with Achinese approval and although they were allowed to rule in Perak they could only do so under Achinese suzerainty. Any attempt at independence was stamped out, as for example in 1619 when the ruler was deposed by Acheh; and royal captives were usually kept as hostages at the Achinese court. It was not until the decline of Achinese power in the middle of the seventeenth century that Perak again became a really independent state.

The capture of Perak meant that the Achinese had now obtained a foothold on the Peninsula and were becoming continually more menacing to both Johore and the Portuguese. Although in 1582 these two states helped each other to defeat a further Achinese attack, this alliance was only temporary for in 1587 the Sultan of Johore, Ali Jalla Abdul Jalil (1570-97), himself decided to make another attempt to recapture Malacca. The city was besieged from both land and sea, but again the fortress held out. The Portuguese were able to repel the attackers and when reinforcements arrived from Goa they went over to the offensive themselves. A strong force was sent to attack Johore Lama and in the fierce battle which followed the Johore capital was razed to the ground. Even today excavations still lead to the discovery of articles lost at this time. The destruction was so complete that it took Johore ten years to recover from this set-back.

THE COMING OF THE DUTCH

It was during the reign of the next ruler of Johore, Sultan Alauddin (1597-1615), that an opportunity occurred to rebuild the fortunes of the royal house with the assistance of a powerful new ally, the Dutch. The arrival of the Dutch further complicated international relations in the Malay Archipelago, but as the Dutch were obviously rivals of the Portuguese, Johore looked upon them as possible allies for the recovery of Malacca. In 1602 a Dutch trading vessel had visited Kedah and in 1603 the new arrivals established a trading centre at Batu Sawar on the Johore River, this being the site of the Johore capital after the destruction of Johore Lama in 1587. Johore hoped to gain Dutch assistance, and the Dutch hoped also to make use of Johore in undermining the position of the Portuguese. The first important result of this 'marriage of convenience' was the 1606 treaty between the Sultan of Johore and the Dutch admiral, Matelief, by which Johore was to assist the Dutch to capture Malacca, after which the city would be kept by the Dutch while Johore could control the surrounding territory.

In 1606 the new allies proceeded to lay siege to Malacca, a siege that lasted three and a half months. The Portuguese defenders had been forced into a precarious position before the allied force of the Dutch and Johore withdrew on the approach of reinforcements from Goa. Although on this occasion they were unsuccessful the Dutch realized that complete blockade was the way to capture the city, for the defenders would then be starved into submission; and they saw that this could only be done by taking control of the sea away from the Portuguese. We shall see below how this in fact did happen, so that the Portuguese were driven out by the Dutch in 1641.

EXERCISES

1 Describe the importance of Brunei in the sixteenth century.
2 Write an account of the way in which the Portuguese administered Malacca.
3 How did the Portuguese eventually lose control in Malacca?
4 Write short notes on:
   A Famosa, St. Francis Xavier, Johore Lama.

5
SEVENTEENTH-CENTURY MALAYSIA

THE sixteenth century had been one of the most eventful in Malaysia's history for it had seen the advent of the Portuguese, the break-up of the Malacca Empire and the rise of states like Acheh, which previously had been no rival to the Malacca Sultanate. And as the century progressed it became obvious to the Johore Sultan that he was not the only ruler who desired the removal of the Portuguese from Malacca; he had a most dangerous rival in the Sultan of Acheh. We have seen how at the end of the century the ruler of Malaysia's largest state, Johore, had come to terms with the Dutch in an attempt to strike at Malacca before the Achinese were successful. The combined attack in 1606 had been a failure and, disappointed with his Dutch allies, the changeable Sultan Alauddin turned away from the alliance. This fickleness was to lose him assistance when he most needed it, especially in the face of renewed Achinese aggression.

In 1612, Sultan Iskandar Muda, also known as Mahkota Alam, became the ruler of Acheh, and he was to become perhaps the most famous of all Achinese rulers. Throughout the sixteenth century Acheh had been growing in power and wealth as its trade had increased. It had made numerous attacks on the key trading centre, Malacca, and it had brought the Malaysian state of Perak under its control. But during the reign of Mahkota Alam, from 1612 to 1636, many more conquests were to be made. His primary object was the capture of Malacca, for it had become obvious that Portuguese strength was declining while a new rival had appeared on the scene, namely, the Dutch. Acheh had to capture Malacca before the Dutch did.

Firstly, however, other potential rivals would have to be eliminated, especially Acheh's old enemy, Johore. The first attacks was made on the Johore capital, Batu Sawar, in 1613. Although Johore was defeated, the Achinese were not able to capture the Sultan, who escaped to Bintan where he died sometime after 1615. The Achinese installed his half-brother, Abdullah, as Sultan with an Achinese princess as his bride. For a time he stayed on at Batu Sawar but because of further Achinese expeditions this place was considered to be rather vulnerable. In 1617 the Achinese defeated Pahang, and the Johore ruler thought it safer to move from Batu Sawar to Lingga, an island south of Singapore. However this move was not to save him from attack, for the Achinese, resenting the independent attitude he was taking, especially by abandoning his Achinese wife, attacked the ruler of Johore again in 1623. He was forced to flee from Lingga and died soon afterwards. His successor had no fixed capital and was to remain away from the mainland until the decline of Acheh later in the century. Johore itself became in effect a vassal state of Mahkota Alam. By this victory Mahkota Alam had virtually succeeded in conquering the whole of the Peninsula including even the Siamese vassal state of Kedah. Pahang had been captured in 1617 and Kedah in 1621, while Achinese control had been more strictly imposed on Perak when the sixth Sultan was deposed in 1619. There only remained the Portuguese in Malacca.

Malacca's position had become increasingly precarious, for the city was now surrounded by Achinese-controlled states on land and was being blockaded by Achinese fleets at sea. Mahkota Alam decided to make the actual attack in 1629. He arrived off the Malacca coast with 20,000 men transported in a fleet of over 200 ships. Landing in the suburbs the Achinese attacked St. John's Hill and after hard fighting they took the strategic position of Bukit China. It was at this point that the timely arrival of reinforcements enabled the garrison of the city to launch a counter-attack which was successful in disrupting the attackers. Now on the offensive, the Portuguese caused the Achinese such heavy casualties that they were forced to withdraw and the city had a further respite.

This was to be the last full-scale Achinese descent on the Malay Peninsula. It took the north Sumatran state sometime to recover from the losses suffered at Malacca, and in 1636 Sultan Iskandar Muda (Mahkota Alam) died. He was succeeded by Sultan Iskandar Thani who was also interested in Achinese expansion but he died too soon (1641) to be able to carry out further conquests. The following four Achinese rulers were women. As a result Acheh's aggressive intentions declined as did her influence in the Peninsula. In fact it was from this period of Acheh's relative weakness in the middle of the seventeenth century that Perak began to regain its independent status.

1641 is thus an eventful year in Malaysian history. Not only does it see the ending of the Achinese menace, but there also occurs the final siege of Malacca, and the capture of the city by the Dutch. At the same time as the Portuguese were driven out of Malaysia the Johore capital returned to the mainland for the first time since 1623.

THE DUTCH IN ASIA

We must now examine the reasons for the arrival of these new Europeans, the Dutch, in the region of South-East Asia. It was these new arrivals who were to take the place of the Portuguese, not only in Malaysia but more especially in the islands which we now call Indonesia.

The Dutch, like the Portuguese, came from a small country in western Europe. In the middle of the sixteenth century Holland was not self-governing but was ruled by Spain. Europe at this time was bitterly divided over matters of religion, and as a result of the Reformation the Christian states of Europe had become either supporters of the new Christianity or the upholders of the old tradition. The former were called Protestants, while the latter came to be called Roman Catholics because they recognized the Pope in Rome as the head of the church. The Dutch were Protestants, while their rulers, the Spanish, were perhaps the most important supporters of the Roman Catholic cause. Religious rivalry led to many wars in Europe in the sixteenth and early seventeenth centuries, and the religious differences between the Dutch and the Spanish only strengthened the desire of the Dutch to throw off Spanish control. While the Dutch wished to throw off the control of Spain, the Spanish wished to stamp out the Protestantism of the Dutch. As a result, in the second half of the sixteenth century, there were frequent Dutch rebellions against Spanish rule.

The Portuguese became involved in this Dutch-Spanish quarrel in 1580 when Spain absorbed Portugal, and the two countries came to be ruled by one king. The Dutch were a sea-faring people and also possessed considerable business expertise. They knew that the best way of striking at Spain was by attacking her trade. They were encouraged in their outlook when in 1594 Philip II of Spain closed the Portuguese port of Lisbon to the Dutch. Up to this time the Dutch had gained a reputation for themselves as the 'cargo-carriers' of Europe. Their ships distributed goods all over the continent and they had built up a lucrative trade distributing the spices which the Portuguese had brought from the East. The Portuguese had been content to bring the spices *to* Europe while the Dutch looked after the distribution *in* Europe. Philip's action, which was aimed at striking at the wealth of Holland, was a definite threat to Dutch prosperity. But instead of coming to terms with Spain, they determined to go East and obtain the spices for themselves, thus bypassing Lisbon altogether. After 1580 the Portuguese possessions overseas and her trading ventures became fair prizes in the Dutch war against Spain.

The Dutch took advantage of Portuguese weakness in the East, and it is rather ironic that it was the Portuguese who were to suffer much more than the Spanish from the Dutch-Spanish rivalry. However, union with Spain was not the only reason for the decline of Portugal in the face of competition. For almost a century the Portuguese had had little competition in their Eastern trade. As a result their administration had become slack and corrupt and their defence forces had become relatively inefficient. Furthermore Portuguese interests were strung out along the sea routes to the East and because of this her strength was dispersed. The retention of these Portuguese fortresses depended upon sea power, the sea power which had originally brought the Portuguese command of the sea in competition with Eastern fleets. But the upkeep of these fortresses needed large fleets and heavy expenditure of resources and men. Portugal was not a country of great reserves, her population was only about one and a half million, and her economy had become seriously overstrained by the tasks which she had undertaken overseas. For example, as well as the Eastern trade, she had also established an empire in Brazil. The union with Spain involved her in defensive operations which she could not adequately undertake, and her naval forces were to prove no match for the Dutch.

In the East the Portuguese were threatened by growing Muslim strength, for the Portuguese had made no attempt to come to terms with Islam. An early sign of this was the siege of Goa in 1569-71 by an alliance of Muslim princes from central India; and only desperate and skilful defence enabled the Portuguese to hold out. As the years passed in the sixteenth century, more and more of India came under Muslim control and thus the Portuguese had even fewer friends, for they made no efforts to obtain Hindu allies. In the Malaysian Archipelago too the same trend was noticeable; in Java there had arisen two powerful sultanates, Bantam and Mataram. These Muslim states had begun to develop the Sunda Straits as an alternative trade route in order to bypass Portuguese Malacca.

DUTCH POLICY AND PRACTICE

The Dutch had decided that they must obtain spices from the

East themselves, for they could no longer use the Portuguese as middlemen. But when the Dutch decided to enter this trade they did it in a most organized manner, for they established the United East India Company. Their expeditions to the East were not to be made in a haphazard manner but, on the contrary, were to be supported by well organized capital resources. Sir Francis Drake's voyage round the world in 1577 had shown that it was perfectly possible for countries other than Portugal to make long distance voyages. His ability to sail through East Asia had also illustrated the weakness of the Portuguese position. Holland, however, was the country which was to take fullest advantage of the new possibilities. Furthermore, although the first expedition in 1596 was not entirely successful and profitable, the Dutch were astute enough to sign a treaty in 1596 with the Sultan of Bantam, who controlled the Sunda Straits.

More trading expeditions soon followed and because the Dutch did not mix religion or piracy with their commerce they became formidable rivals to the Portuguese for they did not find it too difficult to conclude commercial agreements with Muslim rulers. The first persons to benefit were the rulers of the spice islands who were now able to raise their prices because of competition. It was partly to prevent the Dutch competing among themselves that the government decided in 1602 to join together all the companies taking part in the Eastern trade. The government formed the United East India Company which carried out the new trade policy with vigour and success.

In 1609 peace was made between Spain and Holland which had won its independence; and the Dutch could now concentrate their energies on the Eastern trading expeditions. The first rivals to be removed were the English whose own recently established East India Company proved to be no match for that of the Dutch. This was eventually accomplished after the English trading post at Amboina was destroyed in 1623.[1] The Dutch had already decided that, although they had obtained their first foothold in South-East Asia by being competitors to the Portuguese. the best way to succeed was to remove any other competitors and establish their own monopoly over the trade of the area. This was to be done by obtaining possession of key points in the Archipelago, making fortresses into strongholds and establishing Dutch administration.

The man who was largely responsible for the success of this policy

[1] Although the English retained trading stations at Banjermasin until 1651, Jambi until 1679 and Bantam until 1682.

was Jan Pieterszoon Coen who became the Dutch Governor-General in 1618. He established Batavia, close to the Sunda Straits, in northern Java as the centre of Dutch influence. This was the first step leading to the Dutch empire in the East Indies, and was a fatal blow to Malacca and Malaysian trade. Batavia quickly overshadowed Malacca, for it had an extremely good geographical position. Ships could sail direct to Batavia from the Cape of Good Hope via the Sunda Straits, bypassing Malacca and ignoring the Portuguese. At this particular latitude ships could use the permanent trade winds and not the changeable monsoons, while use of the Sunda Straits also made shorter the route to China and Japan. The general plan of Coen was to make Batavia the central market for inter-Asian trade, and the collecting centre for exports to Europe. A centralized monopoly was the easiest to protect and it was the enforcement of this monopoly which led to the acquisition of territory or the establishment of protectorates—in the Banda Islands in 1621, Amboina in 1605, Ternate in 1683, Maccassar in 1667, Mataram in 1682 and Bantam in 1602. Generally only the port towns were ruled directly, other territory being controlled by a system of alliances. The exceptions were the spice-producing areas of Amboina and the Banda Islands which were actually administered by the Dutch. Coen also showed that of even greater importance than the Asia-Europe trade was the inter-Asian trade. He decided that it should be Dutch policy to control this, for herein also lay much wealth. If they were to obtain this wealth the Dutch decided that they had to have a monopoly of all trade in the Indonesian-Malaysian area.

THE CAPTURE OF MALACCA

With the steady growth of Batavia, the trade of Malacca showed a further decline. Not only did the Dutch attract trade to Batavia but they also prevented ships going to Malacca—and the Portuguese had few friends on whom they could rely as allies. The fall of Malacca was inevitable for, as soon as the Dutch showed their superiority at sea—for example in a sea battle at Bantam in 1601 and with the capture of a Portuguese ship at the mouth of the Johore River in 1603—assistance for the Portuguese melted away. These victories greatly impressed the rulers of the Malay states, for, until this time, Portuguese sea power had been thought invincible.

We have seen that although until about 1636 Acheh was the main expansionist power in Malaysia, it was during this period that the Dutch were busy establishing their position in the eastern part of the Archipelago. Although Malacca was not vital to Dutch power it did nevertheless constitute a threat to the establishment of a monopoly as long as the city remained in the possession of another country. Thus once the Dutch had consolidated their control over the spice islands the attack on Malacca became inevitable.

In 1639 the Dutch authorities in Batavia made an agreement with the ruler of Johore, Sultan Abdul Jalil Shah II, whereby Johore would assist in the projected attack on Malacca. Now that Mahkota Alam was dead, Johore was able to reassert its independence from Acheh and was willing to assist the Dutch in removing the Portuguese. With these preparations made, and on the order of Van Diemen, the Governor-General of Batavia, the Dutch forces began the long final siege of Portuguese Malacca in June 1640. The attacking forces commanded by Adrian Anthonisz began by blockading and bombarding the city from the sea. After two months the Johore forces arrived off the port and the Dutch commander ordered the landings to be made on the northern side of the town. The suburbs were quickly taken and the defenders withdrew into the fortress hoping that reinforcements would arrive to break the blockade. Instead of pressing home the attack while the Portuguese were in retreat, the Dutch decided to resort to a full scale siege and as a result the action continued until January 1641. Despite dreadful shortages of food within the fortress, the Portuguese kept up a steady defence, but the longer the siege lasted so the casualties due to disease increased. Plague, malaria and dysentery struck at both defenders and attackers, and more casualties were caused in this way than by the actual fighting. The Dutch had landed with 800 men but, despite reinforcements, by the time the final assault took place in January 1641 there remained only 650. After hard fighting the fortress was finally taken and the Dutch reported that only 400 defenders remained alive. This time the Portuguese had received no reinforcements from their other bases and they had been completely blockaded. After holding out for over five months they were finally forced to capitulate. *A Famosa* had been taken at last, the Dutch were now masters of Malacca, the last important rival European outpost had been eliminated.

The great days of Malacca were now over. Although during the latter decades of Portuguese rule in the seventeenth century its trade and importance had declined continuously, Malacca had nevertheless retained a great deal of its old importance as a trading centre even if only as a competitive alternative to Batavia. But now that it was in the hands of those who also possessed Batavia there was little likelihood of the Dutch tolerating a rival to their capital. In fact the Dutch had captured Malacca not to use it themselves, but to prevent it being used by anyone else. Once they possessed the city it lost its main importance. And so, although the Dutch were to hold Malacca for over a century and a half, the influence which they had on the inhabitants of the Peninsula was possibly even less than that of the Portuguese.

DUTCH TRADE POLICY

However, even though Malacca was never again to experience the importance which she had had in the fifteenth and the sixteenth centuries, the city did not suddenly become of no significance. The Dutch continued to use Malacca as a link in their chain of administration and today Dutch buildings can still be seen in the town. But it was only a link in the chain of Dutch possessions, and not the most valuable link. Batavia was of primary importance, for that city lay in the centre of the Archipelago, much nearer to the source of the spices than Malacca which was now 'on the outside'. The Dutch use of the Sunda Straits only served to emphasize the distance of Malacca from the centre of trade. The Dutch were to use Malacca rather as the subsidiary collecting point for their commerce with the Malay Peninsula and Sumatra and also as their administrative outpost in the Malacca Straits for the enforcement of their monopoly.

The trading profits of the Dutch came from their ability to 'buy cheap and sell dear'—and the ability to do this in the spice trade was a result of the monopoly system which they set up. The Dutch set out to exclude all competitors from the trade in spices so that they became the only suppliers of these goods in Europe. As they were the only traders buying the spices in the East they were able to offer low purchasing prices because, if the producer did not sell to the Dutch, he could not sell to anyone else. The spices were bought cheaply and when they reached Europe they were sold for very high prices since no one but the Dutch could supply Europe's needs. Thus the Dutch were able to charge pretty well what they wished. In this way the Netherlands was able to make enormous profits and the seventeenth century became the 'golden age' of the Dutch.

The Dutch were able to enforce this monopoly while they had command of the sea. They were able to exclude traders from other nations, whether Indian or English, and the few who were allowed to trade in South-East Asia had to obtain permits from the Dutch authorities. Producers were forced to sell to them at very low prices, and it is little wonder that this policy of monopoly was to bring the Dutch many enemies. Unlike the Portuguese, the merchants from the Netherlands were not very interested in making conversions to Christianity—but even though religion did not make many enemies for them, the system of monopoly did.

Malacca therefore became the outpost from which the Dutch attempted to control the entry of traders via the Malacca Straits. It can be described as the headquarters of the Dutch preventive service, that is, of the Dutch ships whose duty was to prevent the Malay states trading with Dutch competitors. Dutch interest in the states of the Malay Peninsula was therefore largely restrictive and was virtually confined to the states on the west coast who were the producers of trading commodities. The most important of these commodities was tin, and, even in the seventeenth century, the most important exporter was Perak.

During the first three or four decades of the seventeenth century Perak was, as we have said, under the control of the Achinese and almost all her tin exports were guaranteed to Achinese sponsored traders. In 1639 the Dutch made a contract with Acheh by which they would purchase all Perak's tin production, but soon after this date the power of Acheh began to decline and the contract could not be enforced on Perak. The Sultan naturally preferred the tin to be sold on the open market rather than to one customer, for, if it was sold openly, a higher price would be obtained. Thus the Dutch found that although they established a trading agency in 1641 at the mouth of the Perak River so that they could make their monopoly purchases, tin continued to be sold to other buyers.

The seventeenth century was to see repeated attempts by the Dutch to obtain a monopoly of Perak's tin exports and equally repeated attempts by Perak to find alternative customers from Acheh and from India. In 1650 the Dutch opened another trading factory at the mouth of the Perak River but in the following year it was attacked by Perak raiders and the occupants killed. In 1653 the Dutch made a treaty with Perak and rebuilt the factory which this time lasted until 1663. But they were still not able to enforce a monopoly, for the tin products were also being taken overland from the Kinta valley and exported from the port which is now Lumut, as well as by means of the Kinta and Perak rivers. Probably because they wished to try to blockade both exits from Perak, the Dutch in 1670 built a fort on the island of Pangkor. This fort, the remains of which can still be seen today, had a garrison of about 60 men. The Dutch occupation lasted for twenty years until in 1690 there was an attack by the local Malays under Panglima Kulup. The fort was captured by the attackers and was abandoned by the Dutch until the middle of the next century.

The Dutch were never able to bring the Perak trade entirely under their control during the seventeenth century although they persisted in their attempts to do so. Dutch attempts to establish the same kind of control in Kedah were even less successful, for Kedah lay too far north from the administrative centre of Malacca. Although Siam was nominally the overlord of Kedah her control was largely ineffective. Thus in 1641 the Dutch made a treaty directly with the Sultan of Kedah by which he agreed to sell all the tin exported through his state to the Dutch. This promise was never kept, for Kedah's geographical position made trade with the Achinese, Indians and Arabs extremely easy and very difficult for the Dutch to prevent. The only part of Malaysia outside Malacca where the Dutch established any territorial administration was in the district of Naning, and this was adjacent to Malacca. During the period of the Portuguese occupation of the port, Naning had been looked upon as a vassal state. The Dutch considered that they had inherited this overlordship and intended to use the territory as a supplier of food for Malacca, which was not itself self-sufficient. The inhabitants of Naning were Minangkabau who had originally come from Sumatra. They were not at all willing to be food suppliers for the Dutch, and, under their chiefs, were not very co-operative. This state of friction continued until 1679 when the Dutch in Malacca decided to interfere directly and appoint chiefs who were willing to co-operate; as a result Naning came to be, for all practical purposes, under Dutch control.

Thus although the Dutch occupied Malacca until the end of the eighteenth century, Malacca itself was never of paramount importance to them. Their main concentration was on the island of Java and the islands further east which were the producers of spices. Later when inter-Asian trade was of equal importance to the trade between Asia and Europe, Batavia was geographically in a much more advantageous position. Malacca ceased to be the leading port in South-East Asia because the city was smothered by Dutch control.

To finish this survey of Malaya in the seventeenth century we must now turn from the Dutch and the states with which they had direct dealings in order to see what was taking place in the other parts of Malaysia, especially Johore and Brunei.

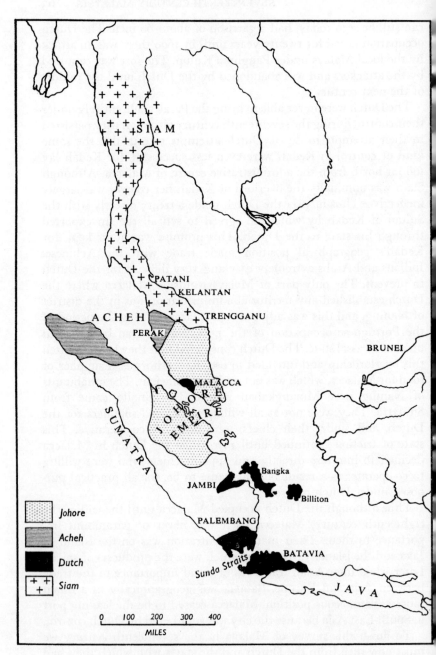

SOUTH-EAST ASIA, c. 1680

THE JOHORE EMPIRE

It will be remembered that the Sultan of Johore, Abdul Jalil, had returned to the mainland in the same year, 1641, that the Dutch had, with his assistance, captured Malacca from the Portuguese. Released from Achinese control, the state of Johore was now able to regain some of its former importance as long as its activities did not clash with Dutch interests. The Dutch themselves were only interested in the states of the Malay Peninsula in so far as these states were involved in exports. Thus the Dutch had little interest in preventing the kingdom of Johore from re-establishing its control over Pahang and the territory inland from Malacca around Klang and Sungei Ujong. The Sultan also exercised some control over various states in Sumatra, for example Rokan, Siak, Kampar and Bengkalis. However it was one of his allies in Sumatra. Jambi, that was to be the main cause of Johore's decline, towards the end of the century .

Sultan Abdul Jalil Shah was ruler of Johore from 1623 until 1677, a long reign, and he himself was aged ninety when he died. As has been said, the influence of Johore in Malaysia increased after the capital was rebuilt on the Johore River at Batu Sawar in 1641. It again became a trading centre collecting imports from all the out-lying areas of the Sultan's domain, from Sumatra as well as from the Peninsula. Pepper was an important product of the Sumatran states and although most of the important exports were sold to the Dutch, other merchants, for example from China and India, traded at Johore when, as it were, the Dutch were 'not looking'. It seemed as though the revival of Johore would result in her regaining a permanent place of importance in South-East Asia when a quarrel with Jambi suddenly led to her downfall. Johore was not as strong as she seemed.

The quarrel arose over a marriage. The Raja Muda was engaged to marry a daughter of the Sultan of Jambi, but instead he changed his mind and married the daughter of the Laksamana of Johore. The Sultan of Jambi refused to be put off by a series of excuses and looked upon this action as an insult to himself and his state. The result was an expedition from Jambi which in 1673 attacked and destroyed the Johore capital at Batu Sawar. The Sultan himself managed to escape to Pahang but over two thousand prisoners were taken by the attackers.

Sultan Abdul Jalil died in 1677 and was succeeded by his nephew, Ibrahim, who established his capital on the island of Riau and remained there for the whole period of his reign. Short of resources and trained men, Sultan Ibrahim was forced to engage mercenary troops to assist him in driving away the invaders who had come from Jambi. The mercenaries whom he engaged were Bugis from the Celebes Islands, in the eastern part of the Archipelago. Renowned as excellent sailors and soldiers, these Bugis under the command of Daeng Mangika accomplished this particular task, but once they had visited the Peninsula they were not so willing to return home. This introduction of Bugis mercenaries was to have far-reaching effects on Malaysian affairs in the eighteenth century.

Johore's obvious weakness after the attack by Jambi caused many of her vassal states to drift away from her control, especially the Minangkabau peoples both in Siak and Sungei Ujong. Sultan Ibrahim's insistence on remaining at Riau did not help him to assert his influence in the Peninsula; furthermore the fact that the Johore ruler had had to call in Bugis mercenaries lowered his prestige.

In 1685 Sultan Ibrahim died; it is said that he was poisoned by three of his wives. He was succeeded by his son, Mahmud, who was still under age, and while he remained in Riau, was very much under the influence of the Laksamana who was also his mother's father and who was the actual ruler of Johore. This did not please the other important chiefs, especially the Bendahara who lived on the mainland. Thus when the boy-king's grandfather, the Laksamana, died in 1688, the Bendahara had the capital moved back to Kota Tinggi on the Johore River.

From 1688 the main influence in Johore's government was the Bendahara—a position of traditional influence, for the holder of this office was considered to be the most important chief in the state. In fact it was also tradition that if the sultan's family could produce no male heir, then the succession would pass to the Bendahara. This was to happen very soon.

When Mahmud did come of age it was quickly seen that he was going to be a most unsuitable sultan. Not only was he a pervert, but he was also mentally unstable and, more especially, sadistic. On one occasion, when given a present of a pair of new pistols, he insisted on trying them out by shooting a man in the shoulder. He was the kind of ruler easily dominated by advisers but at the same time inclined to do things which his advisers could not stop. His madness and general peculiarity made him more and more unpopular until the chiefs of the Bendahara's following decided on his removal and in 1699 he was assassinated. With the death of Sultan Mahmud II the Johore descendants of the Malacca royal family came to an end thus also the direct connexion between Johore and the Malacca Sultanate. The eighteenth century was to open with the first ruler of a new dynasty generally referred to as the *Bendahara Sultans*. When Sultan Mahmud was killed he had no heirs, and so the succession, as was the custom, passed to the major chief, the Bendahara. This family was related on the female side to the old Bendahara of the Malacca Sultanate, and the new ruler's name was Abdul Jalil.

However the line of descent from Malacca had not died out completely, for the Perak royal family was still very much in existence and under the extended rule of Sultan Mahmud Iskandar Shah (1654-1720) the dynasty had once again become much stronger, after the long period of Achinese domination. Perak had had continual friction with the Dutch over the question of exporting tin, but generally the Sultan had been able to maintain his independent position, selling to the Dutch and also selling to others when he wished.

Brunei's political strength and influence had begun to lessen in the seventeenth century and this decline in importance was increased as the Dutch spread to the islands of the archipelago. Between 1650 and 1720 the Dutch had friendly relations with Brunei largely because Brunei was of little interest to them. The Dutch considered that north-west Borneo, far from the centre of trade, had no economic or strategic value. The Dutch policy of trade monopoly diverted legitimate trade away from Brunei and the inhabitants turned to something else, piracy. By the early part of the eighteenth century Brunei town had degenerated into a pirate base, few merchants went there and trade with China was down to seven junks a year. Brunei became the disposal centre for the cargoes captured by the Sea Dyak and Lanun pirates; it became a centre of lawlessness and gradually as the century progressed the sultan was less and less able to control the chiefs. It was this decline in the sultan's power of control which caused the disintegration of the state of Brunei in the next century.

The seventeenth century closed with the political situation in Malaysia showing considerable changes from that of a hundred years earlier. The Portuguese had been replaced by Dutch as the main foreign element. The Achinese had withdrawn but they were soon to be replaced by the Bugis as the most important South-East Asian threat to Malaysia's peace. Johore and Perak were both independent states as they had been in 1600, but the area in which they were situated became less important in both trade and diplomacy as a result of the decline in the importance of Malacca after 1641. Brunei, too, was still independent but had declined considerably from the splendour she had earlier attained. Malaysia itself receded from the world stage during the time that the Dutch East India Company controlled the commerce of the area. And, although the eighteenth century saw the arrival of the vigorous Bugis from the Celebes, Malaysia's political development changed little until the last two decades of the eighteenth century.

EXERCISES

1 Describe the influence which Acheh had on the Malay Peninsula in the period 1612-99.

2 Explain why it was the Dutch rather than Acheh or Johore who captured Malacca in 1641.

3 Describe Dutch trading policies in South-East Asia in the seventeenth century.

4 Write an account of the difficulties facing the Johore Empire in the seventeenth century.

5 Write short notes on:
Mahkota Alam, Pangkor island, the Bendehara Sultans, the siege of Malacca 1640-1.

6

EIGHTEENTH-CENTURY MALAYSIA
AND THE BUGIS

WE have read in the previous chapter how Sultan Ibrahim of Johore obtained Bugis mercenary assistance against Jambi and how these mercenaries had been extremely useful to him. The Bugis were to return to Malaysia again to provide mercenary help to the Johore Sultan in another struggle against invaders from Sumatra. On their first visit to Johore the Bugis had realized how useful had been their help. The second occasion was to confirm their indispensability. As it turned out, the Bugis decided that the Malay Peninsula would be able to provide them with plenty of opportunities for war and wealth, settlement and prosperity. Once they had been brought to Malaysia the Bugis were to prove extremely difficult to dislodge. They were to attack and ravage both Kedah and Perak, they were to cause considerable discomfort to the Dutch, they were to become the rulers of the Johore Empire, in practice if not in name, and finally they were to establish sufficient settlements in the area which is now Selangor for them to establish their own sultanate. Thus it can be seen that a great part of Malaysia's history in the eighteenth century has to do with the Bugis.

The Bugis came from the Celebes Islands in the eastern part of the Indonesian Archipelago, and more especially they set sail from the port of Macassar. They were extremely skilful sailors, and the fleets became well known among the traders of South-East Asia; Francis Light called them the best merchants among the eastern islands. The Bugis were also fierce warriors; this, plus skilful seamanship, enabled their adventurous instincts to be given full scope. From the middle of the seventeenth century, the Bugis fleets had begun to appear in many parts of the Archipelago. They were willing to hire themselves out as mercenary soldiers, but they were also interested in places for settlements, particularly areas that were sparsely populated. Thus, they came to the area (now known as Selangor) lying between the Perak River and the Minangkabau settlements south of Klang and in Sungei Ujong. By 1681 the Bugis had begun to settle in moderately small numbers in this area.

RIVALRY IN THE JOHORE SULTANATE

It was the misfortunes of the Johore Sultanate which gave the Bugis the greatest opportunity to transfer their centre of interest from the outlying area of Selangor to the more central position of Riau. In 1718 Johore became involved in a quarrel with the Minang-kabau state of Siak in Sumatra. The cause of the quarrel is obscure but it may well have been due to the tyrannical rule of Johore by the Sultan's younger brother who had by this time taken over the government of the state. The Sultan's brother was very much a supporter of the Bugis faction at the Johore court and the increasing influence of the Bugis was resented by the other Malay chiefs, especially those who had always opposed the Bendahara family. These same chiefs gained the support of Raja Kechil, a Sumatran prince who now became involved in the affairs of the Johore Empire. The sultan, Abdul Jalil, had been considered a good ruler. He is described by an English sea captain, Alexander Hamilton, as 'a prince of great moderation and justice who governed well while he held the government in his own hands'.[1]

However by 1718 Sultan Abdul Jalil no longer 'held the government in his own hands' and Raja Kechil, the ruler of Siak, descended on the Johore capital with his forces to drive out the Sultan's brother and his supporters. The Johore forces were largely unprepared for this attack—in fact many in Johore were already supporters of the attacking army—and Raja Kechil had little difficulty in overcoming the forces of the Sultan's brother. The Sultan himself, after first submitting to the invader, very soon fled to Pahang where he was assassinated on Raja Kechil's orders. The latter now proclaimed himself Sultan of Johore, a position which he maintained for four years. In 1719 he moved the capital of his newly acquired kingdom from the Johore River to Riau, for he considered the latter easier to defend. This move is noteworthy because the capital of Johore never returned to the vicinity of the Johore River, an area which it had occupied off and on since 1540. The capital was to remain away from the mainland until the final disintegration of the Johore

---

[1] It is interesting that in 1703 the Sultan offered to give the island of Singapore to Hamilton who replied he did not want it himself but that the island would be a suitable place for a trading company to have a colony. The reason which he gave was very similar to that which later appealed to Raffles, namely that Singapore lay in the centre of the trade of South-East Asia.

Empire in 1812. Raja Kechil himself was probably little more than an adventurer, and as it turned out he was not strong enough to stem the rising tide of Bugis influence. However he was the last Malay leader to put up strong resistance to the encroachments of these warriors from the Celebes. In the end he failed, especially in the Malay Peninsula, which very soon was dominated by the Bugis. In 1722 Raja Kechil himself was driven out of Riau and forced back to Siak by Bugis attacks which were aimed at re-establishing a Bugis-supported ruler of Johore. From Siak, Raja Kechil continued the fight until the 1740's, appearing here and there in the Straits to help those who were resisting the Bugis. In 1724 he was active in Kedah where a campaign against the Bugis lasted for two years. He died finally in 1745, the upholder of a lost cause.

THE GROWING INFLUENCE OF THE BUGIS

Meanwhile in 1722 the Bugis had returned in strength to Johore, and their forces led by Daeng Perani and his four brothers—Daeng Merambun, Daeng Merewah, Daeng Chelak and Daeng Kemboja—put back on the throne the eldest son of the Bendahara Sultan. His title was Sultan Sulaiman Badr al-Alam Shah but he was sultan only in name, as were to be all his descendants during the remainder of the eighteenth century. The Bugis placed him on the throne as a puppet ruler, as someone who would obtain the allegiance of the Johore population. They also appointed a Bugis under-King, or *Yang di-Pertuan Muda*, who was in fact the real power behind the throne. All power was in the hands of the Bugis, but they ruled through the figurehead of the Sultan. The first under-King was Daeng Merewah, but although the Bugis were now in control of Johore they were not particularly interested in the state itself. They were far more interested in using it as their base for operations against the other states of the Peninsula. Johore itself they largely neglected, and it was during the Bugis period of dominance that the Johore Empire finally broke up.

Already established in Selangor, the Bugis first of all turned their attention to the northern states on the west coast—Kedah and then Perak—and it has been noted earlier that the Bugis began their campaigns by intervening in Kedah to defeat Raja Kechil. The fighting in Kedah lasted almost two years (1724-6), and the damage to Kedah's trade was enormous. Daeng Perani himself was killed during the fighting but ultimately the Bugis were successful. The first under-King Daeng Merewah, died in 1728, and he was succeeded in that office by his brother, Daeng Chelak. Perak was now in the unfortunate position of being between the Bugis in Selangor and their Minangkabau-supported rivals in Kedah. Neither side was content to have Perak remain a buffer state, but both wished to ensure that their rivals were not established there. As a result Perak was invaded from both quarters. One such Bugis invasion occurred in 1742 and on this occasion, due to quarrels among the Perak chiefs, some of them joined the Bugis. This group was able to capture the regalia, and the Raja Muda was made an alternative sultan. For about eight years afterwards there were two sultans in Perak and as a result of Bugis interference the state was sharply divided.

Another important event took place in 1742. This was the creation of Raja Lumu, a son of Daeng Chelak, as the first Sultan of Selangor. This illustrates the permanence of Bugis settlement in the Peninsula and also the strength of their position, for they were able to establish a new dynasty. Selangor was for some years in the 1740's the centre of their influence and when Daeng Kemboja became the third under-King in 1745 he did not even bother to go to Riau to obtain the Sultan of Johore's approval. This lack of interest in Johore and its dependencies by the Bugis encouraged the Sultan to think about a more independent line of action in liaison with the Dutch.

The Dutch were naturally becoming worried by the expansion of Bugis influence in the Peninsula for they saw this as a threat to their trade monopoly. The fighting spirit of the Bugis made them formidable rivals. Realizing that the Dutch were also suffering from Bugis activity, the Johore Sultan was encouraged to approach them with a view to obtaining Dutch assistance against the under-King. A treaty was in fact made between Johore and the Dutch authorities in 1745, by which, in return for their help, the Dutch were to be given Siak, though it is doubtful whether Johore's control over Siak was strong enough to make this cession definitely possible.

Despite a further treaty between Johore and the Dutch in 1755 the results of the fighting which took place between the Bugis and the Dutch were inconclusive. Johore gained only a temporary respite from the Bugis when the under-King moved to the island of Lingga. However Dutch attempts to aid the Sultan of Johore were sufficient to widen the breach between themselves and the Bugis. In 1756, after the Dutch had made an all-day attack on Lingga, the Bugis landed outside Malacca causing considerable damage in the suburbs, and it was some months before they were driven back into Selangor. The Dutch, although they were successful in preventing the fall of Malacca, began to lose interest in their support of Johore and by 1758 the Bugis were back again in Riau. The following year Sultan Sulaiman of Johore died, leaving his state much smaller than he had found it.

The Johore Empire had by this time virtually ceased to exist; Siak now had its own ruler as did Selangor. The area inland from Malacca was controlled by the Minangkabau inhabitants, Johore was hardly administered at all, and all that remained was Riau itself. The two succeeding sultans, Abdul Jalil and his son Ahmad, both died by 1761, and despite the protests of the Malay chiefs, the Bugis insisted on putting on the throne Mahmud, the infant grandson of Sultan Sulaiman who was one year old. It meant, of course that all administrative power now certainly lay with the under-King Daeng Kemboja, and the interests of Johore were completely subordinated to those of the Bugis. One result of this Bugis domination was the elimination of friction between the Malays and the Bugis and the removal, for the time being, of the Dutch excuse for interference. During the later 1760's and 1770's relations between the Bugis and the Dutch were fairly cordial, for the Dutch themselves were not able to maintain their own monopolistic position against other European rivals.

One of the most remarkable of the Bugis leaders came to the height of his eventful career at this time. His name was Raja Haji, and he became under-King himself when Daeng Kemboja died in 1777. Raja Haji was perhaps the most renowned of all the Bugis warrior captains; as Winstedt says 'the fighter whom every ruler wanted on his side'. He was the son of Daeng Chelak, the second under-King and the brother of Raja Lumu, the first sultan of Selangor—and he might be described as the Bugis mercenary *par excellence*. His early life was in fact spent in fighting in various parts of the Malaysian Archipelago on behalf of an assortment of rulers—Jambi, Indragiri and Pontianak in Borneo, amongst others. He was by the 1760's the principal assistant of Daeng Kemboja, with the title of *To' Klana*.

It was to Kedah that Raja Haji first turned his attention at this time—Kedah being far enough north to be free from much Dutch control and fairly free from the Bugis as well. On his way to Kedah with his brother, the Sultan of Selangor, Raja Haji spent some time on a visit to Perak where he demanded that the Sultan of Perak's niece should marry his brother. The Bugis then continued on to Kedah to demand the payment of money which they said was due from the 1724 campaign.

Kedah in these circumstances could expect little help from her overlord, Siam. The Siamese authorities had not in fact been very interested in their Malaysian vassals for some time. The north Malaysian states were very far from the Siamese capital, and the Siamese exerted little direct influence. Furthermore, during the 1760's Siam was again involved in another round of her long drawn-out quarrel with Burma, and at this stage the Burmese were the more successful. In 1767 the Burmese army had attacked and destroyed the Siamese capital of Ayuthia, situated about forty-five miles from the mouth of the Chao Phraya River. The Siamese were in the process of moving their capital further down stream; in fact they were establishing the beginnings of what is now Bangkok. As a result in the late 1760's and early 1770's the Siamese had little interest in the troubles of Kedah. It was because of this that the Sultan became fairly desperate for help against the marauding Bugis; and he approached an English trader named Francis Light to see whether the English would provide some assistance. This was in 1771. In return for such assistance the Sultan of Kedah was willing to allow the English to establish a trading settlement in Kedah. However the English East India Company did not wish to become involved in the political affairs of the Peninsula by aiding Kedah against the Selangor Bugis, and the Sultan of Kedah withdrew his offer. We shall see below how this first offer to the English was in fact to lead later to something much more definite, the establishment of a British settlement in Penang.

DUTCH CONFLICT WITH THE BUGIS

On this occasion Kedah, without any outside assistance, was defeated by Raja Haji who then retired from the area of the Peninsula to continue his mercenary career in Borneo. It was while he was there that Raja Haji heard of the death of Daeng Kemboja, the under-King, in 1777. He returned immediately and had himself installed as the fourth under-King in place of Daeng Kemboja's son, Raja Ali. Raja Haji established himself in Riau and for some time the new under-King lived on good terms with the Dutch, although he himself was a determined and ambitious man and Dutch power was obviously declining. Then in 1782 a quarrel between the Dutch and Raja Haji broke out over the capture of an English opium ship at Riau: despite an agreement the Dutch refused to give the Bugis any share of the proceeds from the capture. Relations had already become strained because the Bugis were using Riau as a centre for exporting smuggled tin from the Peninsula. As a result the Bugis began to attack Dutch shipping in the Straits of Malacca.

This provoked the Dutch to send a fleet to capture Raja Haji's capital at Riau, but the Bugis put up strong resistance and the Dutch attack was not successful. The Bugis now quickly switched to the offensive, and in 1784 their combined armies laid siege to Malacca. Raja Haji and his men from Riau landed to the south of the city while the Sultan of Selangor and his forces attacked Malacca from the north.

The Bugis siege of Malacca lasted from January 7th to June 24th, 1784, a long siege in which the Bugis were finally unsuccessful because they were unable to capture the fortress. Such failure, as we have seen in the past, always decided the battle. To capture a fortress as strong as that at Malacca the attackers needed two things on their side: either siege guns powerful enough to breach the walls of the fort or command of the sea to enable the garrison to be starved into submission. When the Dutch captured Malacca they had command of the sea; when the Portuguese captured the city they had overwhelming fire power from their ships. But the Bugis in 1784 had neither advantage; they could not breach the walls; neither could they prevent the arrival of Dutch reinforcements.

These reinforcements from Batavia arrived just in time, and they included quite a large number of soldiers. They landed outside the city and as a result the Bugis were caught between the new arrivals and the defenders in the fortress. In the battle which followed, the fighting was very fierce and the Dutch lost over seventy men. Raja Haji himself was killed while the battle was at its height and after that disaster the Bugis began to retreat, having lost nearly five hundred men. Once again the city had been saved by *A Famosa*.

Now that their reinforcements had arrived, the Dutch took the offensive. The same fleet that had come to Malacca from Batavia now moved against the Bugis stronghold in Selangor. Here the Dutch were again successful and the Sultan was forced to escape to Pahang. The Dutch fleet then turned southward against Riau itself where the Bugis fleet was defeated. As a result the Bugis were expelled from the Johore Empire which now came to be protected by the Dutch. By agreement (1785) they were to have a garrison in Riau as well as a Resident. In effect the Sultan of Johore had merely exchanged one overlord for another, although under the new system he and his chiefs did have more control over the actual administration.

In the same year, 1785, the Sultan of Selangor, returning to his state, drove the Dutch out of Selangor with assistance from Pahang and regained possession of his territory. Soon afterwards he was in contact with the newly established English settlement in Penang to obtain further protection against the Dutch. While Selangor was successful in keeping the Dutch away from actual settlement and further interference, the same could not be said of Riau. In 1787 the Dutch took over almost the entire administration of the island and its immediate dependencies, the islands nearby. Administrative control by Johore over the mainland had virtually ceased to exist, and Sultan Mahmud was again no more than a puppet ruler. This was, naturally enough, a position which he did not like, so in the same year he encouraged Lanun pirates (from the southern part of the island of Mindanao) to attack Riau, and they drove away the Dutch garrison. However very soon he had to flee himself when the Lanuns left and the Dutch returned. He was now a wanderer without a capital, a ruler without a kingdom. Sultan Mahmud was to remain in this predicament until agreement was reached with the Dutch in 1795 that the Malays should return to Riau. As it happened, by the time arrangements had been made for this agreement, the Dutch were no longer in control of Malacca, and it was from the British that Sultan Mahmud finally recovered his island capital.

THE DECLINE OF THE BUGIS

The period of Malaysian history with which we have been dealing in this chapter was largely dominated by the Bugis, and the period itself comes to a fairly natural end in the mid-1780's rather than at the end of the century. The failure to capture Malacca, together with the defeats in Selangor and Riau, mark the decline of the Bugis influence in Malaysia. And although there was a Bugis under-King in Johore until the Empire finally disappeared, the Bugis 'golden age' was in fact over. It was the Dutch who finally brought the period of Bugis dominance to an end, but it was not the Dutch who were to benefit from their decline. Those who were to benefit were the new arrivals, the British, who had established a settlement on Pulau Pinang in 1786, and it was the English East India Company which was to replace both the Dutch and the Bugis in the nineteenth century.

The Bugis had left few positive results in Malaysia apart from the establishment of the Sultanate of Selangor. They were not very interested in politics and administration, but rather in wealth and adventure. Although they were immigrants as well as sailors and

merchants, they took little interest in the countries which they conquered. The Bugis by their neglect were largely responsible for the
break-up of the Johore Empire and the fragmentation of southern
Malaya. They were, of course, very interested in Selangor, the state
which they themselves had founded, but the other states of the
Peninsula were only important to the Bugis when they could be
used to further Bugis policy. In the long run Bugis political influence
in Johore was disastrous, for the interests of Johore were largely
neglected, so much so that the break-up of the Empire was presided
over by the Bugis under-King. We shall see in the following chapter
how the division of Johore was made permanent when the British
purchased the island of Singapore in 1819.

Although the Bugis had been the dominant influence in Malaysian affairs throughout the major part of the eighteenth century,
there were also large areas of the Peninsula where they were little
known and they paid little attention to the north-west coast of
Borneo. We have seen above how, on occasions, the Bugis had
attacked Kedah, a state that was nominally subject to Siam. However, during the middle of the century especially, Siamese interest
was largely concentrated on their conflict with Burma. Thus
although Kedah still remained under Siamese suzerainty, the Bugis
were able to interfere there. This policy was also followed in another
west-coast state, Perak, which found itself sandwiched between the
Bugis in Selangor and the Siamese-supported Kedah in the north
and therefore subjected to periodic pressure from the Bugis. The
other main group on the west coast was the Minangkabau in the
territory inland from Malacca—Naning, Sungei Ujong and Rembau. These Minangkabau settlers from Sumatra had been living in
these areas since the time of the Malacca Sultanate when they had
originally been Hindus. They had later become Muslims and
their inter-related tribes had established small states which owed
allegiance to the Sultan of Johore. In the seventeenth century the
Dutch in Malacca had taken over the state of Naning but the others
continued in allegiance to Johore. As a result, during the eighteenth
century they too came under Bugis domination and also suffered
periodic interference. The defeat of the Bugis in the mid-1780's
brought relief to the Minangkabau as to the other Malay states and
enabled these small tribal units to come together to form a loose
coalition—the forerunner of the Negri Sembilan—and because of
the decline of Johore this confederacy was established outside of
Johore's direct control.

KELANTAN, TRENGGANU AND PAHANG

On the east coast of Malaya the northern sultanates of Kelantan and Trengganu were in the same relation to Siam as was Kedah; that is, the rulers acknowledged Siamese suzerainty by sending the annual tribute of the *bunga emas* (the golden flowers). This was a symbolic gift of flowers made of gold signifying the allegiance of the donor, although the states themselves were usually left to look after their own affairs with very little supervision from Siam. Munshi Abdullah's account of his voyage to Kelantan gives an early nineteenth-century account of these two states, which, because of limited trading opportunities, were little visited by foreigners. It is not untrue to say that the east-coast states played little part in Malaysian history at this time. This was because they were nominally under Siamese suzerainty but was also because there was no trading reason why there should be much contact with the other states of the Peninsula.

The other east-coast state, Pahang, was still part of the Johore Empire but was the one part which was not dominated by the Bugis. It gradually became the most independent of the territories subject to the Bugis under-King and as the eighteenth century progressed Pahang's ties with Riau became less and less strong. Pahang itself was controlled by the Johore Bendahara and his family, and the Bendahara himself became virtually an independent ruler in the nineteenth century when the Johore Empire finally disappeared.

EXERCISES

1 Describe the activities of the Bugis in Malaya in the eighteenth century.

2 Account for the fact that the Bugis were unable to capture Malacca from the Dutch.

3 What was the position and status of Johore in the eighteenth century?

4 Assess the contribution of the Bugis to Malaysian history.

5 Write short notes on:
   Raja Kechil, Daeng Perani, the office of Yang di-Pertuan Muda, Raja Haji.

7

THE ESTABLISHMENT OF THE STRAITS SETTLEMENTS

THE political situation in the Malay Peninsula in the last fifteen years of the eighteenth century was one of disunity. In the north there was fairly loose Siamese control over the states of Kedah, Kelantan and Trengganu, although after the end of the Thai-Burmese wars in the 1770's this control began to be tightened up. Further southwards Perak was an independent state suffering sometimes from attacks from Kedah and sometimes from interference by the Bugis in Selangor. Selangor itself was an independent Bugis state. Further southwards again there were the Minangkabau states forming a loose confederation, and, at this period, virtually independent of each other and of Johore. Malacca was still held by the Dutch, and Pahang, though part of the Johore Empire, was controlled by the Bendahara (of Johore) and was rapidly becoming independent of the Johore Sultan's control. The Sultan of Johore also had little influence over the mainland area of Johore itself which, because he was living on the island of Riau, was dominated by another major official, the Temenggong. Finally in Riau itself the Sultan was under pressure on one side from the Dutch and on the other side from the Bugis. The strength of both the Bugis and Johore had declined in relation to that of the Dutch in the latter years of the century, but the Dutch East India Company itself also presented a false appearance of strength. Because of the payment of high dividends in Holland and because of corruption amongst its employees in the East, the Dutch Company's financial position had become very weak. Dutch involvement in the European wars of the 1790's proved to be the final disaster and the bankrupt Company came to an end in 1799.

This picture of a divided Malaysia was to be further complicated in the last quarter of the century by the fact that the British East India Company began to take an interest again in the Malaysian Archipelago; though to begin with it was Borneo rather than the Peninsula which aroused this interest.

The reader will remember that at the beginning of the seventeenth century both the English and the Dutch had begun trading ventures to Asia in order to obtain some share of the spice trade. It will also be remembered that Drake's circumnavigation of the world in 1557-9 had shown that Portuguese and Spanish control could be breached. As a result of this knowledge the Dutch and the English had sent trading ships to Asia and had established trading centres in the Malayan Archipelago. Of the two, the Dutch had been much the more successful for they had concentrated their resources in one company in order to eliminate rivalry amongst themselves and had obtained government support. The English had been much less well organized and eventually had found Dutch competition too much for them in South-East Asia. The English East India Company did not disappear entirely from South-East Asia after Amboina in 1623, as there was a trading post at Bantam until 1682. But thenceforth it concentrated on India itself, the latter's trade being considered more important than spices. The East India Company had an official monopoly of trade between England and the East, while trading ventures to South-East Asia from India were mainly in the hands of free-lance merchants based in India itself like Alexander Hamilton, the English captain, mentioned on page 70.

BRITISH TRADING INTERESTS IN EASTERN ASIA

English concentration in India eventually proved most fruitful and as a result of the Seven Years' War against her main rival, France, England had, by 1763, become the dominant European trading power in the subcontinent. A number of factors now caused that East India Company to show a new interest in South-East Asia. As has been said, the activities of the East India Company were largely concentrated on trade between Britain and India, with the trade in the area of South-East Asia (called 'the country trade') in the hands of merchants who were not directly associated with the Company but who nevertheless had their headquarters in India. However, there was one very vital trading contract which was firmly in the hands of the East India Company, and that was the trade with China, or more particularly the export of tea from China to Europe.

The China trade came to be of very great importance to the East India Company during the second half of the eighteenth century but it was also of very great importance to Britain itself. It was important in two ways: first for the profit it brought the Company and second for the revenue it brought the British Government by means of the tax on tea imports. In 1785, over sixteen million pounds weight of tea was imported into Britain; in 1787, over twenty million pounds; between 1823 and 1833 the tea imports averaged thirty million pounds a year. The British Government obtained a great deal of revenue from this trade and therefore the China trade came to be an extremely important and valuable part of Britain's interests in the East. It was also a temptation to the enemies of England.

Britain therefore became interested in Borneo in the second half of the eighteenth century mainly because of the China trade and it was largely because of this trade that the Straits Settlements were eventually established. However as will be seen below there were other additional reasons which led to the founding of Penang and Singapore; but the British settlement which was established earlier on the island of Balambangan in northern Borneo owed its existence to the fact that it was about the nearest landfall to south China. Britain wanted to have a settlement from which trade could be carried on with Chinese merchants who would be free from the restrictions which were imposed on trade with foreigners in Canton. Chinese merchants had long traded with Borneo and had even settled in Brunei and it was hoped that the prospect of free trade would attract them, and also traders from the archipelago, to the British settlement.

The investigations for the site of a trading post were carried out by Alexander Dalrymple, an employee of the East India Company. In 1761 he made a treaty with the Sultan of Sulu by which he gained permission to set up a factory in north Borneo. The fact that the treaty was made with Sulu and not with Brunei illustrates the decline of the latter sultanate and its loss of of control over the north-east coast. This first treaty with the Sultan of Sulu was confirmed in 1764 and 1769 but in fact the East India Company was never convinced of the usefulness of a settlement on the island of Balambangan. It was thought to be too far east to be able to attract any of the island trade and it had little use as a naval base from which the sea route between India and China could be protected. The island was occupied briefly on two occasions, 1773-5 and 1803-5, and then the settlement was allowed to lapse.

Britain was to continue her search for a suitable place in South-East Asia and the Company was to examine many other possible sites before a decision was made. The matter acquired some urgency when it became obvious that, although France had been defeated in India in 1763, she would try to recover her position at the earliest opportunity. Realizing where Britain's potential weakness lay, the East India Company, as early as 1763, gave instructions to look for a suitable site for a port on the eastern side of the Bay of Bengal.

During the north-east monsoon, from October to May, the eastern coast of India suffers from storms in much the same way as does the east coast of Malaysia. Today Malaysian fishermen cannot put to sea during the monsoon period, and similarly during the days of sailing ships, the British navy could not easily put to sea from the port of Madras at that time of year. The nearest sheltered port which the navy could use while protecting British merchant ships on the eastern route was Bombay. But this was too far away to be of much use for defensive purposes in the Bay of Bengal. Therefore any unfriendly power which had a port on the eastern side of the Bay of Bengal could cause havoc among British ships during the months of the north-east monsoon. From 1763 to 1783 the British looked at many possible places for a port: Acheh, Ujang Salang, the Nicobar Islands, the Andaman Islands, and Kedah. But no decision was made until after the set-backs which the British suffered during the War of American Independence. In this war the Americans were helped by the French and the Dutch and a French fleet commanded by an admiral named Suffren caused much damage to British shipping in the East during 1782 and 1783. The Dutch ports in the East Indies (now Indonesia) were closed to the British in time of war, and the need for a British port on the sea route to China became even more urgent. It was necessary to have a port usable during the north-east monsoon, a port which could be used to protect the China trade route from Britain's European rivals. These factors primarily affected the East India Company and the British Government. But one other factor appealed to the British and Indian merchants engaged in the 'country trade'; they also would have much to gain from the establishment of a British-controlled port which would enable them to break the Dutch monopoly of the South-East Asian trade.

These then are the three main reasons for the renewal of British interest in South-East Asia; first, the need for a naval base on the sheltered side of the Bay of Bengal; second, the need for a port along the China trade route which could be used for refitting, revictualling and protecting the merchant ships; and third, the need for a port which could be used by British and Indian merchants trying to expand their trade in the Malaysian Archipelago and more particularly to obtain tin for the East India Company to sell to China. The Straits Settlements later became the headquarters for these merchants. The primary impulse to establish a British port, then, was strategic and protective, but the fact that Penang was eventually chosen in 1786 was also due to the economic motives of a 'country trading captain', Francis Light, who had found an owner willing to sell a possible site.

Francis Light had earlier considered the establishment of a port in the region of Kedah, a state which he knew quite well and with whose ruler he was on friendly terms. In 1771 Light had written to the East India Company about the possibility of obtaining a trading site in the area of the Malacca Straits. He said that the Sultan of Kedah was willing to approve the establishment of a post in Kedah but that in return the Sultan wanted help against the Bugis from Selangor who, as we have seen, were causing trouble in his state. It will be remembered that Kedah was in fact under the general influence of Siam, whose King was the Sultan's overlord, but at this time Siam was in the process of recovering from the disastrous Burmese wars and had little help to spare for Kedah. It was in such circumstances that the Sultan looked for other sources of assistance. But in the 1770's the East India Company showed little or no interest in Light's proposal, and the matter seemed to have been forgotten.

THE ESTABLISHMENT OF PENANG

Interest in a base on the eastern side of the Bay of Bengal revived after the reverses suffered by the British during the War of American Independence. Light's earlier suggestion was remembered, and the country merchants who wanted to challenge the Dutch monopoly of the spice trade were enthusiastic supporters. This was in 1785, and Light himself was sent to open negotiations with the Sultan of Kedah. The Sultan eventually agreed by letter to allow the East India Company to establish a settlement on the island of Penang which the Company preferred to the mainland because it seemed easier to control. The conditions stipulated by the Sultan included compensation for Kedah's loss of trade, i.e., an annual payment of $30,000 and protection against the Sultan's enemies both from the interior and from the sea. The interior enemy was Siam, for the Sultan viewed with alarm the renewed interest of the Siamese Government in his state. There was little doubt that the Sultan would only be willing to cede Penang if he received protection in exchange, and Light had pointed this out to the authorities in India. Light therefore communicated the Sultan's conditions to his superiors who in the meanwhile authorized him to go ahead with the establishment of the settlement and appointed him as the first Superintendent.

Light landed on Pulau Pinang in July 1786, and on August 11th officially took possession of the island, which was largely uninhabited, in the name of the British Government. He also renamed it Prince of Wales Island, a name which never became very popular. As yet no official treaty had been signed between the Company and Kedah, and as it turned out, Light had obtained possession of the island under what amounted to false pretences. He had virtually promised to assist the Sultan of Kedah against Siam but in so doing had made a commitment which the Company was unwilling to honour. As the East India Company said in a letter to Light in January 1788 'the Governor-General in Council has already decided against any measures that may involve the Company in military operations against any of the Eastern princes'.

The Sultan was now determined to regain possession of the island for it seemed that he had given it away without receiving what he wanted in return, and in 1791 he assembled a fleet in the Prai River for the purpose of attacking Penang. Light took the initiative instead and attacked the Sultan's fleet before it had time to begin the offensive. The forces assembled by the Sultan of Kedah were defeated and the new settlement was preserved, for the Sultan made no further attempt at armed attack. Realizing that it was too late to retake Penang, the Sultan agreed to sign a definite treaty with the Company later the same year (1791). By this treaty the Company agreed to pay the Sultan the sum of $6,000 per year, but there was no mention of providing him with protection against Siam.

Light could now turn his attention to the consolidation of the new settlement. Penang was already a free port by a decision of the acting Governor General in India, MacPherson, in 1787. Light supported this status, writing to the Governor General in 1788 confirming that the only way Penang could prosper was through being a free port. This meant that there would be no tax on imports and exports. Only in this way, he said, could trade be attracted away from the Dutch. Until 1801 Penang was a free port, and its success in building up trade by this means provided the model which Raffles was later to follow in Singapore. By 1794 when he died Light had established the settlement of Penang on firm foundations, and its population had increased to 8,000, a population composed of many immigrant races: Chinese, Indians and Bugis amongst others. There is no doubt that the free-port facilities which Penang offered to this rapid increase in population, but the administration of the Settlement on the other hand did not obtain enough revenue to pay for its expenses. It had to receive financial assistance from the Government of India to meet the annual deficit. Despite the fact that the value of Penang's annual trade was $1½ million, the deficit on administration was about $700,000 per year. The government received little direct benefit from trade, and the officials themselves were more interested in trade than administration. Land was sold so cheaply that it was practically given away and there was little official development of the island. It was therefore decided in 1801 to introduce a 5 per cent. tax on imports and exports to raise revenue and to reduce the expense of Penang to the Indian government. Penang was thenceforth no longer a free port.

In the early days of the new settlement's life the East India Company was not entirely sure of the success of its acquisition. It was expensive and was bringing them little advantage. However, during the French Revolutionary War, Penang proved a useful base: for example, in 1795 when the British took over Malacca from the Dutch and in 1797 when an expedition was sent to capture Spanish-held Manila. Both Holland and Spain had been overrun by France during the French Revolutionary Wars and Britain wished to make sure that the French did not have the use of Dutch and Spanish possessions in the East. The expedition to Manila was able to obtain supplies at Penang on its voyage to the Philippines.

Penang had therefore proved useful and had increased its prospects of permanency; and in 1800 the East India Company bought from the Sultan of Kedah for $4,600 per year a strip of territory on the mainland opposite the island. The purpose of this acquisition (to be called Province Wellesley after the Governor-General of India) was twofold. In the first place it protected the harbour of Penang by giving the Company possession of both shores. Secondly it gave the Company land on which to grow food for the increasing population of the settlement. In the geographical circumstances such food could not be grown on the island. After the Siamese invasion of Kedah in 1821 the Province received a great increase in population, as many people in Kedah fled from the Siamese attack.

The permanent occupation of Penang was now assured, and the East India Company had great hopes for its expansion. Anticipating, rather prematurely, the settlement's increase in importance, the Company in 1805 created Penang the fourth Presidency of India (the others were Bombay, Madras and Calcutta). This made the settlement too important and burdened its administration with large numbers of expensive officials making it even less able to balance its budget.[1] Between 1805 and 1810 the Indian Government had great hopes of developing Penang as a naval base, but the timber available on the island was of little use for ship building, and in 1810 it was decided to use Trincomalee in Ceylon for this purpose.

During the period of the long drawn-out wars between Britain and France (1793-1815) Penang never really fulfilled the hopes which the Company had for it. The picture presented is one of disappointment after hopes had been raised. Nothing seemed to quite work out as expected. Free trade did not bring in revenue, the administration was expensive, it did not have the requisite materials for a successful naval base, and, during the war, the newly established coffee and pepper plantations on the island did not prosper. A further blow in 1811 was the capture of the Dutch possessions in Java by the British, for, instead of using Penang, it was now possible for British ships to use Batavia which was much more in the centre of South-East Asian trade. The Dutch for the time being were removed as competitors, but as a result the greater part of the region's trade still bypassed Penang.

The years 1811-16 were prosperous years for the country traders from India. The removal of the Dutch eliminated the rivals who had previously excluded almost all competition, but Penang which had been established as a trading settlement with the encouragement of these same country traders did not benefit. The country traders preferred to use Batavia, for geographically Penang lay only on the outskirts of the trade of the Indonesian Archipelago. It was in fact too far away from the spice islands and from the main centres of trade. This point is sharply illustrated after the establishment of another British settlement in Singapore in 1819. Singapore because of its geographical position began to prosper immediately while the comparative decline of Penang continued. Throughout the nineteenth century Penang was always less prosperous than Singapore because its trading opportunities were more limited.

While Penang was therefore something of a disappointment to the East India Company, Singapore was an almost instantaneous success. However before relating the circumstances leading to the establishment of Singapore we must first look at the second of the Peninsula settlements to come into British possession—Malacca.

THE BRITISH IN MALACCA

As has been mentioned earlier, the British occupied Malacca in

---

[1] One of the officials sent to Penang at this time in the junior position of Assistant Secretary was a young man named Stamford Raffles.

1795 during the War of the French Revolution. By the Treaty of The Hague (1795) between Holland and France, the former was reluctantly brought into war against Britain, and the French supposedly were able to have full use of Dutch naval bases and possessions around the world, for example the Cape of Good Hope, Ceylon and Java, as well as Malacca. In order to forestall French use of the bases, Britain came to an agreement with the Dutch Government-in-exile that Britain would take over various Dutch possessions for the duration of the war. It was in these circumstances that Malacca was occupied without resistance in 1795. The Malacca that the British acquired for the duration of the war was a town with a population of about 15,000, larger than the newly established Penang. As has been noted in previous chapters, the commercial importance of Malacca had declined while the town was in the possession of the Dutch, and its main use had become that of a 'guard post' for the enforcement of Dutch attempts to monopolize trade in the Archipelago. British occupation of Malacca was to be only temporary; the town was to be returned to the Dutch at the end of hostilities. However the British authorities in Penang did not look forward to the return of Dutch control. It would mean that the Dutch would try to reimpose their monopoly of trade, and Penang's hopes of becoming the centre of the Malaysian tin trade would be thwarted. The East India Company therefore began its administration of Malacca by planning its permanent decline. If the town was to be returned to the Dutch, it would be a town of almost no importance.

In 1795 Malacca had fallen into British hands easily, almost voluntarily, the first time the town had changed hands since 1641. Considering the number of times Malacca had successfully withstood siege after siege this was certainly a quiet exchange. However the significance of this easy acquisition was not lost on the East India Company for they realized that they would never have such an opportunity again; they realized that to capture Malacca from the Dutch would require stiff fighting. The Company therefore decided to remove Malacca's invulnerability by destroying the famous fortress which had for so long been the key to its successful defence. Therefore during the years 1806-7 Malacca's fortress was systematically destroyed. It is ironic that Malaysia's most famous building was in fact demolished without purpose because the British again occupied Malacca by peaceful means in 1824. The fortress took a long time to be destroyed and contemporary accounts in the *Hikayat Abdullah* relate that it was a very difficult job of demolition.

The destruction of *A Famosa* was the first step taken by the British to weaken Malacca. The second was a proposal to move the entire population to Penang so that when the Dutch returned they would find nothing but a derelict 'ghost' town. However, the proposal was easier to make than to carry out for it was very unlikely that the long-established inhabitants of Malacca would voluntarily give up their homes and move to another town. It was at this juncture, in 1808, that Stamford Raffles came to Malacca from Penang on holiday. He had become interested in Malay history and traditions, and this partly accounts for his interest in Malacca. He felt that Malacca was the historical centre of Malaysia and as such should be preserved rather than destroyed. Although unasked, he submitted a report to his superiors advocating the retention of the settlement. He put forward three reasons: firstly, if Britain gave up the settlement someone else would occupy it to the loss of Penang; secondly, Malacca itself was of historical importance and it did not cost money to administer; and finally, Britain had invited the population to remain there after the Dutch departure and therefore this pledge to the population should not be broken. His arguments were well received and as a result of his intercession Malacca was reprieved. The East India Company decided that no attempt would be made to transfer large numbers of the population and that Malacca should continue to be administered as a going concern.

In 1815 the Napoleonic wars in Europe came to an end and Britain's excuse for holding Dutch possessions in Asia ended. She no longer had any need to prevent the use of the possessions by France. As previously agreed by Britain, Holland's overseas territories were to be returned to her when the war was over. In these circumstances Malacca reverted to the Dutch although they did not occupy the town again until 1818. We shall see below, however, that Malacca was only to return to the Dutch for six years.

THE ESTABLISHMENT OF SINGAPORE

We must now turn to the third of the Straits Settlements, Singapore, but first of all a little must be said about the person who was primarily responsible for founding Singapore and whom we have already mentioned as the official who prevented the destruction of Malacca in 1808.

Thomas Stamford Raffles

Thomas Stamford Raffles was born in 1781 on board a ship captained by his father that happened at the time to be in the West Indies. He was brought up in England where he received an average education. At the age of about fifteen he obtained employment as a clerk in the London office of the East India Company. He soon attracted the attention of his superiors by his industry and ambition and was eventually selected to go to the East in the service of the Company. Thus (in 1805) at the age of twenty-four he was posted to Penang as one of the assistant secretaries in the government. Soon after his arrival in Penang he became a fluent Malay speaker; in fact he had begun to study the language on the voyage out from England. As a result he became the administration's expert in Malay and an interpreter to the government. He progressed from language to an interest in customs, history and culture, and it was while pursuing these interests that, as we have seen, Raffles went to Malacca in 1808. He had read about Malacca being the historical centre of Malay culture in the Peninsula, and he had gone there to collect manuscripts. He was astonished that the directors of the East India Company should consider the abandonment of a town of such historical importance and, as we have said, he considered that the Company also had an obligation towards the inhabitants. He outlined these views in a personal dispatch to the Company and at the same time mentioned the possibility of the extension of British influence to other parts of the Archipelago.

This dispatch of Raffles, not the usual thing to be submitted by a fairly junior employee of the Company, brought him to the notice of Lord Minto, the Governor-General of India under whose jurisdiction Penang and Malacca lay. Lord Minto was already considering the further reduction of other Dutch possessions in Eastern Asia after the capture of the Moluccas in 1808, and Raffles impressed him as one who knew more than was usual about the affairs of the Malayan world. Lord Minto was in fact seriously considering the capture of Java from the Dutch, for in 1810 Holland itself had been annexed by Napoleon. In 1810 Raffles was summoned to Calcutta. As a result of this visit Raffles was appointed the Governor-General's Agent to the Malay states with his headquarters in Malacca. From there he was to prepare the way for the invasion of Java. In this capacity Raffles obtained much detailed information about the affairs of the region. In 1811 Lord Minto called at Malacca with the British expedition en route to Java. He took Raffles with him and, after a campaign which proved reasonably easy, he appointed Raffles as Lieutenant-Governor of Java, at the age of thirty.

Raffles' term of service in Java was perhaps one of the most fruitful of his career and his stay in Java was to have considerable effect on the future course of Malaysian history. Raffles wanted the British government to keep possession of the island after the war although he knew that the East India Company would be reluctant to do so because of the expense involved. His administration therefore concentrated on making the government pay its way, something which the Dutch had not been able to do in the latter years of the eighteenth century. Raffles introduced many liberal reforms into Java particularly land reform, the abolition of feudal services and the freeing of trade. But he was not to remain long enough to see his plans mature to success and his administration still did not pay its way by the time he left.

However Raffles was the first British official to consider seriously challenging the Dutch position in the East Indies and even though as Lieutenant-Govenor of Java he realized that the island would be returned to the Dutch after the war, he attempted to establish British influence in Borneo. He considered that the Dutch had no claim to Borneo as they had no settlements there at the time that the British captured Java. In 1812 therefore he appointed a Resident to Banjermasin and in 1812-13 he sent expeditions against the pirates who were based on Sambas in the south-west of the island. He tried to reorganize the trade of the west coast in the face of pirate attacks by making agreements in 1813 with the rulers of Brunei, Pontianak and Banjermasin that trade would be restricted to these three ports which could then be protected. But all Raffles' efforts proved to be of no permanence after 1815 as Britain showed no interest in his plans for expansion; although it is true that the rapidity with which the Dutch moved back to displace the British in 1817-18 helped to convince the Governor-General in India of the necessity for the foundation of Singapore.

THE RETURN OF DUTCH POSSESSIONS

The reason for the return of the Dutch possessions in Eastern Asia in 1815 was almost entirely because of European considerations. Britain had in 1815 brought to a successful conclusion a war which she had been fighting against the French since 1793. At the peace conference in Vienna almost all the countries of Europe wished to make sure that France would never cause so much trouble again; this was one of the main aims of the Congress of Vienna. The British felt that France should not be surrounded by many weak states, for this might tempt her towards further aggression. Holland as one border state therefore had to be strong, and Britain considered that Holland would not be sufficiently strong without her overseas possessions. It was therefore to strengthen Holland's position in Europe that her possessions in east Java, the Moluccas and Malacca were returned to her. Furthermore as the British intended to keep the Cape of Good Hope and Ceylon which had also been captured from the Dutch, there was some embarrassment in London about keeping Java as well. Castlereagh, the English Foreign Secretary wrote, 'I still feel great doubts about the acquisition in sovereignty of so many Dutch colonies. I am sure our reputation on the continent is of more real moment to us than an acquisition thus made.' These decisions were naturally opposed by Raffles who was very much against seeing the re-imposition of the Dutch policy of monopoly in South-East Asia. But his protests weighed little with the British Government, and his supporter, Lord Minto, was no longer Governor-General in India. Thus Raffles' long-term plans for the establishment of British protection over the states of the Archipelago were discarded, and in 1816 he returned to England.

Raffles, now Sir Stamford Raffles, came back to the East again in 1817 as Lieutenant-Governor of Bencoolen, an insignificant British trading post on the west coast of Sumatra. From here he continued to plan for the extension of British influence in South-East Asia. British trade was likely to be completely excluded by the Dutch, who were not only re-imposing their monopoly policy but were extending it. He considered that Britain had to have a centrally located settlement. Before he had left England, Raffles had written to George Canning (the future Foreign Minister) suggesting Bangka or Bintan as suitable places, but the British Government had no wish to antagonize the Dutch by following Raffles' suggestions; and Raffles' attempts in Bencoolen to make treaties with the local rulers only produced reprimands from London. There is little doubt that Raffles had in mind the extension of British control over the whole of Sumatra. But this policy was vetoed in London. However ne was again to be fortunate in finding an influential supporter in the Governor-General in India, this time Lord Hastings. Raffles continued to bombard the Government of India with his suggestions and eventually he was again summoned to Calcutta in 1818 where he outlined his plans for establishing a British settlement to the south of the Malay Peninsula.

The Governor-General was impressed by the arguments put forward and gave Raffles permission to proceed with the establishment of such a settlement. Raffles left Calcutta towards the end of 1818 and proceeded first of all to Penang where he found that his plans for a rival settlement were not well received. He then set sail further south, going first to the Carimon Islands where he found

that there was no suitable harbour, and then to the island of Singapore where he landed on January 28th, 1819.

RAFFLES AND THE RULERS OF JOHORE

What did Raffles know about the island of Singapore? How could
he be sure that there was a possibility of establishing a British
settlement there? We must now return to the history of Johore and
to the point where we left the story in the previous chapter. Raffles
was well informed about Malay affairs, and there is little reason to
think that he was not in possession of the facts of recent Johore
history. In 1795 Sultan Mahmud had returned to Riau and established himself as the nominal ruler of what remained of the Johore
Empire. We saw in the last chapter that large parts of the Johore
Empire were no longer under his real control or even under the
control of the actual ruler of Johore, the Bugis under-King. In
theory Johore now consisted of the mainland area (roughly the
present states of Johore and Pahang) together with a number of
islands to the south, including Singapore, Riau and Lingga. The
capture of Malacca by the British had removed the Dutch influence
for the time being and permitted the Bugis to regain their old
position. Sultan Mahmud disliked the return of the Bugis for they
became the masters of his kingdom in place of the Dutch, and
eventually he moved away from Riau to Lingga where he lived in
semi-retirement.

It was at Lingga that Sultan Mahmud died in 1812, and his death
immediately provoked a crisis over the succession to the throne.
Nothing had been decided about the succession, for the matter was
somewhat complicated. The Sultan had had four wives; two of them
were royal, and two were commoners. Both the royal wives were
childless, but there were two sons by the other wives: the elder was
Tengku Hussein, the younger Tengku Abdul Rahman. Although
Sultan Mahmud had made no official pronouncement over the
succession it would seem that he intended his eldest son, Tengku
Hussein, to follow him to the throne, for he had arranged marriages
for him with relatives of the two major chiefs of the Johore Empire,
the Bendahara and the Temenggong. In fact Tengku Hussein was
with the Bendahara in Pahang when his father died in 1812.

In these circumstances, that is in the absence of the elder son, the
Bugis under-King decided to place the younger son, Tengku Abdul
Rahman, on the throne, probably feeling that the son with the
weaker claim would be more dependent on Bugis support. Tengku
Hussein claimed the throne with the support of the royal wives of

Sultan Mahmud, but there was little that he could do against the Bugis to assert his rights. When the Dutch returned to influence in South-East Asia, after 1815, they recognized the Bugis-selected Sultan and this recognition was also tacitly supported by the British in a treaty with the under-King in 1818. Meanwhile Tengku Hussein lived in lonely exile among the islands to the south of the Malay Peninsula.

These then were the facts almost certainly known to Raffles when he landed on Singapore island in 1819. He discovered immediately that there were no Dutch on the island, that it possessed a most suitable harbour and was in a very favourable geographical position. Also on the island was the Temenggong, the territorial chief of the southern part of the mainland and of the island itself. Raffles knew that he was in fact within the Dutch sphere of influence, for Singapore was part of the Empire of Sultan Abdul Rahman of Johore, who was recognized by the Dutch. The Sultan at Lingga was carefully watched over by the Dutch and would certainly not be permitted by them to give the British permission to establish a settlement on the island, a settlement which would compete with the Dutch.

The only way in which Raffles could obtain some legality for a settlement in Singapore island was by going back on the previous British recognition of Abdul Rahman as Sultan. After discussions with the Temenggong, Raffles proceeded to do just this: he recognized Tengku Hussein as Sultan and on January 6th, 1819, a treaty was signed between the newly installed Sultan, who had been brought from Riau, the Temenggong and the East India Company. Raffles had obtained his site for a settlement. Writing soon afterwards to a friend in England, Raffles stated that 'a more commanding and promising station for the protection and improvement of all our interests cannot well be conceived', and 'it is impossible to conceive a place combining more advantages ... [it is] the Navel of the Malay countries. One fine port in these seas must eventually destroy the spell of Dutch monopoly.'

By the terms of the treaty signed with the Sultan and the Temenggong, the East India Company undertook to pay them $5,000 and $3,000 annually for the right to have a trading settlement on the island. The new settlement was now in existence but its future prospects were not particularly promising. There were two main dangers, in Holland and in England. It was obvious that the Dutch would protest most forcibly against Raffles' activities, and there was also the danger of lack of support in England itself. Even the

Governor-General in India had had second thoughts soon after giving Raffles permission to go ahead, but it had been too late to stop the expedition. Two other points were also important; firstly there was not at first much local Malay support for the British, because it was not definite how long the newcomers were going to remain and there was no wish to antagonize the Dutch. They had already seen the British leave Malacca and hand it back to the Dutch. Secondly Raffles did not receive much encouragement from the other British settlement of Penang whose Governor was jealous of Raffles' influence and success.

THE RAPID GROWTH OF SINGAPORE

The Dutch immediately submitted protests to the British Government who were at first inclined to order Raffles to withdraw. Raffles had also made a treaty with Acheh, and the Dutch were so worried about the prospects of British influence in South-East Asia that they offered to give up their ports in India if Raffles was ordered to abandon his settlement. However communications were slow in those days and it took messages many weeks to pass between Europe and Asia. But the new settlement was saved mainly by its own rapid growth which took place during the long drawn-out Anglo-Dutch negotiations of 1820-3. In February 1819 when Raffles signed the agreement with Tengku Hussein and the Temenggong, the population of the island of Singapore consisted of about one hundred and fifty *orang laut* fishermen, some Malay followers of the Temenggong, together with a small number of Chinese who were planters of gambier. But as soon as it was realized that Raffles at least had every intention of making the settlement permanent, the earlier misgivings of the nearby inhabitants disappeared, and the population increased very rapidly. By June 1819 Raffles was reporting that the population had increased to five thousand and that the harbour was filled with small ships from many parts of the Archipelago. Those that came were Chinese, Bugis, and Malays from Malacca, which had now returned to Dutch control. The existence of a free-trade port naturally attracted the merchants of the area who for so long had been accustomed to the Dutch policy of monopoly. By the end of 1820 the population had grown to ten thousand, and the value of Singapore's trade for that year was over four million dollars. By 1825 the approximate comparative trade figures for the three British settlements were as follows: Malacca: $2,500,000; Penang: $8,500,000; Singapore: $22,185,000. It is little wonder therefore that the Governor of Penang, Colonel Bannerman, had not been very enthusiastic about the establishment of another, and rival, settlement. However, neither is it any wonder that Dutch protests eventually brought little response in England. Singapore had become too successful to give up to the Dutch. It was largely by means of its own remarkable growth and success that Singapore survived the first difficult years. Although as early as August 1819 the British Ambassador to the Netherlands told the Dutch that Britain could not consent to 'all the military and naval keys of the Straits of Malacca being in the hands of the Netherlands government'. Furthermore in 1820 the East India Company told the British Government that it was strongly opposed to abandoning the settlement.

Its position was finally regularized, in Dutch eyes, by the Treaty of London, 1824. This treaty was to be of very great importance to the future of the Malaysian Archipelago and had very far-reaching results. In the first place the Dutch recognized Singapore as a British possession and withdrew their objections to the settlement. Secondly the two powers agreed to try to avoid future conflict by limiting their interests to distinct areas. The distinct areas were to be divided by a line drawn through the Straits of Malacca; areas south and west of this line were to be Dutch, areas north and east to be British. The islands south of Singapore were therefore to be within the Dutch 'sphere of influence', while the Peninsula and Singapore were to be within the British sphere. This rather vague reference to the islands south of Singapore was to lead later to differing interpretations between Britain and Holland over the position of Borneo (see below, page 106). In order to begin this demarcation correctly the settlements of Malacca and Bencoolen (which were on the wrong sides of the line) were exchanged.

These were the immediate decisions, but what were the long term results of the Anglo-Dutch treaty? In return for no further Dutch influence in the Peninsula, the British turned down, for the second time, the chance of establishing a South-East Asian empire by competing with the Dutch in the islands. It is interesting to speculate what would have been the results of Raffles' plans for retaining Java in 1815 and what would have happened if the British had not renounced their interest in Sumatra in 1824 (a renunciation later confirmed in 1871); for Raffles had had the vision of a large area of South-East Asia under British protection, a much larger area than that of Malaysia to-day.

From a Malaysian point of view the fact that the Dutch gave up any interest in the Peninsula meant that there was less likelihood of international competition in the Malay Peninsula, which was therefore removed from the area of international quarrels. A further result was the permanent division of the Johore Empire and the isolation of the Dutch-supported Sultan from the greater part of his former domains. Eventually, as we shall see, an entirely new ruling family (that of the Temenggong) was established in Johore. And finally, as far as Britain was concerned, the agreement also meant that the sea route to China was now secure.

The last step in the consolidation of the position of Singapore was the signing of a further treaty with Sultan Hussein and the Temenggong in 1824. Once the international position of the British settlement had been recognized by agreement with Holland, the East India Company wished to make its local position on the island more secure. The first treaty in 1819 had merely given the Company the right to have a settlement. By the second treaty the Sultan and the Temenggong agreed to cede the entire island to Britain forever. In return the Sultan was paid $33,200 and given a pension of $1,300 a month for life, while the Temenggong received $26,800 and a pension of $700 per month for life. The Sultan did rather better out of this agreement than the Temenggong, for while the latter died in 1825, the Sultan lived in retirement until 1835.

Thus by 1824 the three British settlements, to be known as the Straits Settlements, were well established, and as a result British influence was also established on the periphery of the Malay Peninsula. The Dutch had left the Peninsula for good and had been replaced by the British. But despite the fact that the latter had no trading rivals in the region of the Malay Peninsula, the extension of British influence to the Malay states did not take place for another fifty years. In the eyes of the East India Company the Settlements were primarily for the protection of the trade route to China; but as will be seen below, this was not always the only idea of the merchants in the Settlements themselves.

EXERCISES
1 Why did the British want a settlement in South-East Asia?
2 Describe the events leading up to the establishment of a British settlement in Penang.
3 Did the early history of Penang come up to the expectations of the East India Company?
4 How did the British first acquire and then keep Malacca?
5 Write an account of Raffles and the founding of Singapore.
6 Why was the new settlement of Singapore an immediate success?
7 Write short notes on:
   Francis Light, country traders, Tengku Hussein, the Anglo-Dutch Treaty 1824, Bencoolen.

8

MALAYSIA IN THE EARLY
NINETEENTH CENTURY

BRITAIN'S POLICY OF NON-INTERVENTION

THE establishment of the Straits Settlements did not bring any great immediate change to the states of the Malay Peninsula. At first it merely meant that the British were now in contact with the Peninsula instead of the Dutch; for by the terms of the 1824 Anglo-Dutch treaty the Dutch had conceded that west Malaysia lay within the British sphere of influence. But the British were not particularly interested in extending this influence to the Malay states and in fact for almost fifty years British policy did not look upon the Straits Settlements as beachheads for the 'invasion' of Malaya but rather as 'off-shore' trading posts having as little as possible to do with the politics of the mainland. Looking at Malaysian history in the nineteenth century it perhaps seems odd that although the British had become in 1824 virtually the only European power in contact with Malaysia, it was not until 1874 that Britain officially intervened in the states of the Peninsula. The main reason for this seemingly strange lack of interest was that the East India Company had established the Straits Settlements for other reasons than the acquisition of territory in South-East Asia. The aim was primarily to protect the trade route to China and secondarily to establish trading centres for the whole Malaysian region.

The political pattern of the Peninsula showed no appreciable change in the years immediately following the consolidation of the British position in 1824. The Siamese continued to exercise varying amounts of control over the northern states of Kedah, Kelantan and Trengganu, while to the independent states of Perak, Selangor and the Minangkabau settled regions were now added the newly independent states of Pahang and Johore. These latter had been part of the old Johore Empire but their territorial chiefs, the Bendahara and the Temenggong respectively, had now in practice become independent rulers. This was possible because one Sultan of Johore,

Abdul Rahman, was in Dutch-controlled Lingga and had no contact with the mainland; the other, Sultan Hussein, was living in virtual retirement in Singapore. As has been said, there was no immediate desire by the British to take possession of any of these states, although the British did wish to to make sure that no other power attempted to alter the *status quo*. Thus with a few exceptions, which will be outlined below, the Malayan states continued to pursue their own policies without interference for the first three-quarters of the nineteenth century.

It will be remembered that the initiative for the foundation of the Straits Settlements had been taken in India, by the Government of India. Penang had been established, Singapore had been purchased and Malacca had been taken over by the Government of India which was in fact the East India Company. The Settlements were looked upon as parts of the domain of the East-India Company, and we have seen that Penang had been created the fourth Presidency of India in 1805. In 1826 Singapore and Malacca ceased to be the direct responsibility of Calcutta and were brought under the administration of the Penang Presidency; that is, all the Settlements were then under the charge of one government. However the Indian Government had also begun to realize that it had overestimated the importance and status of Penang and also of the combined Straits Settlements; to equate them with the other Presidencies of Bombay, Madras and Calcutta had been wishful thinking. The Straits Settlements had acquired a top-heavy administration, and this administration was expensive. They had an annual deficit (because of the costs of administration) of about $850,000 per year and this annual deficit was to continue until 1864-5.

The result was that in 1829 the status of the Straits Settlements was reduced to that of Residency under the Governor of Bengal and this, in effect, meant that the three Settlements were to be administered as though they were part of Bengal. As a result they became more dominated by the Indian Government and more subject to the influences of Indian policy. Then in 1832 the headquarters of the Residency was moved from Penang to Singapore. This was in recognition of the relative importance of the two places, for Singapore had by this time developed almost three times the trade of Penang and was rapidly growing in both population and prosperity. The fact that the Straits Settlements were administered as part of India meant that the administration in Singapore had only limited authority and its policies were subordinated to those of India. If there was a clash over policy between Singapore and the

Calcutta authorities, it was the latter's judgement which always prevailed. Almost everything had to be referred to the Indian Government which meant that initiative in the Straits Settlements was curtailed. Even the civil service was dominated by officials who served most of their time in India and only came to the Settlements to do a tour of duty. Their outlook remained India-centred, and they never really had the interests of the Settlements at heart.

The Indian Government also had little or no interest in extending its influence from the Settlements to the Malaysian states. Because Singapore, Penang and Malacca were considered trading centres and protectors of the route to China, there was little likelihood of the Indian Government wishing to become involved in the Peninsula states. The Straits Settlements administration already cost too much money and it seemed likely that the acquisition of more territory would only increase expenses. The official policy therefore was one of strict non-intervention. It was also felt that agreements with the rulers of the Malay states would involve the India Government in the quarrels and civil wars of the Peninsula and at the same time might also lead to war against Siam. The primary aim of the administration therefore was to keep out of the Peninsula. Although this policy was largely successful, there were one or two instances when Britain did become involved.

OCCASIONS OF EARLY BRITISH INTERVENTION

The first occasion arose over the question of Kedah's relations with Siam and the continued refusal of Penang to provide the Sultan with any assistance against his enemies. From the beginning of the nineteenth century the Siamese authorities, in the person of the Governor of Ligor, began to re-impose control over northern Malaysia, control which had been somewhat relaxed while Siam was involved in the Burmese wars. Siam did not like the independence shown by the Sultan of Kedah in selling the island of Penang without consulting the Siamese authorities. At first Siamese control was re-imposed on Kedah itself and then in 1818 the Sultan of Kedah was forced to conquer Perak on behalf of Siam. This was planned as the beginning of the extension of Siamese control over the central (and eventually perhaps the southern) states of the Peninsula. Kedah itself did not remain independent much longer, and in 1821 the state of Kedah was invaded by the Siamese from the north. The Sultan's forces were defeated, and he and many of his followers fled to the territory of Penang. Here he applied to the East India Company for help, but none was forthcoming; the Indian Government had no wish to become emboiled in controversy and a possible war with the Siamese. The Sultan was allowed to reside in the Straits Settlements from 1822 until 1842, and although he had many sympathizers in Penang, he did not receive any official assistance. The East India Company was willing to concede Siamese suzerainty over Kedah and it concentrated its energies on trying to ensure that this suzerainty was not extended further south to Perak and Selangor.

NEGOTIATIONS WITH THE SIAMESE

With this end in view negotiations were opened in Bangkok, and these negotiations eventually led to the signing of the Anglo-Siamese Treaty of 1826. This treaty, which fixed the southern boundary of Kedah as the limit of Siamese influence, was to stabilize the territorial position on the west coast of the Peninsula for the following fifty years. It should be noted that the east coast was not affected by this treaty and friction was later to develop there between Britain and Siam.

In the same year the authorities in Penang sought to reassure the Sultan of Perak in view of the earlier Siamese-supported attacks across the Kedah border. Captain Low, who made a treaty in 1826 with Sultan Abdullah (1825-30), gave Perak British protection against the Siamese and against other Malay states. The Sultan offered the Penang authorities the island of Pangkor and the Dindings coast-line in exchange but the offer was not taken up at this time. There is little doubt that the existence of this treaty helped to preserve Perak's independence in the first half of the century for the state continued to be subjected to threatening pressures from the north.

In 1842 the Sultan of Kedah came to terms with Siam and was permitted to return to his state. He had tried many times to raise forces strong enough to defeat the Siamese but had always been unsuccessful. He had eventually realized that, if he wished to return to Kedah at all, it would have to be on Siamese terms. These agreed terms made the Sultan more dependent on the Siamese authorities who, in order to punish him for his independent outlook, detached the districts in the north of Kedah from the remainder of the Sultan's possessions. These districts were made into the separate state of Perlis. Then in 1843-4 the Sultan of Kedah was forced to undertake a military campaign against Perak on behalf of the Siamese. This campaign was initially successful and was fought over the possession of land in the Krian district. However, British support for Perak brought pressure to bear in Bangkok, and Kedah was compelled to restore the land to Perak. From about this time onward friction between the British in Penang and the Siamese in Kedah decreased, for, as long as the Siamese did not try to extend their influence to the south, the East India Company was prepared to concede Siamese control over Kedah. Also after the return of the Sultan to Kedah in 1842 relations between the Settlement and Kedah became quite good. This was because of mutual trade and because Penang was responsible for paying an annual grant to the Sultan.

THE NANING WAR

Britain also became involved in one important incident in the hinterland of Malacca. This area was mainly inhabited by Minangkabau Malays, a group of people who had originally come from Sumatra and who had many social features which distinguished them from other Malays. The most important of these differences was a matriarchal form of society by which property descended through the female line rather than the male. In the area inland from the town of Malacca these settlers had established many small states one of which was called Naning. During the time that the Dutch were in Malacca, Naning paid annual tithes to the Malacca authorities. In 1831 the people of Naning refused to make these payments to the British authorities who maintained that they had inherited former Dutch rights. Both sides refused to yield, and the result was the Naning War of 1831-2. The British, with regular troops and guns, tried to force their way through the jungle from Malacca but suffered some rather ignominious set-backs from the greatly outnumbered Malays before the campaign was finally brought to an end. Naning itself was absorbed into the territory of Malacca whereas it had previously been on the boundary, while its ruler was given a house in Malacca together with an annual pension for as long as he lived there.

NEGOTIATIONS WITH JOHORE

British connexion with the Malay Peninsula in the first half of the nineteenth century was mainly in those regions which had some contact with the three settlements of Penang, Malacca and Singapore. We have seen this with relation to Kedah and Naning; the third area of contact arose out of Singapore's relations with the ruler of Johore. As a result of the acquisition of Singapore by the East

India Company, the newly installed Sultan Hussein had in fact no territory of his own over which to rule. He was nominally Sultan of the Johore Empire, but in fact the area which is now Pahang was ruled by the Bendahara, Johore was ruled by the Temenggong, and he had ceded the island of Singapore to the British. He thus lived in Singapore as a pensioner until his death in 1835. His successor, a young boy named Ali, continued the same sort of life as his father until the middle of the 1840's. By that time it had become apparent that Temenggong Ibrahim (who succeeded to the position in 1827) was rapidly pushing ahead with the development of his territory. Chinese immigrants were introduced from Singapore to open up gambier and pepper plantation, and the Temenggong became a rich man. He continued to live in Singapore and had very close relations with the government there. In effect his territory of Johore was almost an unofficial 'protected state'.

It happened therefore, that when 'Sultan' Ali began to press his claim to be recognized by the East India Company as Sultan of Johore, he found that the Temenggong had many influential supporters in Singapore. And unfortunately his own indebtedness to merchants contrasted unfavourably with the wealth displayed by the Temenggong. Eventually in 1855 the Company brought its influence to bear on Ali to give up his claims to the state of Johore, of which the Temenggong now became *de jure* as well as *de facto* ruler. In return, Ali was granted a small area of land in north-west Johore between the Muar and Kesang rivers together with a monthly pension. In this particular instance British pressure had been used to bring about the success of the candidate supported by the majority group in Singapore. A little later there developed a further complication when a dispute over the successor to the position of Bendahara in Pahang turned into a civil war. As in Johore after 1842 the major chief in Pahang, the Bendahara, had become the actual ruler of the state. When the Bendahara died in 1857 there was a dispute between his two sons, Tun Mutahir and Wan Ahmad—the latter was supported by Trengganu, the Siamese, and a claimant to the Johore throne; the former was helped by the Temenggong and indirectly by the British.

The civil war in Pahang lasted from 1857 to 1863, when Wan Ahmad was eventually successful. However the course of events is noteworthy for the attempted intervention by Siamese soldiers and warships in Trengganu in 1862 followed by the bombardment of Kuala Trengganu by British warships to discourage this intervention by the Siamese. Thus although the candidate indirectly supported by the British did not win the civil war, there were no further Siamese attempts to extend their influence in Pahang and other places on the east coast of the Malay Peninsula.

THE PURPOSE OF INTERVENTION

From this summary of the occasions of British interference from the Straits Settlements in the affairs of the states of the Malay Peninsula it will be seen that the main purpose of such intervention was generally to prevent another power from establishing or extending its influence in the area. The country generally affected by the British policy was Siam, and as the century progressed, Siamese influence in northern Malaysia began to recede. At this particular point of time, as has been said above, the East India Company did not wish either to become involved in the domestic affairs of the Malay states or to become an administrator of more territory in South-East Asia. On the other hand, the Company did not wish to see possibilities of British trade removed, and it was prepared to try to prevent the exclusion of British interests if this did not mean acquisition of more territory. There is little doubt that the Malay Peninsula had become by 1862 a British 'sphere of influence', and although the East India Company was not responsible for the administration of any of the states, the relationships between the Straits Settlements and some parts of the Peninsula, especially Kedah and Johore, had been quite close. The development of tin-mining in the States of Perak and Selangor was to increase these connexions, especially in the years after 1860.

SARAWAK

However there was one important instance of unofficial British intervention in these years which did lead directly to the acquisition of territory, not by the East India Company, which wanted no more responsibilities, but by a private individual. The individual concerned was James Brooke and his involvement in Sarawak was one of the most extraordinary episodes in the history of nineteenth-century Malaysia.

Born in England in 1803 Brooke had been an officer in the army of the East India Company until 1825 when he was invalided out after being wounded in the first Burmese War. In 1831 and 1834 he visited China and South-East Asia and became a fervent supporter of Raffles' plans for extending British influence in the Malaysian archipelago. After the death of his father in 1835 Brooke inherited £30,000, bought a ship, the *Royalist*, and in 1839 sailed from England to Singapore. This was to be a voyage of exploration, scientific discovery and, if possible, trade. While he was in Singapore Brooke was asked by the Governor and the Chamber of Commerce to carry presents from them to Raja Muda Hasim in Kuching as a token of gratitude for his kindly treatment of some shipwrecked British sailors.

When Brooke arrived in Sarawak he discovered that Hasim was heavily engaged in putting down a revolt by Dyaks and Sarawak Malays against the misrule of the Brunei governor, Pengiran Mahkota. Sarawak was still part of the territory of Brunei although the Sultan, Omar Ali Saifuddin, exercised little control over his governors. We have noticed earlier that during the eighteenth century Brunei had declined into a disposal centre for pirate loot and with the loss of wealth and power by the sultans the feudal structure of government had broken down. The major chiefs were almost independent rulers while Brunei town had become smaller and smaller. In 1730 its population had been 40,000 with many thousands of Chinese pepper farmers. By 1810 the population had shrunk to 15,000 with almost no Chinese and by 1842 Brunei had become little more than a very large village. The revolt in Sarawak had been in progress since 1837 and the Raja Muda, who was the Sultan's uncle, had met with little success in trying to bring it to an end. There was in fact not much love lost between the Sarawak inhabitants and their Brunei administrators.

On this first visit Brooke did not stay long in Kuching and he returned to Singapore in the same year. Hasim then appealed to the authorities in Singapore for assistance but it was obvious that the Straits Settlements government did not wish to become involved. Brooke himself was quite keen and needed little persuading by the merchants in Singapore to go back to Kuching in 1840. Hasim was very pleased to see him again and offered him the governorship of Sarawak if he would help to put down the rebellion. By this time Brooke had become interested in Sarawak and its problems and he accepted Hasim's offer without too much thought for the consequences. The Pengiran Mahkota naturally objected to Brooke's appointment but, as the rebels only agreed to end the revolt if Mahkota left, Brooke was installed as governor in 1841. The rebellion faded away and the Sultan confirmed Brooke's position in 1842 when he ceded to Brooke an area roughly equivalent to Sarawak's present First Division in return for annual payments of tribute.

James Brooke was now the Raja of Sarawak and the Brooke family was to rule there for over a hundred years.

To begin with Brooke had to establish an administration, for the previous system of government had been destroyed by the civil war. There was almost no protection of life and property and the Land Dyaks were permanently plundered by the Sea Dyaks (Ibans) and the Malays. Brooke's immediate aims were three, to stop the oppression of the Land Dyaks, to stop piracy and to stop head-hunting. All these were restrictive aims but until order was established more positive things could not be done. Brooke made no attempt to introduce new constitutions or laws, he preferred to enforce what already existed, basing his administration on custom and consultation with the chiefs. He refused to allow the traditional way of life in its more peaceful activities to be upset by the introduction of foreign capital and his view that 'the activities of European governments must be directed to the advancement of native interests and the development of native resources rather than by a flood of European colonization to aim at possession only' never changed. The financial situation in Sarawak was in complete confusion and it was a long time before revenue came near to meeting expenditure; and by then Brooke had spent all his own money. Brooke himself was not strong on finance and his administration was always in debt. One of the problems of Brooke rule in Sarawak was that it was impossible to 'develop native resources' without capital and Sarawak was never able to generate enough of its own.

At the outset Brooke's main weakness was that he had no official British support. He was to ask for this support throughout his reign but it was only given in grudging instalments for the same reason that the British authorities refused to intervene in the Malay Peninsula. However Brooke was able to obtain some assistance from the British navy in Singapore in his campaigns against the pirates in 1843 and 1845. In the hope of attracting the attention of the British government he also encouraged the navy to take an interest in Borneo as a possible site for a base between Singapore and the newly acquired Hong Kong. And on this latter point he was successful.

In 1846 Raja Muda Hasim, who had returned to Brunei, was murdered with his entire family in a court intrigue by those who were jealous of his support for Brooke. With naval assistance from Singapore, Brooke attacked and captured Brunei forcing the Sultan to make a new agreement with him. Sarawak was now given to Brooke in full sovereignty meaning that no more tribute had to be paid to the Sultan. In the following year, 1847, by a treaty with the

Sultan of Brunei, Britain obtained the island of Labuan for use as a naval base. Brooke was disappointed that Sarawak had not been chosen but Labuan had better port facilities than Kuching, possessed coal, and as an island would be easier to defend. In the same treaty Brunei agreed not to cede any of her territory to another power without the approval of the British government.

Brooke nevertheless received some consideration. While on leave in Britain in 1847 he was knighted and appointed British Consul-General for Brunei and Borneo; and in 1848 he was given the post of Governor of Labuan. This was personal recognition and did not give protection to Sarawak or recognition of Sarawak as an independent state, which was what the Raja wanted. However this was probably the apex of Brooke's career—his rule in Sarawak was well established, the population of Kuching had grown from 8,000 in 1841 to 50,000 in 1850 and exports were worth $250,000. The growth in population was in large part due to immigration; Dyaks, Malays and Chinese came in from over the border. Many Chinese possibly as many as 3,000 came from Pemangkat, in Dutch Borneo, and although they were not miners they joined the gold mining kongsi already working at Bau not far from Kuching.

Brooke's official appointments also impressed the Dutch who had settlements in south-west Borneo. Until this time the Dutch had not been very worried by the activities of a private individual but they now protested that Brooke, and Britain herself in Labuan, were infringing the terms of the 1824 treaty. Britain was unsympathetic, replying that she did not think that Borneo could be considered 'as one of the islands south of Singapore'. The Dutch had to accept this rejection of her protests particularly after the 1848 revolutions in Europe when Holland needed British support. In 1850 the Dutch Cabinet officially agreed to the British interpretation of the 1824 treaty, at the same time exerting greater control over those parts of Borneo which were nearer to Java. However, Britain was not planning any further extension of her influence and between 1850 and 1870 she lost interest in Borneo. Labuan proved to be a failure, its coal was too expensive, it was too far away from the pirates and Kuching was better as an entrepôt for the Borneo trade. Britain was equally unenthusiastic about Brooke's attempts to persuade her to take over Sarawak.

In Sarawak itself the years from 1850 to 1863 (when James Brooke retired) saw the state become larger with the acquisition of more territory from Brunei; almost up to the Rejang river in 1853, the present Second Division, and up to the Bintulu river in 1861, the present Third Division. Brooke's excuse was that the Sultan had no control over these lands and the pirates who lived there were a menace to peaceful trade. During these years Sarawak was not a particularly peaceful place and the administration faced two major threats. The first was from the Dyak and Lanun pirates who lived near the mouths of most of the main rivers and whose established base was in Marudu Bay at the northern tip of the island. With the help of the British navy Brooke was able to inflict a heavy defeat on these pirates in a battle off Tanjong Beting Maru in 1849 and thereafter the pirate menace declined. The help which Brooke received from the navy was later to be questioned in England and the whole matter of the suppression of piracy was the subject of an official British inquiry which was held in Singapore in 1854. The critics maintained that the measures used against the pirates were too harsh and although Brooke was cleared by the investigating commission, he resigned as Governor of Labuan and after this there was a noticeable lack of further naval support for him. But the pirate threat was almost over by 1862 and internal Dyak revolts were only on a small scale after that date. The Dyaks began to accept the prohibition against head-hunting and in 1862 Brooke felt secure enough to form the Sarawak Rangers, a Dyak field force, which became responsible for internal security.

As it happened the most serious danger to the administration during these years came not from the Dyak pirates but from the Chinese gold miners at Bau. This Chinese mining kongsi, mainly Hakka, was also the headquarters of the Triad society in Sarawak and there had been trouble in dealing with the 4,000 miners in 1850 as they resented the government's attempts to lessen their independence. After the Singapore inquiry in 1854 the Bau Chinese felt that Brooke had lost the support of the British government and anti-British feeling had been aroused during the second Anglo-Chinese war in 1856. As a result, in 1857, the Chinese miners rebelled against the Brooke government. Sailing down the river to Kuching they took everyone by surprise, easily captured the town and nearly killed Brooke, who just managed to escape by swimming across the river. The Chinese were in possession of the town for five days while Brooke was gathering together Dyak and Malay support. Then, aided by the arrival of a steamer from Singapore, he retook the town. The Chinese were pursued all the way back to Bau and many were driven over the border; it was estimated that 3,500 were either killed or were forced to leave the country, and for many years afterwards Chinese were not encouraged to settle in Sarawak.

In 1863, because of ill-health, James Brooke finally left Sarawak to retire to England where he lived for another five years. He left a country which was secure from internal and external dangers and made more so by the fact that, in the year he left, Britain at last recognized Sarawak as an independent state and appointed a British Consul to Kuching. Although this was not a guarantee of protection Brooke could leave Sarawak with the knowledge that his small state was firmly established.

EXERCISES

1 Describe Britain's policy towards the Malay States in the first half of the nineteenth century.

2 Write an account of James Brooke's intervention in Sarawak.

3 Give a brief description of Thailand's relations with the Malay States in the years 1818-42.

4 Account for the exceptions to the British policy of non-intervention in the first half of the nineteenth century.

5 Write short notes on:
   piracy in Borneo, Raja Muda Hasim, Naning, the Temenggong of Johore, the Anglo-Siamese Treaty 1826.

BRITISH INTERVENTION

SARAWAK MUSEUM

Sir James Brooke

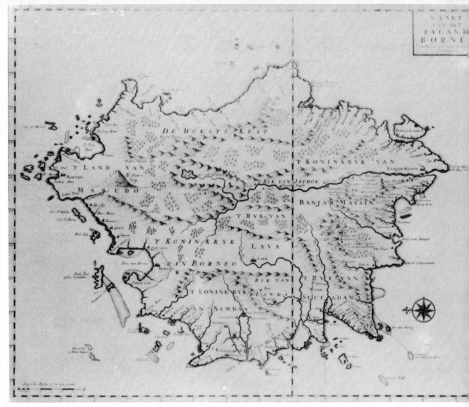

An early Dutch map of Borneo Island

Royalist off Santubong

View of Raja Brooke's house looking across the Sarawak River from what is now Kuching

View from Raja Brooke's house looking across the Sarawak River at what is now the main Bazaar of Kuching

The Battle of Marųdu Bay

First Sarawak Rangers composed of Sea Dyaks. The pictures show them uniform and in mufti. Notice the man in front, he is the sergeant and British. The bandsmen at the rear are Sepoys and not Dyaks

MUN PHOTO

Kuala Lumpur—early days

Yap Ah Loy, Kapitan China

Sir Andrew Clarke

MUN PHOTO

J. W. W. Birch

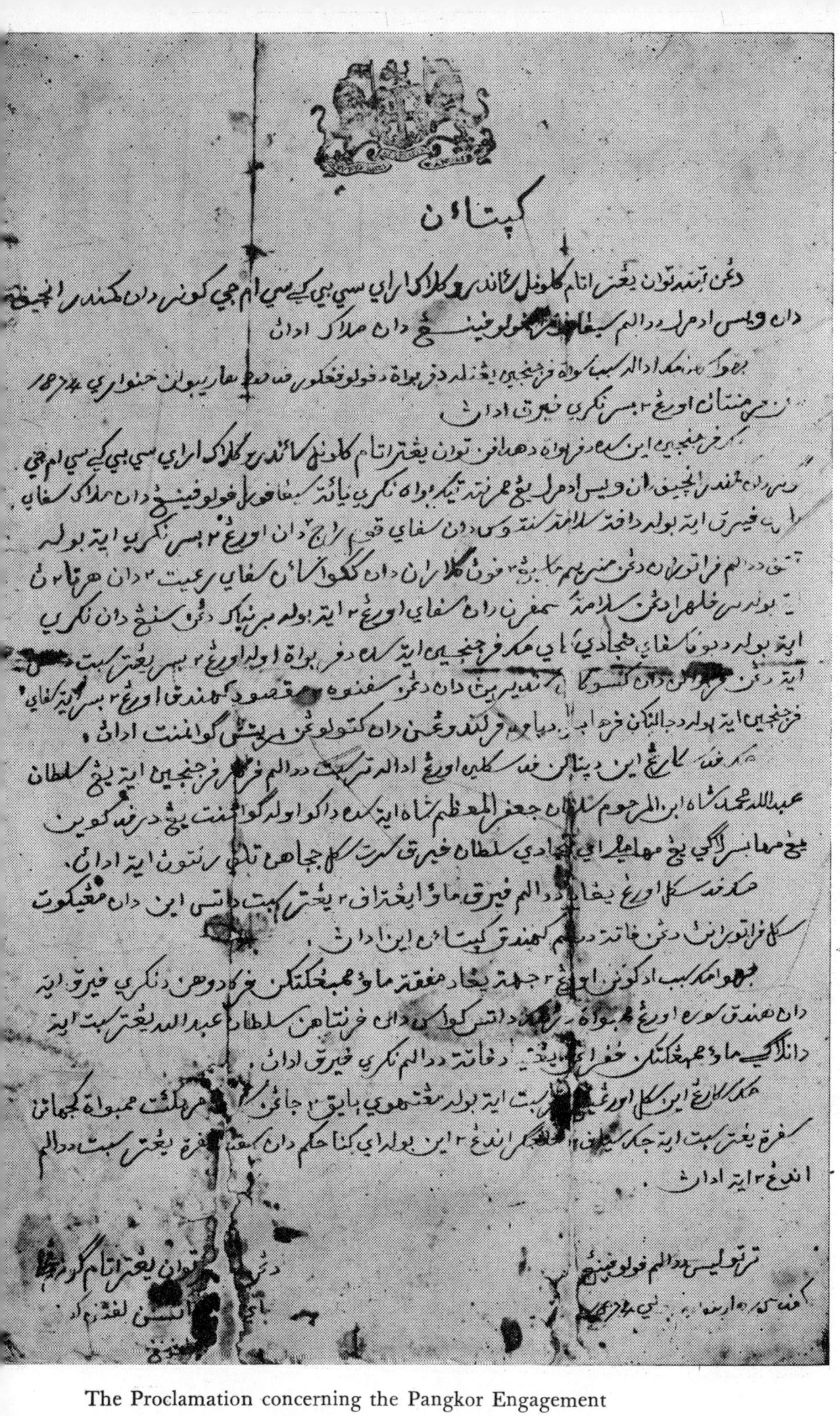

كڤيتاءن

دڠن ايهندق توان يڠ ترااتام كولونل اندرو كلارك اراي سي بي كي سي ام جي ݢوۏرنر دان كمندر انچيف
دان ۏيس ادميرل دالم سيڠاڤورا ڤولو ڤينڠ دان ملاك اداڽ

بهواسڽ كارن اداله سبب دوا ڤرجنجين يڠ تله دڤربواة دڤولو ڤڠكور ڤد ٢٠ هاري بولن جنواري 1874
انتارا منتري اورڠ٢ بسر نݢري ڤيراق اداڽ

مك ڤرجنجين اين ستله دڤربواة دهداڤن توان يڠ ترااتام كولونل اندرو كلارك اراي سي بي كي سي ام جي
ݢوۏرنر دان كمندر انچيف دان ۏيس ادميرل يڠ ممرينته تيݢ بواه نݢري يائيت سيڠاڤورا ڤولو ڤينڠ دان ملاك سڤاي
[illegible] ڤيراق ايت بوله داڤت سلامت سنتوسا دان سڤاي قوم راج٢ دان اورڠ٢ بسر نݢري ايت بوله
تتڤ دالم ڤراتورن دڠن [illegible] دان كڤوڽاءن سڤاي رعيت٢ دان هرتا٢ [illegible]
بوله برخلق دڠن سلامت سمڤرنا دان سڤاي اورڠ٢ ايت بوله برنياݢ دڠن سنڠ دان نݢري
ايت بوله [illegible] منجادي [illegible] مك ڤرجنجين ايت ستله دڤربواة اوليه اورڠ٢ بسر يڠ ترسبوت
ايت دڠن [illegible] دان [illegible] دان دڠن سڤنوهڽ مقصود كهندق اورڠ٢ بسر ايت سڤاي
ڤرجنجين ايت بوله دجالنكن [illegible] ڤرلندوڠن دان كتولوڠن بريتيش ݢوۏرمينت اداڽ

مك ڤد كتيك اين دڽاتاكن كڤد سكلين اورڠ اداله ترسبوت دالم ڤرجنجين ايت يڠ سلطان
عبدالله محمد شاه ابن المرحوم سلطان جعفر المعظم شاه ايت تله داكو اوله ݢوۏرمينت يڠ [illegible]
يڠ مها بسر [illegible] منجادي سلطان ڤيراق [illegible] جاجهن [illegible] اداڽ

حتى كڤد سكل اورڠ يڠ اد دالم ڤيراق ماو ايڠتكن٢ يڠ ترسبوت دالم اين دان منڠكوت
سكل ڤراتورن دڠن [illegible] كهندق كڤيتاءن اين اداڽ

بهواسڽ ادكون اورڠ٢ جاهت يڠ اد منچوب مڠحالڠكن [illegible] نݢري ڤيراق ايت
دان هندق [illegible] اورڠ ممبواة [illegible] ڤرنتاهن سلطان عبدالله يڠ ترسبوت ايت
دان لاݢي ماو مڠحالڠكن [illegible] دالم نݢري ڤيراق اداڽ

مك كتاهوئيله اين سكل اورڠ [illegible] ايت بوله [illegible] ٢ جاڠن [illegible] ممبواة كجاهتن
سڤرتي يڠ ترسبوت ايت جك [illegible] اندڠ٢ اين بولهلاي كنا حكم دان [illegible] سڤرتي يڠ ترسبوت دالم
اندڠ٢ ايت اداڽ

ترتوليس دالم ڤولو ڤينڠ [illegible]
[illegible]

The Proclamation concerning the Pangkor Engagement

Sultan Abdullah of Perak

Raja Yusof

ARKIB NEGARA

Dr. Sun Yat Sen, the founder of modern China and first President of the Republic of China, on a visit to Singapore in 1905 to collect funds for his revolutionary activities.

Collyer Quay as it looked in 1870. Note the tramcars and the rickshaws which provided transport for the common man.

Sir Hugh Low with (seated) Raja Idris, Raja Muda Yusof and his son.
Behind them are Malay Court officials and a Sikh soldier

ARKIB NEGARA

Sir Frank Swettenham

W.A. Pickering,
first Protector of
Chinese.

UNIVERSITY OF MALAYA PRESS

Gan Eng Seng, a member of
the Chinese Advisory Board.

UNIVERSITY OF MALAYA PRESS

Dr. Almeida, Portuguese Consul-
General in the Straits in 1842.

Sultan Idris of Perak in London for the Coronation of King Edward VII in 1902, flanked by Hugh Clifford and Raja Chulan (son of ex-Sultan Abdullah of Perak)

9

THE SUCCESS OF SINGAPORE
1823-1870

FROM its establishment in 1819 until 1823 Singapore was a dependency of Bencoolen where Raffles had his headquarters. Raffles' duties in Bencoolen prevented him from visiting the new settlement very frequently and Singapore's general administration was entrusted to the Resident whom he had appointed, Farquhar. Raffles' second and last visit to Singapore was in 1822-3 when he accomplished a great deal in connexion with town planning, the rules for freedom of trade and other administrative details. In 1823 Raffles returned to England where he died three years later.

ADMINISTRATION FROM INDIA

During the years 1823-6 Singapore was placed under the direct control of the Governor-General in India, and the Resident during this time was Crawfurd. The latter was a hardworking official, extremely interested in the welfare of Singapore and after his retirement to England a consistent opponent of attempts to do away with Singapore's free trade. It was Crawfurd who concluded in 1824 the final treaty with the Sultan and Temenggong of Johore whereby Singapore was ceded 'in full sovereignty' to the East India Company. In 1826 it was decided that Singapore should cease being a separate settlement and it was joined to the other two British settlements in the area, Penang and Malacca, under the general supervision of the oldest settlement, Penang. These became the Straits Settlements, as the three British colonies were to be called. This joining together of the three Settlements was important, giving Singapore a share in an administration which had been in existence for some time. One important result was that in 1827 Singapore obtained a legally established court system by being included under the jurisdiction of the Penang higher courts.

At this time the Straits Settlements were under the administration of the Government of Bengal, one of the three Presidencies of the Indian Government. This was in fact something of a 'come down' from the position Penang had previously held of being the fourth Presidency of India. In the new situation the Straits Settlements had the status of a Residency of Bengal though it is interesting to note that its chief officials still retained the same titles as when its status had been higher. The Straits Settlements still had a Governor in the main Settlement and there were Resident Councillors in the other two.

THE TRADE OF SINGAPORE

The internal history of Singapore during the first fifty years of its existence is told in the story of the rapid growth of trade, its increase of population, mainly Chinese, and in the attempts of the administration to cope with the attendant difficulties. Naturally all the aspects of administration were closely interwoven but any expansion of the activities of Government was closely controlled by Bengal. This control was particularly strict over any increases in expenditure and was so because revenue obtained by the Straits Settlements did not balance expenditure and the Company therefore suffered a loss on the costs of administration. However, although the East India Company itself had a deficit on its administration, many private fortunes, European and Chinese, were made during the early history of Singapore. Companies which have later become famous in the region set up their first offices when their founders came to Singapore at this time—Sime in 1823, Boustead in 1827 and Patterson of Borneo Co. also in 1827.

The secret of Singapore's success in trade lay basically in its geographical position. It was on the main east-west trade route and it was easy for the manufactured goods of Europe and India to be brought to Singapore for transhipment to China or for distribution throughout Indo-China and the East Indies. The fact that Singapore was a free port helped this distribution trade to develop and it also helped the port to become the collecting centre for the produce of South-East Asia. Thus Singapore's trade grew in value from £2,610,000 in 1825 to £3,948,000 in 1830, to £5,851,000 in 1840 and £10,371,000 in 1859. The trade of the other settlements also grew, but much more slowly and even then a great deal of the Penang and Malacca trade went through Singapore.

From 1825 to 1867 Singapore was the key factor in the growth of British trade with the East Indies and, before the establishment of Hong Kong, Singapore played a vital part in the development of the China trade. But prior to this the pattern had been that Singapore's main import/export trade had been with Britain and India, followed closely by China. The main imports from Britian and India were cloth and opium respectively, sold throughout the Archipelago or to traders who came down by junk from China. In the early 1840s between 150 and 250 junks came every year to Singapore from China. They brought with them tea and silk to exchange for the goods they purchased. However, after 1842 Hong Kong and Canton became the main distribution centres for trade with China. Another important type of import was the Straits produce which came from all over the Archipelago; and after 1840 there was a large increase in Singapore's trade with Borneo as a result of Brooke's activities there and the establishment of his influence in Sarawak.

By 1860 Singapore's trade was worth more than £10 million a year while the whole of the trade of the Dutch East Indies amounted to only £14 million. The East Indies were an important source of trade to Singapore and despite Dutch attempts at restriction hundreds of prahus arrived in the port each year—over two hundred, for example in 1840, the majority of them Bugis ships. As yet there was little trade with the Malay Peninsula but many people in Singapore thought that it was rich in mineral wealth—'a great magazine of tin' said Crawfurd, with possibilities of gold in Pahang.

Trade had been the main cause of Singapore's extraordinary success but at the same time the trade which produced success also brought the infrastructure which must develop alongside the actual goods to buy and sell. In the network of international trade, banks and insurance houses are of vital importance if the goods being bought and sold are to be covered by monetary payments and also protected in transit. Singapore thus became the South-East Asian centre for the major banks and insurance companies—the earliest of the present day banks being the Chartered Bank which set up its first branch in Singapore in 1859 though it had been preceded by the Oriental Bank Corporation (1846) which later became defunct.

The founding of many well known agency houses like the Borneo Company has been mentioned above. These European companies, not always British, as some were Dutch and German, were the accepted means (and often still are) through which famous international companies did business in the Far East. Firms like Sime Darby, Henry Waugh, Guthries, etc. obtained the sole agency rights from companies in Europe which did not have branches in Singapore and they became the middle-men of trade between the United States, Europe and South-East Asia generally. Some of these agency houses became extremely influential though none perhaps to the same extent as the Borneo Company which obtained a very special position in Sarawak.

But not only banks and insurance companies are important in a large port—the port also needs facilities for providing food and water for the ships calling there, opportunities for repairing ships and the provision of the host of other services connected with shipping and sailors. These were all necessary in Singapore and by the middle of the nineteenth century the livelihood of a large percentage of the population was bound up with trade, the port and shipping.

POPULATION GROWTH AND PROBLEMS

Singapore had therefore prospered considerably and had grown in fifty years from a small fishing village to the most important trading centre in South-East Asia. This phenomenal development had been due to the right policies at the right time—especially free trade which, in opposition to all the earlier policies of trade restriction, had both attracted people and trade. Without a steadily increasing population there could be little or no trade and the population statistics show how this growth occurred:

1820	5,000
1830	16,634
1840	39,681
1850	59,043
1860	80,792 — and in the last year, out of

this total, 50,000 were Chinese, 13,000 were Indians and 11,000 were Malays.

The population was attracted to Singapore by the fact that while the government provided the framework of administration and protection it nevertheless left the individual free to pursue his own interests in his own way—particularly, to become wealthy from the trade which attracted the majority of the immigrants.

In contrast to the traditional Chinese grading of merchants as fourth in order after scholars, farmers, and artisans, Raffles held the merchant to be the most important class among the Chinese inhabitants of his new city.

The growth of immigration and the consequent development of a plural society is dealt with in some detail in the next chapter. As far as Singapore was concerned the main influx of Chinese provided not only the bulk of the merchant class but also the most numerous social problems. The most serious of these were the riots caused by the activities of the secret societies. These had their origins in Chinese history, see below page 124, but they soon established themselves in Singapore. In some ways they were rather like benevolent societies in that they looked after the welfare of their members but their intention was to set up a 'government within a government' by which they would enjoy the benefits of the stable administration provided by the British, yet at the same time the Chinese would be left free to govern themselves. If they did not like particular British laws they just ignored them!

This extraordinary situation arose because to begin with the British administration knew little or nothing about these societies —in the first place most of the government officers were seconded from India and until the transfer of 1867 few officials, if any, could speak a Chinese dialect. Not only that but until 1832 the police force numbered only eighteen persons and so control was no easy matter. The result was that the headmen of the societies were given considerable freedom of action—in fact the headmen were often prosperous and respectable people. However, the various societies soon quarrelled over the amount of control which they were to have over the majority of the population and it was this rivalry which caused the serious disturbances which took place in Singapore. The first very serious disturbance was in 1851 when the secret societies attacked the Chinese Christians, who were outside their control, and murdered some 500 of them.

Perhaps the most serious secret society fighting took place in Singapore in 1854. In that year fighting in the streets between rival provincial Kongsis of the same Triad Society lasted for ten days and over 400 Chinese were killed. But there were other riots, serious to a greater or lesser extent, in 1831, 1846, 1857, 1863 and 1864. The last ones were made more violent by the new immigrants who entered Singapore after the failure of the Taiping Rebellion in China in 1860. Many of the members of the societies, which may well have had as many as 10,000 members, were in fact criminals and strong-arm men from China. During the 1860s the government had no real means of control over the societies largely because of ignorance, though it did direct that, in the event of further trouble, the headmen of the societies should be sworn in as special constables to help keep the peace! This of course the headmen did not like.

On the whole, although Singapore was growing in prosperity it was for the majority of the new immigrants a hard place to live. Most of the Chinese population was engaged in trade of some kind, though only a minority became rich. Some were in agriculture working on gambier and pepper plantations; but for all of them life was difficult in the face of debt and disease, the necessary to remit money to China and the unnatural ratio in the population between males and females. In 1860 there was one women to every fifteen men, which perhaps helps to explain some of the tensions which existed in Chinese society.

ADMINISTRATIVE CHANGE

Throughout this period, 1823 to 1867, the administration of Singapore was controlled from India, the local government had little initiative and we have seen that the civil service, which had little experience in non-Indian problems, lacked expertise for providing an able administration for the people, the majority of whom were Chinese. There was also a continual struggle between the local administration for an increase in the size of the civil service and the desire of the Government of India to decrease its size and thereby its costs. The latter was primarily concerned to reduce the annual deficit incurred in the Straits Settlements—anything that cost money was strictly controlled and problems which needed expenditure, for example the suppression of piracy and the control of secret societies, were for a long time left unresolved. It should perhaps be noted that Singapore had no Commissioner of Police until 1856. Little was done about piracy, a serious threat to Singapore trade, before the arrival of a Royal Naval ship in 1836, though it was the advent of the steamship which finally ended the pirate menace in the 1860s.

While the basic policy of the government supervising the Straits Settlements remained largely unchanged from the departure of Raffles to the arrival of Sir Andrew Clarke in 1873, changes were made in the authority responsible for this supervision. In 1831 the Straits Settlements had been placed under the Government of Bengal. The Settlements were to stay under the control of the Indian Government until 1867 although one change was made in 1851 when they were removed from the administration of Bengal and placed under the supervision of the Governor-General himself. In 1858 after the 'Indian mutiny', the Government of India passed from the East India Company to the India Office in London and as a result the Straits Settlements also were no longer administered by a trading company but by civil servants. Although such changes did occur between 1831 and 1858 they had only the minimum effect on the overall attitude of the supervisory authority towards the affairs of the Straits Settlements. Throughout the period control remained in India, and as has been shown India showed only the slightest interest in South-East Asian affairs. This lack of concern by the East India Company was emphasized after 1833 when it lost its monopoly over the China trade, for the Settlements no longer brought any real benefit but rather the reverse, for they still were costly to administer.

The establishment of Hong Kong in 1842 as the transhipment port of the China trade, meant that Singapore was even less important in this respect, and the Settlement itself was forced to become more interested in the trade of South-East Asia. Although Singapore had a larger trade with China than with India nevertheless the establishment of Hong Kong meant that the merchants were forced to look for alternative trading areas. They found that competitors from other European countries were beginning to establish closed markets: the Dutch in the outer islands of the Archipelago, the Spanish in the Philippines and the French in Indo-China. As a result they became more interested in the Malay Peninsula itself. As early as 1844 newspapers in Singapore wanted the annexation of the Malay States but the merchants were to have to wait some time before they were able to persuade the British Government to support them. In fact they were to have almost no immediate success in bringing about changes in the non-intervention policy of the Indian Government.

That the transfer of control from the India Office to the Colonial Office took place at all was due to the agitation begun in the Settlements about the year 1835 and to the willingness of the post-mutiny government in India to be rid of these long-distance responsibilities. It was the merchants of Singapore who were in the forefront of those who wished to be rid of Indian control. Some of their reasons have been outlined above, but the main reason was the general lack of Indian interest in the problems of the Settlements; these reasons were to be reinforced in the middle 1850s because of attempts by the Indian Government to interfere in matters of trade and currency.

What initiated the main agitation was the Currency Act of 1855. In 1855 it was suggested that the standard currency should become the Indian rupee rather than the Straits dollar, this despite the fact that for years the dollar had been the generally accepted currency in South-East Asia. Furthermore the Indian Government in 1855-6, in an attempt to balance the budget of the Settlements, suggested that there should be taxes on trade. The fact that this would have put an end to Singapore's free-port status made no impression in Calcutta. These two matters, however, really brought criticism of the Indian Government to the point of action. They were reasons on which the merchants of Singapore could base a fight, but in fact discontent had long been simmering in the Settlements over the Indian attitude of disinterest. The Settlements were a long way from Calcutta, and by continuing the policy of non-intervention, the Indian administration seemed to indicate a complete lack of interest in the welfare of its own possessions. They can be illustrated for example by the reluctance of the Indian authorities, as outlined above, to spend money on the suppression of piracy in South-East Asia. It was also true that the problems of Singapore bore little resemblance to those of India and were in fact more akin to those of Hong Kong and China. Thus it appeared that India was not concerned over the future welfare of the merchants of the Straits Settlements and was willing to forgo the extension of British influence (as well as the increased prosperity of these merchants). The extension of British influence could only be brought about if treaties were made with the rulers of the Malay states, but the Indian Government was unwilling to do this.

The European merchants also wanted the establishment of a Legislative Council in Singapore by means of which they would have a greater voice in the administration of the Colony. The inhabitants of the Settlements also resented the fact that the Indian Government seemed to consider the Settlements as a dumping ground for convicts. All these factors, together with the controversy over free-port status and currency, led to the presentation of a petition to the British Parliament in 1858 asking for transfer from the Indian Office. As had been said the transfer was supported by the Indian Government which wished to be free of these Settlements which cost money; the fact that the transfer was not effected until 1867 was partly due to the reluctance of the Colonial Office to take them over. The Colonial Office had some misgivings about the over-enthusiastic forecasts of the potential prosperity of the Straits Settlements as outlined by the merchants of Singapore.

Britain set up a Commission in 1863 headed by Robinson, the Governor of Hong Kong to investigate the revenue position of the Settlements. After the Commission reported that the revenue position was such that the transfer would be no drain on the British Treasury there were no further objections.

The Straits Settlements were transferred to the Colonial Office in 1867 and by good fortune their prosperity and importance did increase after 1869. This seemed to vindicate those who had proposed transfer but was in fact due much more to the opening of the Suez Canal in that year. As Bogaars states, 'The Suez Canal revived the flagging trade of the Port and brought a new era of prosperity.' This can be seen from the followiny trade statistics:

Tonnage of ships using Singapore

1869	600,000 tons
1873	1,030,000 tons
1878	1,600,000 tons

General trade

1870	1879
Imports $39 millions	$56¼ millions
Exports $31½ millions	$49 millions

Singapore became more prosperous because with the opening of the Suez Canal the trade route between Europe and Asia became shorter and freight charges decreased. Moreover the trade route was now re-directed through the Straits of Malacca which brought more trade to Singapore and Penang. Also of value was the increasingly important route to Australia and New Zealand on which the Settlements were useful ports of call. Thanks to the Suez Canal, the Straits Settlements' annual deficit was replaced by a surplus, but it was still a few years before the expected change of policy towards the Malay Peninsula was brought about. Until September 1873 the Colonial Office continued to follow the same policy of non-intervention, but we shall see below the reasons for the important change when it did take place.

The first six decades of the century show a Malaysia which was very sparsely populated and not very developed in terms of international trade, but at the same time it was an area gradually subjected to influences both direct and indirect from the British Settlements around her coasts. Despite the dominating position of the British Settlements, no open move had yet been made to bring the Peninsula under any political control. However connexions between the Malay states and the Settlements had been increasing, especially as numbers of Chinese immigrants began to enter the tin-mining states on the west coast. The Malay Peninsula was about to become a plural society.

EXERCISES

1 Account for the rapid growth of Singapore between 1824 and 1867.
2 Describe the activities of the secret societies in the early history of Singapore.
3 Why were the Straits Settlements transferred from the control of the India Office to the Colonial Office in 1867?
4 What effect did the opening of the Suez Canal have on the prosperity of Singapore?
5 Write short notes on:
Free port status, secret society riots, J. Crawfurd.

10

THE BEGINNINGS OF A PLURAL SOCIETY

UNTIL the middle years of the nineteenth century the inhabitants of the Malay Peninsula were almost all of the Malay race. Some of them had been settled along the coasts and the rivers of the country for a very long time. Some had come from Sumatra at the time of the Malacca Sultanate; and in the years that followed, other Malay immigrants came to Malaysia—the Bugis from the Celebes and the Minangkabau from Sumatra. At the beginning of the nineteenth century the Peninsula was only sparsely inhabited;[1] apart from the Straits Settlements there were no large towns, and the population lived mainly in villages scattered along the banks of rivers or on the coast. It was a pattern of society which had changed little over the years and only occasionally had much contact with the complications of the rest of the world. The establishment of Penang and Singapore and the importance of the tin trade was to alter this rather static situation by bringing Malaysia very closely into contact with the outside world. The development of this trading relationship led also to the growth of a plural society, for new waves of immigrants came to the Peninsula to take part in its economic development. Malaysia became a plural society because these new immigrants were not Malaysians from Sumatra or the Celebes but were Chinese who had come from China via the Straits Settlements. Chinese immigration was eventually to change completely the pattern of society in the Peninsula, and in the future the Chinese were to number 40 per cent. of the population. This large-scale immigration has been probably the most important event in modern Malaysian history, and we must therefore examine how and why it happened.

---

[1] Even in 1874 a British Government paper (Cd. 111) estimated the Malay population at only about 150,000.

CHINESE IMMIGRATION

There had been some contact between Malaysia and China for many centuries. We read about it during the period of the Malacca Sultanate when the Malacca rulers sent delegations to the Chinese Emperor and when the Chinese ruler dispatched envoys such as Admiral Cheng Ho to Malaysia. However these political contacts were spasmodic and did little to affect the Malay Peninsula in any permanent way, though in the early years of the Malacca Sultanate they did bring Chinese protection against attacks from Siam. Generally the Chinese Empire had little interest in other countries, and over the centuries China always had much less cultural impact on Malaysia than had India. Although Chinese political and cultural influences had little effect in Malaysia, which did not become part of a Chinese political system and was not affected by Chinese religion, there was some economic influence. Trade led to the growth of small Chinese merchant communities in the trade centres of the Peninsula and Borneo. This was especially so, of course, in Malacca and Brunei where there were *kampong2 China*[1] and permanent settlements of merchants. Contemporary accounts mention Chinese ships being in Malacca harbour at the time of the Portuguese attack in 1511. The oldest Chinese graves at Bukit China in Malacca, graves which belong to the Tan's and the Tay's, date back to the early part of the seventeenth century, to the days of the Ming dynasty in China. The Dutch estimated that there were between three and four hundred Chinese in the town when they captured it in 1641; in the census of 1678 the Chinese population had increased to 892, and by 1750 it had reached 2,161. In Brunei the Chinese were not only merchants but also, in the seventeenth and eighteenth centuries, farmers who controlled the pepper plantations. Other places of settlement were at the mouths of the Johore and Pahang rivers. Alexander Hamilton, who was a visitor to Johore Lama in the early 1700's, speaks of about one thousand Chinese families living there; and from the *Pelayaran Abdullah* we learn that in 1838 Munshi Abdullah found a number living at the mouth of the Pahang River and also in Kuala Trengganu. 'As regards the Chinese community,' he states, 'I found that all the Chinese in Kampong China (Kuala Pahang) were Khehs. Their houses were all thatched and each man kept some goods, such as foodstuffs, cloth, etc., in his house and buyers inquired for what they wanted. All of them had married Balinese or Malay women

[1] Chinese quarters.

though I noticed that their children preferred to speak Chinese rather than Malay. However in Trengganu the Chinese appeared to be all Hokkiens and Khehs, mixed together; and most of them speak Malay in preference to Chinese.'

None of these communities was large but as long as there was trade in the area, they were reasonably permanent. This was especially so in Malacca where due to intermarriage between Chinese men and local women a distinct element in society appeared. This group, known as the Babas, eventually spoke a language which was a Chinese version of Malay, although in general they retained Chinese traditions in the form of Chinese dress, religion and customs. Throughout the years following the foundation of Malacca and the period of the Johore Empire, the Chinese settlements were mainly merchant communities in places where there were opportunities for trade. For example, by the beginning of the nineteenth century most of the Chinese had left Brunei because the opportunities for trade had declined. They had no more influence or importance than the other merchant communities, Arab, Indian, or Javanese, and usually they had considerably less.

Then at the beginning of the nineteenth century came the foundation of Penang and Singapore by the British; the rapid growth of population which took place in both places was largely due to the immigration of Chinese. It was these new nineteenth-century immigrants who were to add a distinctive element to the existing Malayan social pattern. Why did these large numbers of Chinese leave China and why did they come to the Straits Settlements?

ATTITUDE OF THE CHINESE GOVERNMENT

The traditional practice of the Chinese Imperial Government had always been to discourage emigration, largely because it was felt that China herself would gain nothing by having citizens overseas. This feeling was strengthened during the time of the alien Manchu (Ch'ing) dynasty (1644-1911), for the Manchus, who were never wholly accepted by the Chinese, did not want emigrants from China to set up centres of disaffection overseas. The Manchu Government was most unpopular in south China, and it is noticeable that when government control began to relax, it was from this region of China that most of the emigrants came. South China was also the centre of disturbance during the Taiping Rebellion in the middle of the nineteenth century, and Canton was always a meeting place for would-be rebels as well as China's main point of contact with the outside world.

Emigration was thus actively discouraged by the Manchu Government and when emigrants did leave China their families had to be left behind, rather like hostages. The Chinese people themselves did not particularly want to leave China, for there was always the possibility of being buried abroad with no one to perform the various ceremonies connected with ancestor reverence. These factors help to explain why there was so little Chinese emigration before the nineteenth century.

But towards the end of the eighteenth century conditions began to change in Manchu China. The government had become a petrified autocracy afraid to introduce change for fear of undermining its own position. China's population was increasing while neither food production nor opportunities for employment were keeping pace with this increase. The government exercised strict supervision over trade with foreigners, and only a few merchants received any benefits from foreign trade. As has been said, south and south-east China were not areas of particularly strong support for the dynasty, and it was from these regions—Kwangtung, Fukien, Kwangsi—that emigrants began to leave to look for better opportunities in the lands across the China sea. These emigrants went to all parts of South-East Asia, to Siam, Java, the Philippines, parts of Borneo, as well as to the newly established Straits Settlements. This first trickle of emigration became a flood in the middle years of the nineteenth century when political conditions in south China became more unsettled with the outbreak of the civil war known as the Taiping Rebellion. When the Rebellion was put down in 1861 many rebels fled overseas to escape the wrath of the authorities.

THE ATTRACTION OF THE STRAITS SETTLEMENTS

What was it that attracted these emigrants particularly to Penang and Singapore, for it was to these two places that many of them came? In the first place, there were obvious opportunities for advancement in these new towns where labour was scarce and trade was expanding rapidly. Secondly, the Settlements offered an acceptable amount of law and order, in comparison to many other places; and of equal importance, protection for goods and property. Finally administrative restrictions by the government were much milder than in China itself. The immigrants had considerable control over their own affairs, and in practice were administered by their own headmen. They thus had the best of both worlds: protection and at the same time almost no interference in their way of life. It was not until the secret-society riots in Penang and Singapore in the 1860's that the Straits Settlements administration began to take much interest in the Chinese population. It was for almost similar reasons that the Chinese population of Sarawak had increased in the 1840's and the earlier attempts by Brooke to bring the Chinese under control had led to the rebellion in 1857.

Most of the Chinese who came to the Settlements came as labourers or craftsmen, single men without their families who hoped to do sufficiently well to retire rich to China or bring their families and relatives to their new homes. The immigrants were usually brought to the Settlements by a shipowner who gave them free passages; in return they had to work for one year for the employer who purchased their services from the shipowner. A labourer was sold for between $17 and $20 while the passage from China cost about $14. In Perak a labourer might work for 360 days for $42 in the first year, from which would be deducted his passage money. He did however receive free food and lodging. After they had worked in this tied employment for twelve months the newcomers were then free to select their own type and place of work. As a result, most of the labourers and craftsmen remained in the Settlements, but an increasing number drifted over to the mainland to try their luck in the tin mines, first in Kasang and Rasa near Malacca, then later in Selangor and Perak.

CHINESE LABOURERS FOR THE TIN MINES

But the great influx of Chinese into west Malaysia came after mid-century. In the 1850's, new tin fields were discovered in Larut (Perak) and in the 1860's in that part of Selangor which is now Kuala Lumpur. In the 1860's also came a great increase in the demand for tin ore to supply the rapidly expanding tin-plate industry in Europe. (This was expanding because of the growing popularity of canned food.) The ore was in the ground, the world wanted the ore, and the Chinese immigrants provided the labour which was necessary to supply the demand. Called in first by the Malay chiefs who owned the mines, the Chinese soon proved to be uncontrollable under the old feudal system of government, and their inter-clan quarrels led to civil wars in which the Malay chiefs took sides. The Malay chiefs could not control the flood of Chinese even if they had wanted to do so—and it is doubtful that they did, for they were growing rich on the revenue from tin. The result was that by 1870 the Chinese in Larut outnumbered the Malays, and though they were not yet a fully settled population, Malaysia was well on the way to becoming a plural society. Penang island (though not Province Wellesley) was almost entirely Chinese populated as was the island of Singapore. Chinese were also entering Johore with the encouragement of the ruler, all this activity taking place mainly on the west coast. Not all the Chinese who came to Malaysia worked in the tin mines; as the numbers increased, so did the diversity of their occupations. They worked for the contractors making roads and railways, but most important, they took over, almost completely, the position of retail traders and small shop-keepers. They became the ubiquitous middlemen.

With them the Chinese brought their customs, religion and language. Unlike the earlier traders in Malacca and elsewhere who had undergone some assimilation and become the Babas or Straits Chinese, these immigrants came in such large numbers and kept so close together in family and clan groups that there was little or no chance for assimilation to take place. They remained a separate community, self-sufficient, independent, but to some extent temporary; for although the numbers of Chinese in Malaysia in the nineteenth century continued to increase, the majority continued to regard their stay in the country as a prelude to retirement to their villages in China. Thus the Chinese communities were always transient and rapidly changing. Large-scale Chinese immigration into the Peninsula coincided with the great development of tin production in the 1850's and 1860's; although in about 1860, while it was estimated that the Chinese population in the Straits Settlements numbered about 97,000 the Chinese in the Peninsula still only totalled about 25,000. Tin mines were subsidized and provided with labour by businessmen who lived in the Straits Settlements, many of whom had by virtue of residence become British subjects. The chain of command between Penang and Larut, Malacca and Lukut and later Selangor was closely linked, and it was not long before the quarrels between the rival groups of miners in the tin fields began to spread to their backers in, for example, Penang, where there were dangerous riots in 1867. Chinese immigration was therefore one of the reasons the British were to be drawn into closer contact with the Malay states. The Straits Settlements Government felt obliged to stop the fighting in the tin fields because there was a danger that the fighting could cause serious trouble in the Settlements.

EXERCISES

1 Write an account of the emigration from China in the early nineteenth century.

2 What did Chinese immigrants find attractive about the Straits Settlements?

3 Describe the changes which took place in the tin mining industry in the Malay States in the middle of the nineteenth century.

BRITISH INTERVENTION IN THE STATES OF THE PENINSULA

AFTER the establishment of the Straits Settlements the main trend of British policy had been one of non-involvement in the affairs of the Malay Peninsula. This policy had been forced on the Government of the Straits Settlements by the Indian authorities, often against the wishes of influential groups in Penang and Singapore who had, for exampe, wished to assist Kedah against Siam. Although as we have seen there were occasions for intervention in Perak, Johore and Trengganu, the policy did in fact continue unchanged until 1873.

The transfer of the Straits Settlements in 1867 from the India Office to the Colonial Office did not bring about any immediate change, though it was significant that pressure from the Straits Settlements had helped to bring about the transfer. It was therefore likely that in the future similar pressure might be brought to bear on the British Government to pay more attention to the wishes of those living in Penang, Singapore and Malacca, especially those having trade connexions with the states of the Malay Peninsula.

It has been stated above that the Chinese who had come to live in the Straits Settlements had begun to cross over to the Peninsula to work in the tin mines which were opened up, especially in Larut and Selangor, in the 1860's. Quarrels between the miners had spread to their supporters in the Settlements, and rival branches of the Chinese secret societies had been involved in large-scale riots in Penang in 1867. Unstable conditions in the mining areas were a direct cause of law-breaking in the Straits Settlements and a source of much concern to the government there.

The Penang riots occurred in the same year as the transfer of the Settlements to the Colonial Office and the arrival of the first Governor, Sir Harry Ord. Ord himself arrived in Singapore with no clear instructions regarding the Malay Peninsula, and being rather an obstinate man he did not like to listen to advice which conflicted with his own views. Experienced as a negotiator in West Africa, Ord hoped that he might intervene as an arbitrator to help solve the disputes in various states. Thus during the first two years after his appointment negotiations were carried on with Perak, Kedah, Kelantan, Pahang and Johore as well as Siam. He tried unsuccessfully to bring about a new treaty between Siam and Kedah and in 1868 he acted as an intermediary in a boundary dispute between Johore and Pahang. This policy of Ord is described by Cowan as 'one of limited interference' and was in fact a conscious attempt by the 'man on the spot' to extend British influence. However it did not have the support of the Government in Britain who, when they came to hear of Ord's activities, discouraged and prevented them. In 1869 the Secretary of State wrote, 'I should not be disposed to approve of any proceedings which would extend the responsibilities of Her Majesty's Government in the neighbourhood of the Straits Settlements.' Ord's initiative was abrupty curtailed.

ATTITUDE OF THE BRITISH GOVERNMENT

The general outlook of the British Colonial Office was greatly influenced by the policies which it had inherited from the India Office. However the British Government was in principle opposed to the acquisition of fresh responsibilities overseas. Since the 1840's Britain had been ruled for most of the time by the Liberal Party whose ideas of free trade placed little importance on the value of overseas possessions. Earlier thinking in relation to colonies, in America for example, under the old colonial system, had been conditioned by their importance as protected markets and suppliers of raw materials. The Industrial Revolution had given Britain great advantages in competitive trade and protected markets were no longer thought to be essential, for her goods could compete favourably in open markets. For example, British trade with America increased rather than declined after the colonies became independent.

Colonies and overseas possessions were thus not considered very valuable by the Liberal 'free traders'; such possessions were in fact considered by some to be a needless expense to the mother country, which was responsible for their defence. The more extreme groups in England thought that the remaining colonies could well be disposed of; but although the Liberal Government did not go so far as to subscribe to this view, it nevertheless considered that the acquisition of any further overseas responsibilities was unnecessary and to be avoided. The success of the policy of free trade depended to a large extent on the preservation of 'open' trading areas. Naturally enough Britain's trading competitors did not see in free trade these same advantages for they wished to establish protected markets to keep out British competition. Once this policy of setting up areas of protected trade began to enter Asia—the Dutch in the East Indies, the French in Indo-China and the Spanish in the Philippines—the British merchants in Singapore began to see many trading opportunities being closed to them. They turned in the first place to the Malay Peninsula as an alternative trading area and wished to make sure that the British Government was not going to allow other powers to establish themselves there. It was in this way that commercial pressure began to exercise increasing influence in Britain. This pressure also found an ally in the Conservative Party which, though at this time in Opposition, favoured a policy of commercial expansion as did many of the younger Liberals who were not what was called 'Little Englanders'. The influence of these supporters of commercial expansion was to grow in importance during the 1870's; this was the decade which was to see British expansion in West Africa and Burma as well as intervention in the Malay states and Borneo.

THE REASONS FOR INTERVENTION

What then were the reasons for 'those on the spot' in the Straits Settlements to think that intervention was necessary?

As we have said, the merchants in the Straits Settlements viewed with some concern the possibility of markets being closed to them by other powers who were extending their territorial acquisitions in Asia. After 1858 the French began to expand their area of control in Indo-China and the Anglo-Dutch convention of 1871 recognized Sumatra as being within the Dutch sphere of influence. These merchants therefore began to look towards the Malay Peninsula as an area which would provide suitable alternative trading opportunities. The Malay Peninsula possessed tin, the importance of which had greatly increased in the late 1860's with the growth of the canning industry. The development of the use of tinned food in Europe and America was in fact to have far-reaching effects on Malaysian history.

Tin had of course been mined in Malaya for centuries, but the relatively small amounts which had been exported had been sent mainly to China to be beaten out and used on joss-sticks where the tin had the appearance of silver. Only when the demand for tin-plate became so great that it could not be supplied from the old sources did mainland Malaysia become directly involved in the complexities of world trade. It was the great expansion in the use of tin-plate rather than any other use of the tin ore which had such startling repercussions in Malaysia. There had been a tin-plate industry established in Britain, in South Wales, since the 1740's, and this industry had obtained its supplies of tin from the mines which were situated in Cornwall, England. Tin-plate was used for making kettles and pots and pans but there was not a big demand. However the possibilities of its greater use increased with the invention of the sealed tin container in 1810. In England this container was called a *canister* and later referred to as a *tin can*. The purpose of this invention was to preserve food, for the acids in food would not eat into a container that was lined with tin. However the use of tinned food developed slowly, and in Europe, for example, only luxuries to be eaten by the rich were put into tin cans. But in America, the civil war of 1861-5 produced new uses for tinned food. In this war, common foods like meat and fish were preserved in tins and distributed to the Federal armies. Tinned food became common and popular during the war and was also used extensively after the war by the migrants who moved across the country to the west.

This new use for tin-plate naturally increased the demand for tin. At first, although the actual canning of food was done in the United States, the tin-plate was imported from Wales where there was a doubling of output between 1865 and 1871. But from about 1860 it became obvious that the supply of tin from the mines in Cornwall was not going to be sufficient to meet the demands of the tin-plate industry, and new sources of supply were sought. It was therefore from the middle 1860's that the demand for Malaysian tin caused a new interest in the Peninsula to develop among the merchants of the Straits Settlements. It was these merchants who began to invest money in the new mines that were opened up in Selangor and Sungei Ujong, and it was these merchants who, from 1872, began to ask for British intervention in the states of the Peninsula in order to safeguard their investments. They did not consider that conditions in the states were conducive to successful investment, and they thought that British intervention would make everything much safer. The attitude of the Straits Settlements Government is well expressed in the following reply to the merchants by the first Governor, Ord: 'If persons, knowing the risks they run, owing to the disturbed state of these countries, choose to hazard their lives and properties for the sake of large profits which accompany successful trading, they must not expect the British Government to be answerable if their speculation proves unsuccessful.'

It is now necessary to describe why British intervention was considered important by these investors and to do so we must examine the 'disturbed' conditions in those states which were producers of tin, especially Perak and Selangor. The system of government in the Malay states had long been a form of feudalism. The ruler, or sultan, was the head of the state but he was dependent for both administration and defence on the major chiefs. The chiefs not only administered great areas of territory but they also collected taxes and had their own private armies. For example, when goods travelled on the Perak River, taxes had to be paid to each chief through whose territory the boat passed. There was in reality no centralized administration, and each sultan maintained his position by keeping an uneasy balance between the major chiefs. The sultans collected what taxes they could and with this revenue they tried to make sure that no one chief became too powerful.

A feudal system of government is typical at certain stages in a country's history, for instance in a period before the development of a centralized government; before one man can effectively govern the whole country he must delegate powers and privileges to his greatest followers. This was so in Europe in the eleventh and twelfth centuries, in Japan before the Meiji Restoration (1868), and in Malaya in the eighteenth and early nineteenth centuries. However for feudalism to work effectively the administration must not be too complicated and the ruler must not have smaller financial resources than the chiefs. The 'overmighty subject' can become very dangerous, and the result can be civil war, as happened in Malaysia in the middle of the century.

Malaysia had reached this particular stage in her history by the middle of the nineteenth century, for increased contact with the world outside Malaysia had increased the complexities of government in the west-coast states. These administrative difficulties could not be adequately dealt with through a feudal system in which no Malay middle class had developed. More important, however, was the fact that a number of chiefs—for example the Mentri in Perak and Raja Mahdi in Selangor—had control of greater revenues than the Sultan himself. This situation had arisen as a result of the development of tin mines, and this development had introduced a further factor—a large group of aliens which the system was quite unable to handle. By 1872, for example, there were between thirty and forty thousand Chinese in Larut, originally introduced by the Mentri to open up the mines, and some officials in the Straits Settlements even feared the establishment of a Chinese republic in Larut if the two rival groups of Chinese should ever combine. The existing system of administration was unable to deal with such large numbers. In both Selangor and Perak there was endemic civil war between two groups of Chinese miners who were struggling to gain control of the tin mines. These civil wars were out of the control of the sultans, and the Malay chiefs themselves were taking sides. It was in these circumstances that administration was breaking down, and the local Malay government proved unable to provide protection for those who had investments in the mines. The government was no longer able to restrict the influx of Chinese immigrants to the mines and of course had no means of stopping the secret-society wars which soon followed.

Thus we can say that in the middle of the nineteenth century effective administration had disappeared in Perak and Selangor. It had disappeared because the old feudal structure had proved incapable of dealing with the political and economic stresses and strains to be met in the nineteenth-century world. Conditions in these two states must now be examined in a little more detail.

CIVIL WAR IN SELANGOR

It was in 1858-9 that Chinese miners from Rasah and Lukut in Negri Sembilan began to arrive in quite large numbers in the vicinity of the Klang and Gombak rivers. Here they joined other miners who in 1857 had made their way up the Klang River and, where the two rivers joined, had built a small village. That village is now the city of Kuala Lumpur. These were the miners who began the mines in the vicinity of Kuala Lumpur, while others moved further north across the Kanching Hills to the area near present-day Rawang. The former were mainly Hakka and Hokkien and were members of the Hai San secret society; the latter were Cantonese and members of the Ghee Hin Society. These societies were already rivals in Larut and this antagonism was transferred to Selangor, especially after the arrival of mining refugees from Perak in 1862.

One year later, in 1863, a man destined to be very famous as a Chinese leader arrived in Kuala Lumpur. He was Yap Ah Loy and under his leadership the town was to grow in both size and prosperity. However his arrival also brought more fighting between the rival groups, for Yap Ah Loy was an ambitious and determined man. This rivalry with the Chinese miners coincided with quarrels between the Malay territorial chiefs, for whoever controlled the land containing the tin mines would obtain much revenue from taxes.

The Sultan, Abdul Samad, was rather an easy-going old man whose main aim was to be left in peace. He lived first of all at Klang and then at Kuala Langat, and he took little interest in the administration of his state. As long as he received the revenues to which he was entitled he was content to let the other Selangor chiefs quarrel amongst themselves. The main quarrel was in fact over the control of Klang. One chief, Raja Abdullah, was appointed territorial chief, but another, Raja Mahdi, considered that he should have been so appointed. To make matters worse, Raja Abdullah was supported by the Sumatran element in Selangor while Raja Mahdi was backed by the Bugis.

In 1867 Raja Mahdi captured Klang but, though he was able to hold it, fighting still continued with the sons of Raja Abdullah. In 1868 Sultan Abdul Samad's daughter married Tengku Kudin, brother of the Sultan of Kedah. The Sultan appointed his new son-in-law viceroy and Tengku Kudin tried to arbitrate between the two factions fighting over Klang. Raja Mahdi, who was in possession of Klang, refused to accept this arbitration and as a result Tengku Kudin joined Raja Mahdi's opponents. Some troops were brought in from Kedah and with these reinforcements Tengku Kudin and his allies recaptured Klang, forcing Raja Mahdi to flee inland, where his allies were the Chinese miners at Kanching.

Meanwhile there had been serious fighting in 1869 and 1870 between the two rival groups of Chinese miners. Yap Ah Loy of course realized that it would be disastrous for the Kuala Lumpur miners if Raja Mahdi should win the Malay struggle for supremacy and so he threw his support behind Tengku Kudin. The two sides, then, were composed of Raja Mahdi and the miners at Kanching against Tengku Kudin and the miners in Kuala Lumpur led by Yap Ah Loy. It should be said that the latter group had little support in Selangor, for both leaders were foreigners and they had to import mercenaries of all races for their forces. Outside Selangor, Raja Mahdi was supported by Johore while Tengku Kudin was assisted by Pahang.

The fighting itself continued on and off throughout these years; it was mostly inconclusive, neither side obtaining an outright victory. Raja Mahdi's first attack on Kuala Lumpur in 1871 failed, but his second in 1872 succeeded after a siege, and Yap Ah Loy fled to obtain more reinforcements. When these were obtained he took the offensive again, and with the assistance of further reinforcements who came over from Pahang, Kuala Lumpur was recaptured in 1873. After this Raja Mahdi's resources were exhausted, the interior of Selangor was gradually cleared, and the war was virtually over by mid-1873.

Throughout the period of the civil war the export of tin had dropped to a slow trickle for it was not really safe to work the mines. Yet in 1872 the the price of tin reached its peak because supply could not keep pace with the demands of the tin-plate industry. The Sultan's administration, itself short of money, could not guarantee protection to the miners nor could it guarantee protection to the ships sailing off Selangor's coasts. There had been a case of piracy in 1871 which had led to an unauthorized intervention in Selangor's affairs by Lieutenant-Governor Anson of Penang while Ord, the Governor, was absent on leave. These then were the conditions in Selangor at the time when, in 1873, Sir Harry Ord was replaced as Governor by Sir Andrew Clarke.

RIVALRY IN PERAK

In Perak, where Clarke first intervened officially, conditions were even more complicated, for here there was also a dispute over the succession to the throne. In Perak the line of succession to the throne was not from father to son; that is, when a Sultan died he was not succeeded by his eldest son. There were three major offices of state: the Sultan, the *Raja Muda*, and the *Raja Bendahara*. When the Sultan died he was succeeded by the Raja Muda, the Raja Bendahara becoming the Raja Muda, and the eldest son of the late Sultan becoming Raja Bendahara. Thus a ruler had generally to go through two lower positions before becoming Sultan. This system should have ensured that the ruler was a man of experience; it helped to prevent young boys inheriting the throne, with the attendant difficulty of a regent until the child came of age. Yet even this procedure was not automatic for the Council of Chiefs could exclude from the succession anyone who was obviously unsuitable.

The difficulties in Perak began in 1857 when Sultan Abdullah died. In the 1850's as a result of virtual civil war in Perak the chiefs had broken the power of the Sultanate. The ruler's son, Raja Yusof, naturally disliked the chiefs responsible for lessening the Sultan's powers and was unpopular with them. Therefore because he would probably have been a strong ruler, he was not appointed to the position of Bendahara. In his place the new Sultan Ja'afar appointed a favourite of his named Raja Ismail who was not even a Perak Malay. Sultan Ja'afar did not reign long and the succession was further complicated when he died in 1865. The Raja Muda moved up to become Sultan Ali but neither Raja Ismail, the Bendahara, nor Raja Yusof was appointed Raja Muda. Yusof was still unpopular, while the chiefs did not intend the throne to be eventually inherited by a foreigner. Raja Abdullah, a son of Sultan Ja'afar, was therefore appointed directly to the position of Raja Muda.

In 1871 Sultan Ali died and there were then three possible claimants to the throne—Abdullah, Ismail and Yusof. Any reconciliation of this situation was made more difficult by events in the tin-mining area of Larut.

Tin had been discovered in quantity in Larut by a man called Long Ja'afar in the 1850's. It was he who first brought in Chinese miners to work the mines for him; as a result he soon became quite a rich man. Of greater importance, however, was the number of Chinese who flocked into the district. Very soon they outnumbered the Malays and were extremely difficult to control. This was because the two rival groups of Chinese, from the Ghee Hin and the Hai San secret societies, established themselves in the mining area. Long Ja'afar himself died in 1856 leaving his interests to his son, Ngah Ibrahim, who got over the immediate difficulty of controlling the Chinese by playing off one faction against the other. Initially he was successful, and because of his riches and power he was appointed territorial chief of Larut. Very soon, however, rivalry between the Chinese groups became so great that fighting broke out in 1861. In the first clash the Ghee Hin were defeated and were forced out of the mines by the victors. Ngah Ibrahim was now in too dangerous a position to play off one side against the other, and he threw in his lot with the Hai San. The losers went back to Penang and complained that they had lost the mines because of the duplicity of the territorial chief. The Governor of Penang on behalf of those who were British subjects asked the Sultan for redress but the Sultan was quite incapable of forcing Ngah Ibrahim to come to terms. The British therefore blockaded the Larut River until payment was made and in effect the authorities in Penang dealt directly with Ngah Ibrahim. The Sultan then gave the latter full powers in Larut and the title of Mentri. Ngah Ibrahim, with his control over the tin revenues, had become by far the most powerful chief in Perak and virtually an independent ruler. It is estimated that his revenues were never less than $100,000 per year and while the other chiefs lived in their wooden houses along the Perak River, the Mentri had a large bungalow in Larut and another house in Penang.

It was no surprise therefore that the Mentri was no friend of either Raja Muda Abdullah or Raja Yusof; if either of them became Sultan they would try to exert rights over the Larut district. Abdullah and the Mentri had already quarrelled over the possession of land in Krian, and Abdullah was also a supporter of the Ghee Hin faction of the Chinese miners who spent most of the 1860's trying to regain possession of the mines lost in 1862. Unable to make a landing in Larut itself the Ghee Hin turned on their rivals in Penang, and the result was the terrible riot in 1867 when the Penang authorities completely lost control of the situation for ten days.

There was little doubt therefore that in the quarrel over the succession, the Bendahara, Ismail, had a strong supporter in the Mentri, for Ismail would, if he became Sultan, owe his position to the Mentri who could become the actual ruler of Perak with Ismail as puppet. In 1871 Ismail had the support of the Mentri and the up-river chiefs, Abdullah the support of the down-river chiefs, for he lived in Lower Perak. Unfortunately for Abdullah, Sultan Ali had died at Sayong near Kuala Kangsar and, as was customary, the Bendahara kept the regalia at Sayong until the installation of the Raja Muda should take place. However Abdullah was afraid to venture upstream for the burial and installation; after waiting for some time the chiefs who had assembled there declared Ismail the Sultan. Abdullah retaliated by proclaiming himself the rightful Sultan and nominating Raja Yusof as Raja Muda in an attempt to gain his support. This then was the position in Perak when Abdullah sent a letter to the Governor of the Straits Settlements setting out his claim to the throne and asking for his support. Meanwhile what had been the general reaction of the British to these events?

THE NEED FOR STABLE ADMINISTRATION

By the 1860s there was considerable British capital, both European and Chinese, invested in the development of the tin mines in Selangor and Perak. The unsettled conditions in both states, due primarily to quarrels between the rival Chinese factions, upset the profits to be obtained from the investments. Therefore the merchants wanted effective administration to return as soon as possible. Many had lost large sums of money in the fighting between the factions and as British subjects they had often lodged complaints with the Straits

Settlements authorities. But in the light of the earlier warning given by Ord these complaints could only be unofficial. However the Penang Government became directly involved as a result of the fighting in Larut, for this fighting between the Hai San and Ghee Hin was also carried out in Penang. There had been the riots of 1867, and Penang was also the source of supplies for both groups as well as being the base for the Ghee Hin blockade of the tin mines.

Fighting became more serious in 1872-3 especially as a result of the Ghee Hin interfering with the passage of ships to Larut. Eventually in 1873 Ord decided to support one side in the hope of bringing the fighting to an end. The Mentri was recognized as the independent ruler of Larut and no obstacles were placed in the way of the employment of a British officer, Captain Speedy, as the leader of a small Indian police force recruited to restore order in the tin fields. By the end of 1873 peace had been brought to Larut. However it was at this point that Ord was replaced as Governor by Sir Andrew Clarke who had arrived in Singapore with instructions to look into the affairs of the Malay Peninsula.

> Her Majesty's Government have no desire to interfere in the internal affairs of the Malay States but looking to the long and intimate connection between them and Her Majesty's Government, Her Majesty's Government feel it incumbent to employ such influence as they possess with the native princes to rescue these fertile and productive countries from the ruin which must befall them if the present disorders continue unchecked.

This was the policy behind Clarke's instructions; how had the change from non-intervention been evolved?

The 1870's in England saw a noticeable change in the attitude of many members of the ruling Liberal Party towards overseas possessions. These were mainly the younger members of the Party and they were not so confident of the benefits of free trade in the face of growing commercial competition from Britain's rivals. The same feelings also affected the officials of the Colonial Office after 1870-1 and gradually these officials came to support the idea of some kind of intervention in order to stop the fighting in Larut and Selangor. Cowan points out that this change of outlook was not entirely due to pressure from the merchants of the Straits Settlements but was also due to British fear of intervention by other powers. He quotes from a minute by the Colonial Secretary:

> We would not see with indifference interference of foreign powers in the affairs of the Peninsula, on the other hand it is

difficult to see how we should be justified in objecting to the native states seeking aid elsewhere if we refuse to take any steps to remedy the evils complained of.

There was the fear that if Britain did nothing the merchants with investments in the Peninsula might obtain assistance from another power (perhaps Germany) in order to stabilize conditions.

It was still true however that the Liberal Government would never agree to annexation. Therefore the instructions given to the new Governor, Sir Andrew Clarke, were to investigate and report on what steps could be taken to restore peace in the states of the Peninsula. This was in 1873. We shall see that when Clarke reached Singapore he exceeded his instructions to 'investigate and report' by actively intervening.

BEGINNINGS OF BRITISH INTERVENTION

The new Governor reached Singapore towards the end of 1873, and within a short time seems to have decided that intervention was the best policy. He was given the opportunity to intervene by the letter from Raja Abdullah asking for British support for his claim to the Perak throne. This letter was obtained by a Singapore resident W. H. Read through a Chinese merchant friend of Abdullah's named Tan Kim Cheng who was a member of the Ghee Hin; and while Abdullah probably never considered the implications of what he was doing, the request for help was just what Clarke wanted. Abdullah thought British support would gain him the throne; afterwards the support would be unnecessary; Clarke saw this as an opportunity to institute a complete change of policy, a change which he carried out without reference to London.

Clarke therefore arranged for a meeting to be held at Pangkor to which the disputants to the Perak throne, the major chiefs, and the leaders of the Chinese factions were invited. It is interesting that the Governor was at first inclined to support Ismail as Sultan but, when only Abdullah came to Pangkor, where he had the support of all the chiefs who were present except the Mentri, the Governor changed his opinion. (Yusof was not even invited to the meeting.)

The quarrel between the Ghee Hin and Hai San miners was dealt with first. This presented little difficulty as preliminary agreement had already been reached. It was decided that both groups would disarm and that a commission of British and Chinese would settle all claims to the mines. The more important Pangkor Engagement between the Governor and the Malay chiefs was signed on January 20th, 1874. The treaty stated that Abdullah should be Sultan while Ismail should be given a pension and the title of Sultan Muda. All the other chiefs would retain their offices and the Sultan recognized the Mentri's special position in Larut. The cession to Britain of the Dindings (including a strip on the mainland) by the 1826 treaty was also confirmed. It was agreed that all revenues were in future to be collected by the Sultan, not by individual chiefs who were to be paid allowances from a civil list. Finally the Sultan was to accept the appointment of a British Resident and, though the Resident was to have no executive powers, his advice 'must be asked and acted upon on all questions other than those touching Malay religion and custom'. An Assistant Resident was also to be appointed in Larut.

Such was the Pangkor Engagement and it was in this way that the British first actively and officially intervened in one of the Malay states to the extent of appointing an official to reside there. Clarke quickly followed up this initial success by turning to affairs in Selangor and Sungei Ujong. In Selangor there was an excuse for intervention in the attack by pirates on a Malacca trading ship in in November 1873. Nine people from Selangor were identified as having been involved in this attack, and in February 1874 Clarke took them back to Selangor for punishment. Negotiations thereupon took place between Sultan Abdul Samad, his viceroy, Tengku Kudin, and the Governor. First of all friendly relations were established, the pirates were dealt with, and in August 1874 the first British official, F. A. Swettenham, was accepted by the Sultan at Kuala Langat. The actual appointment of a Resident was to come later in the year.

British intervention in Sungei Ujong, a small state just south of the Selangor border, came in support of one of the chiefs, the Dato' Klana. He had recently succeeded to this position but having lived long in Malacca he was on good terms with the British authorities. Trouble in Sungei Ujong was centred on control of the Linggi River, which, because it was the means of communication to the tin mines at Rasah, gave its controller an important source of revenue. By an agreement signed in April 1874, the Governor agreed to support the Dato' Klana in his quarrel with the other major chief in Sungei Ujong, the Dato' Bandar, a quarrel which was intensified by the fact that the two Dato's supported rival claimants to the position of major chief in Rembau. The agreement did not envisage the appointment of a Resident but did give the Dato' Klana the 'moral and material guarantee and protection of the British

Government'. In fact it was not long before Clarke had to come to the help of the Dato' Klana with armed force.

Between January and April 1874, Sir Andrew Clarke had thus made agreements with the rulers of the states of Perak, Selangor and Sungei Ujong and had done far more than was warranted by his original instructions 'to investigate and report'. Almost immediately after Clarke had reported the signing of the Pangkor Engagement to the Colonial Office he received instructions to delay the appointment of Residents until the steps which he had taken had been fully considered. Although Speedy and Swettenham had been sent to Larut and Kuala Langat, the appointment of official Residents was delayed by a change of government in England. The British elections, held in February 1874, saw the defeat of the Liberals and the return to office of the Conservatives led by Disraeli. It was therefore some time before the new government came to any decision about Clarke's activities in Malaysia. Eventually, after four months delay, approval was given by the government and Clarke was told to proceed with the appointment of Residents. He nominated J. W. W. Birch for Perak, with Speedy in Larut; Davidson in Selangor, with Swettenham in Langat; and an Assistant Resident named Tatham to Sungei Ujong. The procedure of government by advice had begun, and British protection was now officially extended to three of the Malay states.

EXERCISES

1 Describe the situation in either Selangor or Perak in the 1860s and 1870s.

2 Why did Britain change its policy of non-intervention in 1874?

3 Was the British decision to intervene in the Malay States a result of events in the Peninsula or a change in imperial policy?

4 Describe the effect which the expansion of tin mining had on the administration of the Malay States.

5 Write short notes on:
Sungei Ujong, tin plate, Yap Ah Loy, Ngah Ibrahim, Tunku Kudin, the Pangkor Engagement, Sir Andrew Clarke.

12

THE RESIDENTIAL SYSTEM

WHEN the British intervened in West Malaysia in 1874 there was virtually no possibility of direct annexation of the Malaysian states for the government in England was almost certain to prohibit such action, if only to prevent itself being responsible for the administration of such states. Responsibility for administration probably meant expense, and extra expense was the last thing that the British Government wanted in 1873-4. While it was therefore improbable that Britain would become directly responsible for the administration of the states of the Peninsula in the same way as it was responsible for the administration of the Straits Settlements, it was nevertheless necessary to at least establish some system of political advice. For various reasons, which will be outlined below, it was decided that British officers should be appointed to advise the rulers of the states on how to improve the administration of their countries. These officers were to reside in the states and to be permanent advisers. In the first instance they were not intended to be executive officers, although the Pangkor Engagement had stated that the Residents' advice 'must be asked and acted upon on all matters save Malay religion and custom'. As will be seen it is easy enough to give advice but rather more difficult to ensure that such advice is followed.

THE IDEA OF 'INDIRECT RULE'

Later in the century, in northern Nigeria, Lord Lugard established a system of administration which was called *indirect rule*. This meant that British control was to be exercised through existing Nigerian political institutions. These institutions were to be preserved and used rather than swept away in a flush of reforming zeal. British officials, though ultimately responsible for the administration, would exercise their authority in an indirect way. The alternative was outright annexation and the imposition of direct control by the British Government. Although the phrase *indirect*

THE DEVELOPMENT OF BRITISH INFLUENCE
AND MALAY NATIONALISM

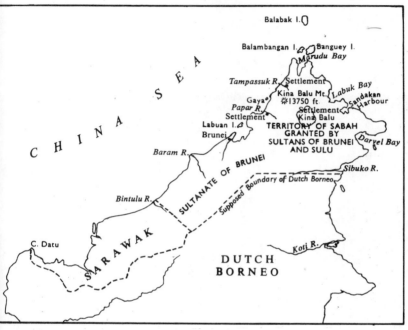

Borneo in 1878

The Borneo Company's Offices, Kuching

Sir Alfred Dent

(reproduced with kind permission of his son L. A. Dent, Esq.)

Sir Charles Brooke

SARAWAK MUSEUM

The First Rulers' Conference, Kuala Kangsar, in 1897

First rubber trees in Kuala Kangsar

Kuala Kangsar about 1880

H. N. Ridley

MUN PHOTO

The Malay College, Kuala Kangsar

NATIONAL ARCHIVES. SINGAPORE

Raffles Institution, Singapore's old
between 1835-41. Teaching bega

Malay Students Society, London, around 1925. Seated Tengku Abdul Rahman, then the President of the Society, now Prime Minister of Malaysia

It was completed by Coleman

Sir Cecil Clementi

Vyner Brooke

SARAWAK MUSEUM

Malay Members of the Supreme Council, Sarawak

BY COURTESY OF OSMAN HASSAN

Eunos Abdullah

Dato Sir Onn bin Ja'afar

BY COURTESY OF AHMAD BOESTAMAM

Ahmad Boestamam

Thomas Braddell, first
Attorney General of the
Straits Settlements and
author of many of the
state's laws.

UNIVERSITY OF MALAYA PRESS

rule is usually associated with the activities of Lugard in the Emirates of northern Nigeria, the same type of government was in fact introduced into the Malay Peninsula in the 1870's, though in Malaysia it was called the *residential system*. This system was based upon the same ideas of indirect control.

Residents and their subordinates were sent to the Malaysian states to persuade the rulers of those states to follow certain lines of policy. In the first place there were certainly not enough British officials to carry out very much direct administration by themselves; and secondly there existed in the states an administrative hierarchy which had long been in use. It was felt that this administrative structure could continue to be used to carry out the new policies proposed by the Residents. Thus it was originally intended that the Resident would advise the Sultan who could then use the traditional system to administer his state. The essence of indirect rule is that change is introduced slowly and by means of existing political institutions. However the early residential system in Malaysia had one important drawback: if the Sultan did not take the advice offered by the Resident there was no way of forcing him to do so, apart from sending an army. A ruler might be pleased to have a Resident at his court for prestige value, for example to illustrate a special relationship with Britain; at the same time he might have no intention of listening to the Resident's advice. The Resident, in fact, had an extremely difficult task, for he had to work almost entirely by personal influence. The success or failure of his appointment depended on how great his influence was with the Sultan and the chiefs. Above all he had to be diplomatic and tactful for it was not easy to give advice and at the same time refrain from giving the impression that he was really running affairs.

All the advisers, when appointed to the Malay Peninsula in the 1870's, had three general aims which they hoped to see accomplished by means of their advice. The first was to restore and maintain peace and to establish regulations of law and order. This had to come first. Second was the development of the resources of the state so that its wealth could be properly used. Finally there was the the setting up of a sound system of taxation so that the wealth of the state could help further development. Naturally the various Residents had different methods, some successful, some not. The careers of Birch and Low in Perak provide good examples of both types. At the conclusion of the previous chapter, we saw that by the end of 1874 Residents and assistants had been appointed to Perak, Selangor and Sungei Ujong. During 1875 the residential system functioned quite satisfactorily in Selangor and Sungei Ujong, where the rulers wished to follow the advice given and where both rulers had reasonably firm control over their respective territories. In Selangor, especially, Davidson and Swettenham were personal friends of Tengku Kudin and Sultan Abdul Samad. In Perak, however, things were different.

FAILURE IN PERAK

The Resident appointed by Clarke to Perak was J. W. W. Birch, previously Colonial Secretary in the Straits Settlements with earlier service in Ceylon. Although Birch was an efficient public servant, he was not a tolerant man; neither was he a fluent Malay speaker. He was not able to get on to terms of personal friendship with the Perak chiefs, and he considered that most things in Perak were 'of such an irregular character as to require immediate alteration'. Despite warning from Governor Clarke about the necessity of going slow and having patience, Birch was the sort of man who lectured the Sultan in public and did not hesitate to interfere in Malay customs. He provoked many clashes with Sultan Abdullah and the chiefs because of his interference in matters concerning debt slavery, a custom rather widespread in Perak at that time.

Birch's task was not made easier by the fact that he was appointed ten months after the Pangkor Engagement, and during that time Sultan Abdullah contracted out the collection of the Perak customs duties to a Singapore Chinese for $26,000 per year. Most of the money which he obtained he spent on himself, including the purchase of a military uniform from Europe for $4,000. When Birch arrived and attempted to curtail these extravagances he was naturally resented by the Sultan. It is doubtful whether the Perak ruler and chiefs understood the implications of accepting a Resident, and they quickly objected to being deprived of their sources of revenue, for their right to collect taxes was the basis of their social position in the state.

In May 1875 Sir Andrew Clarke was replaced as Governor by Sir William Jervois, and thereafter matters in Perak came rapidly to a state of crisis. A forceful and pushing man, the new Governor very soon decided that the residential system of giving advice was not working properly in Perak, and he proposed that the administration of the state be taken over by British officials who could govern directly on behalf of the Sultan. Sultan Abdullah was not pleased with this suggestion but so much pressure was put upon him that with great reluctance he eventually agreed. This substitution of a more direct form of British influence might have succeeded if the Resident in Perak, Birch, had not tried to make the Sultan sign proclamations giving finality to the agreement to allow direct British control. Abdullah objected to this step and only signed the proclamations on the threat of being deposed. He now decided that Birch would have to be removed. Agreement was made with Ismail and his supporters, and in effect the Perak chiefs were at last united in their desire to be rid of the Resident. Birch's death was brought about at Pasir Salak, on the Perak River, through the agency of the Maharaja Lela on November 2nd, 1875. The murder of the Resident came as a great shock to Jervois who visualized a full scale insurrection all over the Peninsula. Thinking that matters were more serious than they were, he panicked and asked for troops to be sent from India and Hong Kong as reinforcements. Many of these did arrive and took part in the events which followed, and which are known as the Perak War.

As it turned out there was no national insurrection, not even in Perak, for the chiefs had primarily wished to remove Birch. It is doubtful that they had any further plans. Jervois' reinforcements poured into Perak from north and south but there was remarkably little fighting. Those implicated in the death of Birch were captured and tried. Abdullah and Ismail were both exiled, the former to the Seychelles and the latter to Johore. With his two rivals removed, Yusof was appointed Regent and later became Sultan. He had therefore finally achieved the position from which he had earlier been excluded, an exclusion which had begun the Perak quarrel over the succession and indirectly led to British intervention.

The Colonial Office in England disapproved of Jervois' action in Perak which it heard about after he had tried to enforce it. The result was to discredit completely a policy of more direct rule, for the British Government considered that Jervois' change of policy had caused the Perak War. As a result the residential system was to be given a further trial though unfortunately the powers of the Residents were still left rather vague and ill-defined. In Perak, particularly, where the Malay framework of government had been largely swept away in the aftermath of the Perak War, British officials came to be much more executive officers than mere advisers. However personal influence still played a very large part in deciding how much control over policy a Resident would have. In 1878 the Governor told the Residents:

> The Residents have been placed in the Native States as advisers not as rulers, and if they take it upon themselves to

disregard this principle they will...be held responsible if trouble springs from their neglect of it.

The difficulty, as Low point out in reply, was,

If fully understand the wishes of Government and intend to carry them out, but we must first create the government to be advised and that is what all along I have been trying to do.

SUCCESS IN SOME AREAS

The new permanent Resident appointed to Perak was Hugh Low, formerly Colonial Secretary at Labuan in Borneo. A good Malay speaker, he had had considerable experience in South-East Asia and proved to be an extremely capable administrator and adviser in Perak. He was on good terms with the new generation of Perak chiefs, he was easily approachable and made no attempt to interfere in Malay custom. He got on with the job of restoring order in the state and developing Perak's resources. He began by moving Speedy, the rather extravagant Assistant Resident, from Larut to Lower Perak, and he brought the revenues of the tin mines under his direct control. This revenue was henceforth to be used for the benefit of the whole state. Chiefs no longer collected revenues for themselves but were given official salaries; in six years Hugh Low liquidated a Perak debt of $800,000. The Resident made no attempt to abolish debt slavery but allowed the practice to die out over a period of ten years, for it was estimated that in 1874 there were three thousand debt slaves in Perak. He tried to ensure that the policies which he initiated would not give the ruling class in Perak legitimate grounds for complaint. At the same time his policies tried to ensure that the resources of the state were used for the benefit of the many rather than the few.

In Selangor and Sungei Ujong, the residential practice was similar, though Low is generally considered to be the model Resident in the 1880's. In all three states revenue for the first twenty years depended almost entirely on the duties obtained from the export of tin ore. Thus much emphasis was placed on making the development of the tin fields easier; for example the first railways in Malaysia, between Taiping and Port Weld (1885) and Kuala Lumpur and Klang (1886), were to connect the mines with the places of export. During the same period most surplus revenue was spent on roads, thus expanding communications and leading to further development in the tin fields.

Another similarity in practice was the setting up of State

Councils to discuss the policy that was to be implemented in each state. These Councils were small and the idea may have been copied from the Indian Councils Act of 1861. The members were the ruler, the major chiefs, one or two Chinese leaders, and the Resident, and the purpose of the Councils was to institute some method of judging local opinion. The Councils discussed all aspects of policy and helped to gain the confidence of the Malay people through their chiefs by keeping the chiefs informed about government policy. Only in this way could the Residents hope to have their proposals accepted and carried out.

Begun first in Selangor in 1877, the same system of State Councils was also established in Perak and Sungei Ujong. The retirement of Tengku Kudin to Penang in 1878 left authority undivided in the hands of the Sultan, and the appointment of Frank Swettenham, a friend of the Sultan, as Resident in 1882, enabled matters to proceed smoothly in Selangor. At the same time British influence was expanding outwards from Sungei Ujong to the surrounding small states. British protection and advice was extended to Jelebu and Rembau in 1883 and 1887 and also to the Confederation of Sri Menanti in 1887. Finally in 1889 all the states which composed the Negri Sembilan accepted the appointment of a British Resident. Just as the success of the residential system in Perak and Selangor owed much to the individuals involved, Low and Swettenham, the success of the policy in Negri Sembilan owed much to the appointment of Martin Lister.

THE SYSTEM IN PAHANG

The only other state in the Peninsula which lay outside the Siamese sphere of influence and which had not yet come into direct contact with the British was Pahang. Johore, the state nearest to Singapore, did not have an official Resident but its ruler had very close connexions with officials in Singapore and received a great deal of unofficial assistance. A new treaty between Johore and Britain in 1885 recognized the Maharaja as Sultan of Johore and gave definite British protection against external attack.

Pahang, however, came to British attention at a later date than Perak and Selangor for a number of reasons. In the first place Pahang was not on any of the trade routes used by the Straits Settlements whose merchants therefore had no direct interest in the state. In the second place it had no export trade, no Chinese immigration on a large scale, and therefore no need for British interest. This did not mean that Pahang was a state without problems and troubles, for in fact, as it was a large state, the Sultan's administration did not extend very far up-river from the coast. It will be remembered that there had earlier been a long drawn-out quarrel over the right to be ruler, a quarrel which had only been settled in 1863.

In the 1880's the Sultan Wan Ahmad was not on good terms with the up-river chiefs; he had no control over them and as a result was short of revenue. In order to remedy this the Sultan began selling large land concessions to foreigners, many of whom were British subjects. These concessions were so large that there was a danger of dissipating Pahang's resources, and the Straits Settlements authorities feared the establishment of British-owned concessions which were outside official supervision. They also feared that similar concessions might be obtained by Germany or France. Swettenham after visiting Pekan suggested the appointment of a British agent there, and in 1887 the Sultan was persuaded to accept a British Consul-General, Hugh Clifford. At first Clifford had very limited influence, but in 1888 after the murder of a Chinese British subject in Pekan the Sultan was persuaded, with the help of the Sultan of Johore, to accept a Resident on the same terms as the three west-coast states. The immediate reaction of the up-river chiefs was to oppose this appointment. They realized that it would bring about a strengthening of the Sultan's position and consequent weakening of their own independence. Therefore when the attempt to increase the centralization of administration was begun, the territorial chief of Semantan, named Bahaman, rose in revolt in 1891. The campaign to end this insurrection proved to be long drawn-out affair due to the jungle terrain in which it was fought. It was not until 1895 that the rebellion eventually collapsed when the leader fled to Trengganu.

By the end of the 1880's British influence was dominant in all those states of the Malay Peninsula which lay outside Siamese claims of suzerainty. Perak, Selangor, Pahang and the Negri Sembilan states had British Residents, while Johore had a special relationship with the Straits Settlements authorities with as yet no Resident.

The residential system was used to exercise British influence because it was the only practical one in the circumstances. Outright annexation of the states of the Malay Peninsula was impossible because of the trends of British policy at that time, and furthermore the British Government considered the appointment of Residents by far the cheapest way of exercising influence. But, as is often the way when things are done cheaply, policy did not work out as originally intended. As it turned out the British Government had no specific instructions to give the Residents apart from telling them that their duty was 'to give advice'. How their advice was to be implemented was left almost entirely to them, and it says much for the competence of the Residents that there were no more 'Birch incidents'. In all the states to which they were sent the Residents found conditions in which advice alone was not enough. Often also, while they intended to work through existing institutions by suggesting lines of policy, they found that these institutions were not always able to carry out their innovations and suggestions. As a result the Residents developed a tendency to do things for themselves, to take short cuts in administration, and they became executive officers rather than advisers. However, they were, after initial set-backs, successful in accomplishing their three aims: the establishment of law and order; the centralized collection of revenue; and the development of the resources of the states.

THE BRITISH NORTH BORNEO COMPANY

At the same time that the British government was intervening directly in the Malay Peninsula, British influence was also being extended indirectly in Borneo; not only in Sarawak but in a more northerly part of the territory of the Sultan of Brunei, present-day Sabah. In the 1870's interest was revived in the same areas which Dalrymple had hopefully obtained from the Sultan of Sulu in 1761. Brooke's success in carving out a private kingdom for himself in Brunei territory was bound to give others ideas, particularly in view of the weakened condition of Brunei in the nineteenth century. This condition was very similar to that in the states of the Peninsula, the feudal structure had almost collapsed. The Sultan, Abdul Mumin (1852-83), had no real power, he was an old, weak man (over one hundred when he died) and therefore controlled by his *pangirans* (major chiefs) and easily influenced by a persuasive talker.

In 1865 the sultan met a persuasive talker in the person of the United States consul in Brunei, an adventurer named Moses, to whom he gave a grant of all the present area of Sabah in return for annual payments. Moses did not really intend to do very much on his own and he soon sold his rights to the Hong Kong based American Trading Company, headed by two Americans and two Chinese. One of the Americans, Torrey, was made Raja of Ambong by the Sultan and the company established a settlement on the Kimanis river, sixty miles north of Brunei town. But the settlement did not prosper and this attempt to start an American colony in Borneo ended in failure in 1866.

This lack of success caused Torrey to sell his rights in turn to Overbeck, the Austrian Consul-General in Hong Kong, who eventually formed a partnership with the British company of Dent Brothers. This new organization made a further agreement with the Sultan of Brunei in 1877 by which they were given possession of Sabah in full sovereignty together with the right of administration. In return the company was to make annual payments of $10,000 to the Sultan and $3,000 to the Temenggong. This was a fairly good bargain for the Sultan as it was doubtful whether Brunei was in control of the land in question, especially the north and north-east areas which were claimed by the Sultan of Sulu. Overbeck realized this and to make doubly sure he made another agreement with Sulu in 1878 by which he obtained an outright grant of sovereignty from the Sultan, Mohammed Jamalul Alam, in return for $5,000 a year. This second treaty was a safety precaution as there is no documentary evidence that Brunei had ever ceded the area to Sulu and the amounts of the two payments to be made to the two sultans perhaps indicates the contempory view of the strength of the rival claims.

In 1881 Dent bought out Overbeck and formed a new company in London for the development of North Borneo. He realized that he could do little without the support of the British government, for the agents of the company were quickly opposed by the Spanish in the Philippines. The Spanish had forced the surrender of Sulu six months after the treaty with Overbeck and they had tried to eject the Resident whom Dent had appointed to Sandakan. As has been seen with the events in the Malay Peninsula, the policies of the British government had changed in the 1870's, intervention was allowed, although the undertaking of responsibilities was discouraged. At this time Britain was afraid of German or French settlements in Borneo and therefore Dent was able to obtain the support he wanted; in 1881 he was given a Royal Charter to bring into being the British North Borneo Company, the first such charter since that given to the East India Company. By this charter the Company was allowed to administer the territory of Sabah and in return it was agreed that facilities would be provided for the British navy. No monopoly of trade would be set up, there would be no interference with local custom and religion and the company could not transfer its rights without the approval of the British government. Finally, the Governor was to be appointed with the latter's approval and the first one was Treacher, from the Civil Service of the Malay States. As far as Britain was concerned this was an extension of influence on the cheap and British approval for Dent's acquisition of territory from the Sultan of Brunei marked a definite change of policy from that previously maintained against the Raja of Sarawak. The latter had been prevented from extending Sarawak's borders after 1861 but this attitude could no longer be justified and in 1882 Brooke was allowed to acquire land up to the Baram river, the present Fourth Division. These moves in 1881-2 set in motion a scramble between Sarawak and North Borneo for the remaining territory of Brunei, which became even weaker in 1888 because of a disputed succession. Weld, who was then Governor of the Straits Settlements, did not wish to see Brunei swallowed up, as he believed it should be treated in the same way as the Peninsular Malay states. On his advice, therefore, Britain decided to preserve the *status quo* and in 1888 declared a protectorate over Brunei and also over Sarawak and North Borneo. At the same time Labuan was handed over to the administration of the North Borneo Company, and the Governor of the Straits Settlements became High Commissioner for the Borneo states.

Meanwhile the international position of the territories of east Malaysia was secured by agreements with Spain and Holland, both of whom had raised objections to the activities of the North Borneo Company. In 1885 Britain recognized Spanish rights in Sulu and Spain 'renounced all claims of sovereignty over the territory of the continent of Borneo which belongs or has belonged in the past to the Sultan of Sulu'. So far as Holland was concerned the difficulties were over boundaries; the border between Sabah and Dutch Borneo was defined by treaty in 1891 and finally fixed in detail in 1912.

EXERCISES

1 Write an account of the Residential System in the Malay States.
2 In what circumstances did the British establish themselves in North Borneo?
3 Explain the reasons for British intervention in Pahang.
4 Write short notes on:
   debt slavery, J. W. W. Birch, the Perak War, Sir Hugh Low, State Councils.

13

THE CONSOLIDATION OF BRITISH INFLUENCE

THE NEED FOR INTER-STATE CO-OPERATION

WE have seen how the residential system was set up in the Malay Peninsula, and it has been remarked that although the process may be called the residential 'system' there was in fact very little system about it. It is fair to say that conditions in no two states were the same, and the methods used by the Residents to bring about improvements in these conditions were not the same either. Each Resident worked, more or less, in his own way; though all of them had the same basic aims, the methods which they used varied from state to state depending on local feelings and local customs. Each state was an independent unit, each Resident dealt directly with the Governor of the Straits Settlements who was responsible to the British Government. In theory the Governor was responsible for over-all control of policy in the states, but he was usually far too busy with the affairs of the Straits Settlements to take much interest in day-to-day administration. Although there was a subordinate official in Singapore responsible for the administrative details of the Residents' policy, he was junior to the Residents and was unlikely to exercise much influence over them.

Therefore, although the policy of sending Residents to the states was successful in achieving the immediate aims of the British Government, as the system developed, certain obvious faults began to appear.

In the first place the Residents had become too independent in their own states; they carried out the administration in their own way and by the 1890's the four states were drifting apart. This trend was increased by the second factor, a lack of over-all control by the Straits Settlements authorities. There was little or no attempt made to co-ordinate policy in the various states or to plan for developments which affected more than one state—for example, the linking up of roads and railways. Finally, the growing power of, and lack of control over, the Residents had removed much influence from the ruler and the State Councils. As administration became more complex, with the economic development of the west-coast states in particular, the rulers and the Councils were by-passed by the Residents, who were more eager to get things done than to delay matters with consultation. As far as administration was concerned each state was beginning to develop its own laws, as well as land and taxation policies, and there was a likelihood that in the future, co-operation between the states would become extremely difficult.

THE FEDERATED MALAY STATES

These dangers became more apparent in the 1890's and both in Malaysia and Britain consideration began to be given to some form of closer association between the states. Swettenham, the Resident in Perak, was an early supporter of these ideas, and in 1893 he submitted some draft proposals for the consideration of the Governor. However other Residents had also supported such proposals, particularly J. P. Rodger in Pahang for this State was short of revenue for development. The project for closer association eventually received the agreement of the British Government, and in 1895 Swettenham was directed to obtain the agreement of the rulers for a federation of Perak, Selangor, Negri Sembilan and Pahang. With the encouragement of Sultan Idris of Perak, the other rulers agreed to the proposals if only because Swettenham explained that more control would be exercised over their respective Residents. However as it turned out, although the Residents were to be less independent, this control was not to be exercised by the Sultans but rather by the new Federal Government. The Treaty of Federation was agreed to in 1895, and in the following year the Federated Malay States came into being.

The significance of this step was perhaps not appreciated at the time, but today we can see that this Federation introduced for the first time since the days of the Malacca Sultanate some measure of unity among the central states of the Malay Peninsula. It was also the first step in the emergence of the Federation of Malaya as we knew it prior to 1963. The importance of this 1896 movement towards unity should not be underestimated, for although the immediate system of federation discouraged other states from joining, in the long term view it was to serve as the nucleus of modern Malaysia. An example of the significance of this closer association was the Rulers' Conference held in Kuala Kangsar in 1897. This

MILES

0   50   100

SIAM

PERLIS

KEDAH

PENANG

PROVINCE
WELLESLEY

KELANTAN

TRENGGANU

PERAK

DINDINGS

PAHANG

SELANGOR

NEGRI
SEMBILAN

MALACCA

JOHORE

SUMATRA

SINGAPORE

After 1909 Unfederated Malay States	Independent with unofficial British advice
	Under Siamese suzerainty
	Straits Settlements
	Federated Malay States

THE MALAY PENINSULA IN 1895

was the first time that the rulers of the four states had ever met each other and was therefore a great step forward towards mutual agreement. What then were the immediate changes and results brought about by the establishment of the Federated Malay States? Firstly the rulers agreed to accept the appointment of a Resident-General, who would be responsible for controlling the activities of the Residents and whose advice they would also accept. The purpose of the appointment was to have a senior official, second only to the Governor, to supervise the co-ordination of policy for all the states. Secondly, therefore, the four states would submit to some uniformity of policy especially in matters which affected more than one state. All the main departments of administration would have a federal head who would supervise the work of the departmental branches in all the States. The Governor of the Straits Settlements became the High Commissioner of the Federated Malay States and was the channel through which communication was made with the British Government. Finally it was intended that the richer states with greater resources should help in the development of the poorer states. In this way the revenue collected from the export of tin from Perak and Selangor would assist in the opening up of the resources and the improvement in the administration of Pahang and Negri Sembilan. For the first time the 'have' states conceded that they had a responsibility towards the 'have-not' states. From this closer association there also developed a common outlook and this was helped by the establishment of a unified civil service and police force which could serve in the four states. Later there also came into being a federal education policy, a standard postal system, and a common code of land regulations.

These were the changes which were intended when federation was introduced; and in practice most of these changes took place. But of equal importance were the unintended changes, bringing results which had not been forecast or foreseen.

FAULTS OF THE NEW FEDERATION

Although called a federation, the constitutional and administrative system established in 1896 was not a federation in the strict sense of the term. There was no division of power between the states and the federal government, no division of sovereignty by which some functions were allocated to the states and some to the central government. Little attempt was made to decide which aspects of government were the responsibility of the states and which the responsibility of the federation; and most important of all, the major sources of revenue, export duties, came under the control of the central authority. As a result the latter, because it controlled the sources of revenue, also effectively controlled the administration. Although the intention was to create a federation, the result was in fact a union. This tendency towards centralized control was also helped by other factors, although constitutionally the failure to establish a real federal structure was the main reason for turning a federation into a union.

It was quite true that the independence of the Residents was curtailed, for the appointment of a Resident-General (the first one was Swettenham himself) did much to limit their individuality and establish greater conformity of policy. In effect the Resident-General became the initiator and the co-ordinator of policy. But the powers which the Residents gave up did not go back to the Sultans, as the latter had hoped, but rather to the new super-authority in Kuala Lumpur which was even more remote from the rulers. Very soon it was seen that whereas the aim in 1895 had been to enhance the position of the Sultans in relation to the Residents, in fact the real powers of the Sultans further declined for much initiative now rested with the central government which was established in Kuala Lumpur, the new federal capital. All major decisions affecting all the four states were made in Kuala Lumpur and the state governments had fewer and fewer opportunities to exercise initiative.

Another important result was the increase in the number of British officials in the Malay states. All departments of government began to expand rapidly and as a result administration came to be taken over by British engineers, doctors, educators, and administrators. The older aim of indirect rule, to associate the traditional Malay officials in the business of government, was lost sight of, and the states came to be run almost entirely by British officers. The traditional Malay official was not at ease with this new type of administration with its emphasis on economic development, and it was not until a new generation of civil servants had been trained that the Malays took part in administration once more. Little was done to interfere with Malay custom and tradition—the British had learnt that lesson—with the result that although the Sultans and chiefs lost most of their actual power to the new bureaucratic set-up, they still retained their prestige and appearance of power. The Sultans were preserved by the British for their ceremonial functions, just as the British had preserved their own monarchy for the same purpose. The pomp and circumstance of monarchy remained in the

Federated Malay States but as time passed the political power of the Sultans became almost non-existent. It was this change, unforeseen in 1895, which discouraged the rulers of the other states in the Peninsula from associating themselves with their colleagues who had agreed to federation. Therefore, the whole trend of federation was towards centralized control and unification rather than mere association. This followed from the fact that there was no clear delineation of sovereignty between the states and the federal authority. Since the latter controlled the more important sources of revenue it soon exerted considerable control and influence over almost all state policy, and the four states were soon directed from Kuala Lumpur.

THE FEDERAL LEGISLATIVE COUNCIL

The main result of federation was the loss of power and initiative on the part of the states. What did they get in return for this loss of authority? In the first place they obtained more efficient government, efficient not only because there was more uniformity of policy but also because there was more continuity. Good ideas used in one state could now be communicated to the others; policy would not now change every time the Resident changed, because all Residents would have to conform to over-all direction from Kuala Lumpur. Development could be planned on a wider scale, economic resources could be more efficiently utilized and communications, especially, could be co-ordinated. The resources of the Federated Malay States could be used for the benefit of all the individual states and the states with less-developed resources would benefit. There is no doubt that the establishment of the Federated Malay States ushered in the era of the development of modern Malaysia. Political and constitutional problems were put on the shelf, and all the energies of the government were directed to the economic development of the four states.

The fact that the administration proved efficient; the fact that the development of the country proceeded rapidly as there was plenty of money for development because of the revenue from tin and later rubber, both these facts served to disguise the general trend of centralization in the years before the First World War. The Sultans themselves did not immediately notice what had happened. They had enough money for themselves, and some were not particularly interested in government. Even the establishment of a Federal Council in 1909, of which they were members, did nothing to enhance their position. The Council was composed of the four Sultans, the four Residents and four unofficial members together with the Resident-General. In this Federal Council the Sultans were no longer the rulers of their own states but advisers to others who were ruling their states for them. The wheel had come full circle very quickly. Originally the British had come to the Malay states to advise the Sultans on how to administer their states; now the Sultans were advising the British.

The powers which the rulers had within the Federal Council were purely advisory for they could have no executive authority outside their own states. Thus the actual administrative powers possessed by the Sultans suffered a further decline. However the new Council established in 1909 was to be of great importance for the future. From this Council, as time passed, grew the traditional assembly which was established in all countries under British influence. As the Federal Council in West Malaysia expanded in size it came to represent more and more interests in the four states. It came to contain not only officials actively concerned with administration but also businessmen and representatives of the professions who may be called 'unofficials'. The practice was for the unofficials to be consulted on many aspects of government and they often exercised quite considerable influence over policy decisions. It was from these beginnings in the Federated Malay States in the early years of this century that the Federal Legislative Council containing representatives of all the states of the country developed. This happened after 1948 and, not long afterwards, this Federal Legislative Council became the Federation Parliament, for which the first elections were held in 1955.

THE UNFEDERATED MALAY STATES

1909 is an important year in the history of the Federation of Malaysia, not only because it saw the creation of a council in Kuala Lumpur from which developed the Legislative Council and Parliament, but also because in that year the present geographical limits of West Malaysia were finally drawn. In 1909 the British made a treaty with Siam by which Siam transferred to Britain whatever rights she possessed over the four states of Trengganu, Kelantan, Kedah and Perlis. As a result of this treaty the border between Malaysia and Siam was fixed along the lines of the present boundary.

The rights which Siam possessed over the four northern states were somewhat vague and differed considerably from state to state.

and were also differently interpreted from generation to generation. The rights were generally referred to in the phrase 'Siamese suzerainty' which to the Siamese meant that the states recognized the general overlordship of the King of Siam. This subordination was conceded by the sending of the symbolic *bunga emas* to the Siamese capital. Suzerainty was sometimes strictly enforced by the Siamese while sometimes the Malay states were ignored for many years. However, with regard to Kelantan, Kedah and Perlis, the Siamese claims were not really disputed by the inhabitants, whereas Trengganu always maintained that she was not in the same position as the others, being much less under Siamese control.

British relations with Siam during most of the nineteenth century were governed by the Anglo-Siamese Treaty of 1826. By this treaty the British recognized that Kedah and Patani (the State to the north of Kelantan) were virtually Siamese provinces and were almost directly under Siamese control. The position of Kelantan and Trengganu was stated to be more difficult to define although Britain again recognized that Siam exercised some kind of authority over the area. In Trengganu the authority was often little more than nominal whereas in Kelantan, which was nearer to Siam, control was more rigorously exercised.

As far as Britain was concerned her policies towards Siam were governed by two factors. Firstly the Government of the Straits Settlements did not wish to see any extension of Siamese control in the Malay Peninsula, and its plans were directed to seeing that this did not happen. But the British Government was also concerned with the preservation of Siam as an independent buffer state between the British in Burma and French expansion in Indo-China. In order to prevent Siam falling under the influence of the French, Britain had to retain friendly relations with her. For this reason Britain was willing to concede Siamese suzerainty over the northern states of the Peninsula and was generally most reluctant to provide any assistance for those rulers who wished to be rid of Siamese control. Britain was not willing to aid, for example, the Sultan of Kedah, at the risk of antagonizing the Siamese, for the latter might encourage the extension of French influence in their country. Therefore throughout most of the nineteenth century there was almost no British initiative for the acquisition of the Siamese controlled Malay states.

Towards the end of the century Anglo-French rivalry began to decline and there was less competition over the extension of a dominating influence in Siam. Although it was not really until the signing of the Anglo-French Entente in 1904 that overseas rivalry between the countries ceased, at the turn of the century there was a development which hastened the conclusion of a pact of friendship between Britain and France. This was the growing power of Germany.

Germany was building a navy which was intended to rival that of Britain, and the latter looked with alarm at any attempts by Germany to build naval bases near her trade routes around the world. In 1897 Britain signed a secret convention with Siam by which, in return for protection, the Siamese agreed not to grant any land or concessions in the Malay Peninsula to another power. This could apply equally well to France or Germany.

Siamese suzerainty was not exactly popular in the northern Malay states and during 1898-9 there was discontent in the Patani group of states which tried to obtain British intervention and protection against their Siamese overlords. However in continuation of her previous policy, Britain refused to have anything to do with movements which would weaken and antagonize the government in Bangkok. On the other hand, Britain did not have things all her own way for there were other powers to whom the anti-Siamese groups could appeal. In 1899-1900 the Germans made attempts to obtain Pulau Langkawi from the Siamese Government, but the attempts were rebuffed. By 1901 it was rumoured that those groups in Patani and Kelantan who wished to break away from the Siamese were looking to foreign powers—the Germans—for assistance. There were also reports that the United States was interested in the islands off the Trengganu coast.

The British Government viewed with alarm the possibility of German and United States settlements being established in the Malay Peninsula, and in 1902 another agreement was concluded with Siam. Both Chamberlain in the Colonial Office and Swettenham, who was by then High Commissioner, were in favour of what was called the 'forward policy' in the Peninsula. By this convention, the Siamese agreed that they would exercise much stricter control over the Malay states so that all dealings with foreign powers would be through the Siamese Government. There were to be no concessions to foreigners, and Kelantan and Trengganu were to have resident Siamese advisers to supervise foreign relations. These advisers, when appointed, were Englishmen who were working for the Siamese government. In 1905 they were also appointed to Kedah and Perlis. Britain's special interest in the northern states was thus recognized in 1902 and was made formal by the 1909 Anglo-Siamese Treaty.

BRITAIN GAINS CONTROL FROM SIAM

In 1909 Siam handed over to Britain whatever rights and powers she possessed in the states of Kedah, Perlis, Kelantan and Trengganu. She thus transferred the rights of suzerainty so that these states became British protectorates, following the other states of the Peninsula. British advisers were appointed to the states instead of Siamese advisers, and they were in much the same position as the Residents in the Federated Malay States had been before 1895.

The Siamese also agreed not to allow any other power to lease land or build bases in any part of the Malay Peninsula which remained under Siamese control (i.e. south of Monthon or Rajaburi) for the British were still a little alarmed at the revival of French interest in 1893-4 in building a canal across the Kra Isthmus. British interests in the Peninsula and on the sea routes to China were adequately protected by the 1909 treaty, for the possibility of other powers establishing settlements was now ruled out. By 1909 the present boundaries of West Malaysia had been set and the Peninsula was all under British protection. (The last state to obtain an adviser or Resident on the same lines as the others was Johore. In 1914 the Sultan was pressed to accept an official adviser in place of the numerous unofficial advisers he had previously obtained from Singapore.)

ADMINISTRATION IN EAST MALAYSIA

(a) Sarawak and Brunei

When James Brooke retired in 1863 he left the administration of Sarawak to his nephew, Charles Brooke, and when he died in 1868 Charles became the second Raja. Charles was less of an adventurer and more of an administrator than his uncle and it was he who finally brought Sarawak out of debt. The first Raja had established law and order, the second began the development towards prosperity. James had always wanted Sarawak to become a British colony or protectorate rather than remain an independent state relying on its own resources. And when Britain had showed no interest in his proposals he had, at various times, unsuccessfully offered the territory to France, Belgium and Holland in return for protection. (It had also been suggested that he approach Greece but Brooke replied that he thought Sarawak would be better able to support Greece than Greece Sarawak.) However the second Raja intended to maintain the independence of his state and made no suggestions that Sarawak should be taken over by Britain. He also wished to expand the area of his territory at the expense of Brunei but until 1882 this was prevented by the British government.

But between 1882 and 1910 the final encroachments were made on the territory of Brunei by both Sarawak and North Borneo. The Brooke family had extended its boundaries northward in a series of steps, 1853, 1861 and 1882; on the other hand the British North Borneo Company had obtained almost all its land at the time of the original cession in 1877. The remaining part of the sultanate of Brunei was to be a source of conflict between Brooke and the Company both of whom wanted to acquire it. Both were jealous of each other and the Company had welcomed British protection in 1888 not so much from a desire to preserve Brunei as from a wish to prevent the expansion of Sarawak.

However the expansion of Sarawak continued, the Trusan valley in 1884 and the Limbang valley in 1890; both areas now make up the present Fifth Division. The Limbang valley was annexed by Brooke without the consent of the Sultan; the valley split the sultanate into two parts and for many years the Sultan refused to accept the compensation offered. There is no doubt that the Raja's rough and ready method of dealing with the Sultan provoked resentment in Brunei and suspicion in Britain. It seemed to be mere aggrandizement, especially to those Malays who held high position in Brunei and did not want to lose their privilages by being absorbed into Sarawak. It was not long after this that Brooke had the opportunity to obtain all the territory administered by the North Borneo Company. In 1894 the Company was going through an unprofitable time, the 'great wealth' of Sabah was non-existant, and so the directors offered the territory to Brooke, hoping to get it off their hands.

But Brooke was in fact more interested in gaining possession of the rest of Brunei than in taking over Sabah and the terms which he offered to the Company were not considered to be acceptable and the Company withdrew its offer. Brooke's hope was that the Sultan of Brunei would become so weak and his state would become so disorganized that the ruler would be willing to hand over his lands in return for compensation. This might easily have happened but once again Brooke's plans for expansion were frustrated by the British government. Following the advice of Swettenham, the High Commissioner in Singapore, and Birch, the Governor in North Borneo, Britain in 1906 at last appointed a Resident to Brunei to help reform the Sultan's administration. Brunei was to be the model later followed in the appointment of advisers to the Unfederated Malay States in 1909 and the Sultan of Brunei's position in relation to the British government was similar to that of the rulers of those states. It can be said that if a Resident had been appointed with the granting of protection in 1888 the subsequent difficulties between Brunei and Sarawak might have been avoided. Two final adjustments brought the boundaries of east Malaysia to those that are in existence to-day. In 1905 the Company transferred control of the Lawas valley to Sarawak and in 1906 the Company gave up the administration of Labuan; the island became part of the Straits Settlements until 1946 when it reverted to North Borneo.

(b) Progress in North Borneo

At first the North Borneo Company had to proceed slowly with the extension of its influence over the river basins of Sabah, which were the inhabited areas, for naturally the chiefs were reluctant to give up their independence. There was a certain amount of resistence, the most serious being the Mat Salleh rebellion 1894-1900. Mat Salleh was a leader with a commanding personality who was largely provoked into rebellion by the ineptitude of the Company's policies. The rebellion lasted as long as it did because of Mat Salleh's skill and because the police force only numbered 300 men, most of whom were Sikhs who had been obtained from Hugh Low in Perak. At one stage Mat Salleh had 1,500 followers and in 1897, although he lived on the east coast, he attacked and sacked Gaya on the west coast. He was a formidable opponent for the Company until he was killed in a battle in 1900, after which the rebellion faded away.

Generally the North Borneo Company followed an administrative policy which was similar to that of a British colony; the governors had to be appointed with the approval of the British government and the first two governors were seconded from the Malay States Civil Service. Although the administration was in the hands of a Chartered Company there was no policy of extracting much wealth from the inhabitants in order to pay large dividends and in fact dividends were often not paid at all. From 1899 to 1904 the dividend was 2½ per cent., from 1909 to 1925 it was 5 per cent., then 1½ per cent. until 1928; there was no dividend at all from 1928 to 1937 when 2 per cent. was paid until the outbreak of war. Throughout the whole period there was general supervision by the Colonial Office and the administration followed Overbeck's advice in the early days, 'conciliate the native authorities and secure their goodwill'. Thus in 1889 it was laid down that no title deed to any land could be given by a native to a foreigner without the chiefs' consent, and until 1928 almost all the interior of Sabah was declared a prohibited area to aliens. The early administration owed much to Treacher, who was Governor from 1882 to 1887. He divided the territory into two residencies, each sub-divided into provinces under the supervision of district officers. The capital was Sandakan on the east coast and an Advisory Council was set up in the capital in 1883 modelled on the Legislative Council of Ceylon. Treacher also made a start with the problem of eradicating slavery. The slave trade was stopped almost immediately in Sabah but it was difficult to eliminate it entirely in the surrounding area until the United States took over Sulu from the Spanish in 1898. The ending of slavery itself took rather longer. Treacher issued a proclamation in 1883 formally abolishing the practice but in fact it was another twenty years before slavery became extinct.

In North Borneo's early years the revenue for the government came from a 10 per cent. tax on imports and exports as was the practice in the Straits Settlements and Hong Kong, and between 1881 and 1895 the return from this tax increased from $20,000 to $349,000. During the same period exports increased in value from $145,000 to $2,130,000 and imports from $166,000 to $1,664,000. In these years trade was mainly with Hong Kong—birds' nests and timber, the latter being used for building railways in China. Attempts were made to start the growing of tobacco as a cash crop and for a time the crop was successful, exports of tobacco reaching a value of $2 million just before the collapse came in 1902. Economic progress was not spectacular but it was steady.

1893 to 1910 were difficult years for the Company mainly because of long distance interference in the administration by the directors in London, who also appointed as governor a man named Beaufort who had no previous experience of Asia. Much money was wasted with an over-optimistic scheme for the building of a railway; the administration instituted a tax on rice which resulted in the hoped-for Chinese immigrants being reluctant to go to Sabah and so the labour shortage continued; and finally there was the Mat Salleh rebellion. These were not years of great progress although one constructive event was the building on the west coast of the town of Jesselton now called Kota Kinabalu and the capital of the state. Eventually the Company realized its mistakes and once again in 1900 returned to the practice of obtaining its governors from the Malay

States. But because of the interference from London they did not remain very long, Clifford who came from Pahang stayed six months and Birch from Negri Sembilan stayed for only two years. However after 1910 interference from the London directors began to decline and the North Borneo Company was able to return to the task of developing the state.

This was not an easy problem as the territory had few natural resources, little available capital and a shortage of labour. In 1911 the total population was only 208,183, far too few for any rapid development of a plantation-type economy which it was hoped would make up for the lack of minerals. Attempts were made in 1882 to recruit Chinese workers in Hong Kong but they were so badly selected that the first arrivals were shopkeepers rather than farmers. They took one look at the uninviting conditions in North Borneo and went back to Hong Kong. Health conditions were so poor in the rural areas that both Chinese and Indian workers were much more attracted to the Malay Peninsula and they preferred to go there.

(c) Progress in Sarawak

In Sarawak, too, progress was slow. But because development had begun earlier than in Sabah, more had been achieved by 1914. Like Sabah, Sarawak had few natural resources, some gold and antimony, pepper and sago (*kalimantan* means raw sago) but despite this deficiency the export-import trade was worth $13½ million by the end of the century and most of this trade was channelled through Singapore. However it was a fact that the Brookes had never encouraged the opening up of the state by foreign capital. Only one company, the Borneo Company, established in 1856, was allowed to do business in Sarawak and in the early years of Brooke rule the Company had given the Raja a great deal of financial support. The search for new crops in Sarawak was not very successful, sugar, tobacco, tea and coffee were all tried but only gambier was a revenue earner until the advent of rubber at the end of the century.

The second Raja concentrated on consolidating the régime and instituting a solvent administration with the result that after 1880 there was no public debt. James Brooke had never been really interested in the details of administration which he had left to his subordinates. Charles, on the other hand, set up a more modern system of government, dividing the state into divisions which were in turn divided into Residencies. Although the Raja's rule was very paternalistic—for example the Raja himself often sat in court to hear cases—there was also considerable consultation by means of advisory councils. A Supreme Council had been in existance since 1855 to advise tht Raja; meeting once a month, it consisted of the Raja, the Datu Bandar, the Datu Halim, the Datu Imam and also the four Divisional Residents. There was also the Council Negri, formed in 1865, whose members were the leading chiefs of all the various races and tribes and which met in Kuching about once every two years. Each Divisional Resident also had his own council of local chiefs. Until the end of the century the Malays were the largest community in Kuching; Malay was the official language of the Raja's administration, Islam was the official religion, and the government service was mainly staffed by Malays. By the 1880's Brooke's prejudice against the Chinese as a result of the Bau rebellion began to lessen and the government started assisted immigration schemes to bring Chinese labourers to Kuching and Sibu to relieve the shortage of workers. Many of the first arrivals were Christians, for example the 1,000 Foochow who settled in Sibu in 1901 and the 5,000 Cantonese, all Methodists, who arrived in Sarawak between 1902 and 1911. Although the Chinese came relatively late to Sarawak they are to-day the largest racial group in the state because they have had a greater natural increase than the others, of whom the Sea Dyak community is the next most numerous.

To sum up the Brooke administration before the First World War it can be said that it concentrated on preserving customary practices rather than encouraging the introduction of western ideas and methods. The Brookes made haste slowly, perhaps a little too slowly for the well-being of their subjects in the twentieth century.

A SUMMING UP

On the occasion of the outbreak of war in 1914 the Malaysia of today was divided into the main areas of the Malay Peninsula and Borneo and there was little in common between the two. In the former, British influence was direct and official; in the latter, it was, with the exception of Labuan and Brunei, indirect and unofficial. The Malay Peninsula was divided into the three groups of states, and these divisions continued until the establishment of the Malayan Union in 1946. These were the Straits Settlements, the Federated Malay States, and the other Malayan states which were known as 'Unfederated'.

The differences between the three groups in West Malaysia were legal and constitutional rather than political, for in fact the control of power lay with Britain. However the legal and constitutional differences did affect the way in which this power was exercised. The Straits Settlements were British territory. Here Britain ruled directly and those born in Singapore, Penang and Malacca were British subjects. The Settlements were British colonies ruled by a Governor (who was also High Commissioner for the Federated Malay States), and three Resident Commissioners. There was no limitation on British rule, and British control was absolute.

The Federated Malay States were individually 'protected states'. They were not colonies and those born in them were not British subjects. British power was intended to be exercised indirectly through the Sultans of the states, but when the states of Perak, Selangor, Negri Sembilan and Pahang formed a closer association in 1895, British control (and it was control) was exercised through a Resident-General in Kuala Lumpur. He was subject only to the High Commissioner in Singapore. The government tended to become more and more centralized, and the powers of the Sultans declined.

The so-called Unfederated States had in fact very little in common, except that their relations with Britain were carried on by means of the High Commissioner in Singapore and also that they each had a British adviser. The states of Johore, Kedah, Perlis, Kelantan and Trengganu were also protected states, not colonies, but they were separate entities, having no formal ties with each other and no administrative association with the Federated States. Because they were not associated with any form of centralized government, the rulers tended to retain rather more independence than their counterparts in the Federated States, and their advisers remained more like advisers and less like executive officers. All these states even today have their own civil services, and while the former Federated States and the Straits Settlements have Saturday and Sunday for the week-end, the former Unfederated States have Thursday and Friday. The Unfederated States always had fewer British officials in their governments, and because they were less closely associated with the centralizing tendencies in the Federated States they retained their characteristics as 'Malay states', being less subjected to Western influences.

As the rulers of the Unfederated Malay States saw the way in which, with more centralization, the rulers in Perak, Selangor, Negri Sembilan and Pahang became less and less influential, they had no incentive to enter into any closer political association with the Federated States. Thus the division in west Malaysia continued until the Japanese occupation in 1942. This non-association helps to explain why Kelantan and Trengganu are today relatively undeveloped compared even with Kedah and Johore. Until 1946 all these states were entirely dependent on their own revenues, and whereas Kedah and Johore had already established connexions with the trading ports of Penang and Singapore and were linked by the west-coast railway, the states on the east coast were still largely isolated. Being dependent on their own resources, the economic development of Kelantan and Trengganu was a slow process.

By 1914 therefore the political pattern of the Malay Peninsula had been settled, and it did not change for thirty years. Changes involving closer association between the two groups of Malay states were suggested, but because this would involve a decrease in the powers of the rulers of the Unfederated States, the suggestions had borne no fruit at the time of the Japanese invasion in 1941. The great changes which took place in west Malaysia after 1914 were to be economic rather than political.

Permanent boundaries had also been fixed in Borneo and the only link between the different territories was the over-all British protection guaranteed by the treaty of 1888. Sarawak was a well-established kingdom of the Brooke family where the second Raja was coming to the end of a fifty-year reign (he died in 1917). Government was paternal and uncomplicated but there was considerable consultation with the inhabitants, North Borneo (Sabah) was the possession of a British Chartered Company, but because of Colonial Office supervision it was administered on much the same lines as an official British colony. The Company itself was almost entirely concerned with administration and had nothing directly to do with trade.

Of the two smaller areas, Brunei was a Malay state in a similar relationship to Britain as the Unfederated States of the Peninsula. British officers were gradually appointed to advise the sultan whose state was about to become the richest part of Borneo with the discovery of oil in 1903. There is a nice touch of historical irony in the fact that, although the sultan lost the greater part of his lands to the Brooke family and the North Borneo Company, the small area which he did retain was the only area rich in mineral deposits. The last territory, Labuan, was the only actual colony in British Borneo; it was of little value and unlikely to be of much use to the government of the Straits Settlements which administered it from Singapore.

To sum up our discussion of the period of British intervention and the consolidation of British influence, we can say that in the first instance the concern of the British Government was trade, not only with China but also with Malaya. The British were concerned with the protection of this trade and did not wish to see any other power established in strategic positions in Malaya and Borneo. Intervention on the west coast of the Peninsula in the 1870's, in Borneo in the 1880's and again in north Malaya in the 1900's was not so much to acquire colonies as to create a situation in which it would be impossible for other powers to do so.

In theory the British Government did not intend to become involved in direct administration but in practice it became impossible to suggest a given line of policy without eventually being responsible for seeing that such a policy was carried out. Thus the British administrators in Malaysia carried intervention farther than was originally intended, and ultimately in both the Federated and Unfederated States, British officials became directly responsible for administration.

EXERCISES

1 What were the reasons for the bringing into being of the Federated Malay States?

2 Describe the advantages and disadvantages of the Federation which was established in 1896.

3 Write an account of how the Unfederated Malay States came under British influence.

4 Describe the way in which the Brookes enlarged the territory of Sarawak.

5 Compare and contrast the administrations of Sarawak and North Borneo.

6 Write short notes on:
   F. A. Swettenham, the Federal Council, Abu Bakar of Johore, the Anglo-Thai Treaty of 1909, Charles Brooke.

14

THE DEVELOPMENT OF MALAYSIA'S ECONOMY

WE have told the story of Malaysia's political problems and political changes up to the outbreak of the First World War. We will now turn to another story which was going on at the same time as the events which have been described in earlier chapters—a story which is as important as the political changes.

The economy of Malaysia today is based almost entirely on primary products: in the Peninsula tin and rubber—one indigenous to the country, the other introduced into Malaysia in the last quarter of the nineteenth century. Possession and production of these two raw materials enabled the Peninsula to become the richest country in South-East Asia, and today the revenue which is obtained from these exports pays for almost all the capital development which is taking place. Malaysia's economic history has shown little variation in type during the last century though it has shown great changes in volume. Tin, and later rubber and tin together, have for almost a century provided the revenue for the development of the Penin-sula while in Borneo the states of Sabah and Sarawak have been dependent on revenue obtained from timber, pepper and copra as well as rubber. Sarawak has benefited to some extent from the oil wells but the main wealth from this discovery had gone to Brunei. These primary products have been and still remain the pillars of the economy. The changes in political conditions, which have already been outlined, brought about a situation in which it was economically feasible to expand the production of tin and later to introduce the growing of rubber.

Little change took place in the economic pattern of West Malaysia from the early years of this century up to the time of the Second World War. Almost all attention was concentrated on tin and rubber, although the effect of the slump of 1929-31 showed the dangers of complete reliance on these two products. As a result of this concentration, the development of the country was largely confined to those areas which had facilities for these two industries. Roads and railways and other amenities like water, light, education, and hospitals were established in places where there was tin and rubber. In the first instance roads and railways were built to facilitate the export of the two raw materials, and the other amenities later appeared to cater for those living and working near the centres of industry.

It is for these reasons that pre-war economic development in Malaysia was unbalanced. There was little over-all planning, and attention was paid mainly to these extractive industries. Agriculture was considered less important, for rice could always be imported from Burma or Siam; and little attention was paid to those people who were directly or indirectly connected with the growing of food. To some extent this explains why so much effort is now required in Malaysia to develop the rural and agricultural areas. Since 1946 attempts have been made to diversify the economy of Malaysia, and the production of palm oil, copra, and pineapples has been encouraged; more recently we have seen the establishment of secondary industries and the encouragement of padi-planting and fishing. However it is still true that without the pillars of tin, rubber and timber, the Malaysian economy would collapse.

TIN

We have already seen in earlier chapters that tin ore had been exported from the Malay Peninsula for many centuries. It had been mined in fairly small quantities, mainly by alluvial methods, and sold to Chinese and Indian merchants. In the Peninsula itself the metal was often used as currency. In the eighteenth and early nineteenth centuries the ore was found in sufficient quantities in the Kinta valley and in the hinterland of Malacca to supply this limited trade. The tin was mined by the Malay inhabitants of the Peninsula, largely by using swift-flowing river-water to separate the ore from the earth. It has been estimated that at the beginning of the nineteenth century Perak produced about five hundred tons per year.

The increased use of tin-plate in the latter half of the nineteenth century caused a rapid rise in the demand for tin ore, and as a result many more mines were opened up with Chinese labour in the areas of Larut, Kuala Lumpur and Rasah. We have seen how these developments led to the influx of large numbers of Chinese to the Peninsula and later led to intervention by the British.

The mines, which had been set up in the tin-mining areas in the

1870's provided the revenue for the early development of the Malay states. Although some revenue was obtained from opium and gambling licences, in the early years of British influence the tin mines were certainly the main source. Until the late 1880's tin-mining was almost entirely in the hands of the Chinese, although the land was leased from Malay chiefs, and some European merchants in the Straits Settlements had invested capital. The majority of mines were open-cast workings dependent on a plentiful supply of water. The methods used were somewhat like the gravel-pump method of today; the practice was to wash away the ore-bearing earth and then bring about the separation of the ore and the waste earth. These mines were owned by a small number of Chinese capitalists who employed imported and indentured labourers. The labourers were under the direction of a headman who, acting as a middleman, arranged the labourers' terms of employment. The workers usually received nine-tenths of the profits, the owner one-tenth, though the owner also supplied his workers with food and clothing, often at exorbitant prices, and many workers who were often already in debt to the mine for their passage money to Malaya found it very difficult to get out of debt.

It was not until the late 1880's that European capital began to take a direct interest in mining the ore rather than purchasing it from the Chinese, though it was only in the early years of the twentieth century that large-scale British investment took place with the establishment of British registered companies. These were often registered in Cornwall and connected with English tin-mining companies. European-owned mines were first established in the Kinta valley rather than in Larut—seven mines with their registered offices in Redruth, Cornwall, opened in the Kinta valley between 1901 and 1906. However, it is of interest to note that the pioneer of European enterprise was a French company established in 1883, the Société des Mines d'Etains de Perak. By 1890 Kinta had replaced Larut as the centre of mining enterprise in Perak; in that year total production in Perak was 15,101 tons, and of that amount 8,289 tons came from Kinta. There were also 46,711 Chinese living in the Kinta valley, almost as many as in Larut.

Steam pumps and gravel pumps were in use before the end of the century but dredging with buckets as we know it today began in 1913. The introduction of dredges, which are expensive, meant that more capital had to be invested in tin-mining. As a result of the success already achieved the capital was forthcoming, and Malaysia very rapidly became the world's largest producer of tin. In 1904 her production was 51,733 tons, or half of the total world output at that time. There were, of course, other tin-producing countries which greatly expanded their own exports in the years that followed. As a result, by 1929, although Malaysia produced 69,366 tons of tin, this only accounted for 36 per cent. of the total world production. The remainder was largely supplied by Bolivia, Indonesia, and Nigeria.

The major part of Malaysia's tin exports, even from the time of the late nineteenth century, was sent to the United States. Britain obtained most of her tin from Bolivia, which was less distant than the Malay Peninsula, while the demand for tin increased more rapidly in the United States than anywhere else. Malaysia thus came to depend a great deal on the prosperity of the United States economy, for, as we shall see below, rubber was also a major export product sent to that country. Exports meant export taxes, and it was with the revenue obtained from the tax on tin exports that the Malay states were able to finance the building of roads and railways and later the establishment of hospitals and schools.

Tin therefore began Malaysia's modern history, for not only did it provide the revenue for the modernization of the country; it also gave the country its first industry, tin-smelting. The fact that smelting plants were set up in Singapore and Penang meant that Malaysia was able to export the tin concentrate rather than the ore, and in this way was not dependent on any foreign country for the processing of her own raw materials. It also resulted in increased trade, for much ore from Indonesia and Siam was brought to Malaysia for smelting. The first smelting plant was built in Singapore in 1887 and the second at Butterworth in 1902. In 1900 American buyers attempted to gain control of the tin industry by insisting that the smelting be done in the United States. Swettenham, who was the High Commissioner, frustrated the attempt by imposing a prohibitive duty on the export of tin ore. As a result the duty on smelted tin was much less than the duty on the unsmelted tin ore. In this way Malaysia retained control of this important part of tin production and attracted a great deal of extra trade by smelting tin for other countries.

RUBBER

While the production of tin is one of the most important success stories in Malaysian history, the train of events connected with rubber is probably even more spectacular and its effects more widespread. There was no tin in the ground in Borneo but the states of Sarawak and Sabah both followed the Peninsula in rubber planting, though not on such a large scale. Malaysia had always had tin ore in the ground, and in the events which have been related the most important factor was the question of making the supply of the existing raw material meet a new demand. But rubber was a different matter. It was a new plant introduced into Malaysia on a rather speculative basis, for at first it was not introduced to meet any real demand. Then suddenly the popularity of the motor car resulted in entirely new uses for rubber (as tyres, for example), and what had started as speculation became a successful financial investment.

Rubber had always been grown in a wild state in many parts of the world and *gutta percha*[1] had long been a Malaysian jungle product, as well as a jungle product of other tropical regions. Brazil was possibly the best known of these regions, for the authorities there had progressed quite far in rubber cultivation. Some of the seeds of these rubber trees were obtained from Brazil and sent to the Royal Botanical Gardens at Kew in England. It was hoped that the rubber plants, known as *Hevea brasiliensis,* would prove to be a successful crop in Britain's possessions in Asia. After some of the seeds at Kew had germinated, the young plants were sent to Calcutta in 1873. However, Calcutta did not turn out to be a suitable place, and later plants were sent to Ceylon. It was in 1876 that the first seedlings from Kew arrived at the Botanical Gardens in Singapore. Some were successfully planted in Singapore while others were planted by Sir Hugh Low in the garden of his Residency in Kuala Kangsar. From these few seedlings have developed the millions of rubber trees that are in existence in Malaysia today.

However the development of the rubber-planting industry was slow and owed much to H. N. Ridley, who was appointed to the Botanical Gardens in Singapore in 1888. After the establishment of British influence in the Malay states in 1874, some investment had been made in coffee plantations in Perak and Selangor by planters who had come to the Peninsula from Ceylon. The growing of Liberian coffee had not been entirely successful for the price fluctuated a great deal, and the coffee trees were prone to attack by disease. It was to many of these planters that Ridley tried to sell the idea of growing rubber, distributing rubber seeds when he visited their plantations. Little came of his efforts until 1896 when the price of coffee fell and some estates planted rubber as an alternate crop with coffee. Ridley had shown that the rubber tree would flourish

[1]Strips of rubber (from a wild rubber tree).

in Malaysia although by 1897 only 345 acres had been planted. The success of those who had followed Ridley's advice was assured when the world demand for rubber increased rapidly at the beginning of the twentieth century with the increasing popularity of the motor car. This became even more certain after Henry Ford in the United States introduced mass production, thus lessening the price of cars and increasing the demand. By 1905 40,000 acres in the Peninsula were planted with rubber, 85,000 acres in 1906, and by 1920 West Malaysia was producing 196,000 tons of rubber which was approximately 53 per cent. of total world production. The area planted with rubber had, by 1920, increased to 2,475,000 acres. The great boom years for rubber producers were 1910-12 when the price of rubber reached just over five dollars a pound. Fortunes were made during these years and an interest in planting rubber passed to the small holders as well as to the capitalist. During these years many Malay farmers gave up padi cultivation for the more profitable rubber trees.

The rapid expansion of rubber production and its export to the United States and Europe furnished the governments of the Malay states and especially the Federated Malay States and Johore with a growing additional source of revenue. Later, plantations were begun in other parts of the Peninsula and in Borneo, and small-holders were influenced to plant the crop also. Thus for example, by 1917, 35,000 acres of rubber had been planted in Sabah. Together with tin, rubber provided the Peninsula governments with the money needed for the provision of the many amenities of a modern state. The establishment of plantations meant that greater areas of the country were cleared of jungle and opened up for settlement; and further- more the road and railway system was extended to keep pace with this economic activity. In turn better communications stimulated further economic development. The rather un-coordinated Peninsula railway system was linked up so that by 1909 there was a continuous line from Prai to Johore Bahru (and to Singapore after the building of the Causeway in 1923). The road system was also extended so that there was a trunk road from north to south and branch roads were linked to this main system, to Pahang for example, and to Teluk Anson and Malacca.

REVENUE PUT TO USE

By 1920 in the economic sphere West Malaysia had utilized two extremely valuable primary products, tin and rubber. Through the revenue obtained from these products, the administration had been able to establish not only roads and railways but also hospitals and schools.

Health Services. One of the most important uses to which the revenue from tin and rubber was put was in the work of the Medical and Health Departments in the Peninsula and more especially in the control of malaria. An Institute of Medical Research had been established as early as 1901. The Malay Peninsula was probably one of the first regions in the world where successful use was made of Sir Ronald Ross's early research and the Italian Giovanni Grassi's discovery that malaria was spread by the anopheles mosquito. This discovery was made in 1900, and in 1901 Dr. Malcolm Watson, the District Surgeon of Klang, put into practice new methods of dealing with this mosquito. The essential thing was to destroy the breeding places of the mosquito which were in swampy areas. The swamps were drained, and within two years, Klang, which had been a very malarial town, was almost free of the disease.

The same methods were applied at Port Swettenham which was being built about this time. The success achieved in these areas led to these techniques being used elsewhere, and the almost complete eradication of malaria in the urban areas was one of the first accomplishments in the realm of health improvement. Later other methods were developed by Watson to deal with the disease-carrying mosquito, for example, the draining of subsoil and the spraying of breeding areas with a mixture of oil and kerosene. The death rate from malaria was reduced from 62.9 per 1000 in 1910 to 18.57 per 1000 in 1920. In 1921 Sir Malcolm Watson (who was knighted for his work) estimated that over a hundred thousand lives had been saved in west Malaysia by the wide-spread anti-malarial campaign. The Peninsula became one of the healthiest of all tropical countries and so was able to carry out the development of tin and rubber in rural areas. In Borneo control took longer because of fewer resources but also because it took until the 1930's to find out that in Sabah the main carrier of malaria was a mosquito which was harmless in the Peninsula.

Education. While government revenue was spent in good measure on the development of communications and the improvement of health standards, in the sphere of education government activity was rather limited until after the First World War. In the Malay States to begin with the government's main concern was Malay education, the immigrant communities being left to take care of themselves. Free compulsory primary education for Malay boys had begun in Selangor in 1891 but the Malay population was not very keen on sending its children to secular schools until religious instruction was included in the curriculum. For the same reason the Malays were not much attracted to English education and it was to overcome this reservation that religious instruction was made a compulsory subject at the Malay College when it was started in 1905. However the aims of Malay education provided by the government were strictly limited. According to Swettenham it was to make the children 'better farmers rather than offer to them any wider view of life'. This rather patronizing attitude towards education was echoed in Sarawak—'the longer he [the Sea Dyak] is kept away from the influences of civilization the better it will be for him, for the good cannot be introduced without the bad'; while 'reading, writing and a little simple arithmetic' were considered sufficient for the Malay boy.[1] The restricted list of subjects (there was no English) excluded the Malays from the middle levels of government employment and the instruction received at the Malay primary school led nowhere. Unfortunately, on the advice of Winstedt in 1921 the North Borneo authorities set up the same type of vernacular education in Sabah. Certainly, it did nothing to enable the Malays, Dyaks and Kadazans to compete with the forceful Chinese. Even the training of teachers had left much to be desired before the opening of Sultan Idris Training College in Tanjong Malim in 1922. An attempt to train Malays for work in the civil service had resulted in the establishment of the Malay College in Kuala Kangsar but this opportunity was limited to a very few pupils. Malay education in the kampong schools was so restricted in content that the rural Malay was isolated and even divided from the minority who were English educated. This helps to account for the divisions which arise in Malay nationalism (referred to on p. 196) often described as a division between the graduates of Sultan Idris Training College (Malay educated) and those of Malay College (English educated).

As will be mentioned in a later chapter the government neither aided nor controlled Chinese schools, which were left largely to themselves, although for political reasons control was imposed in the 1920's. Education in English had been begun mainly on the initiative of Christian missionary bodies, though the government had established seventeen English medium schools in West Malaysia by 1919. Thereafter the numbers receiving education in English increased, though because these schools were situated in towns it

---

[1] *History of Sarawak under its Two White Rajas*, by S. Baring-Gould and C.A. Bampfylde. London, 1909.

was generally only the urban dwellers who had the opportunity to use them.

Higher education was provided by the King Edward VII College of Medicine in Singapore (originally established in 1904 as a Medical School with twenty-two students) and arts and science courses were later provided at Raffles College, Singapore, which was opened in 1928. After the Second World War these two Colleges were joined together to form the University of Malaya. This institution later established a separate section in Kuala Lumpur which took the name University of Malaya, the original foundation becoming the University of Singapore.

Of equal importance to this progress was the fact that many of the inhabitants of Malaysia were benefiting materially by working in the production of tin and rubber, timber and pepper. It seemed likely then that tin and rubber would be responsible for the Peninsula entering a long era of prosperity. Until the 1920's the horizon seemed to have no threatening clouds, but the fact that Malaysia was now closely tied to the world trading market meant the possibility of difficulties later. Dependence on primary exports meant that Malaysia was not and could not be master of her own economic destiny. To a greater extent than many other countries, she was closely involved in the economic booms and slumps of countries on the other side of the world, especially the United States.

LABOUR

Between 1901 and 1921 the population of the Malay Peninsula doubled from approximately 1,600,000 to 3,300,000. This was largely due to the entry of Chinese and Indian labourers to work on the mines and plantations and also to the great improvement in public health. We have seen in an earlier chapter how Chinese immigration had risen steeply between the 1850's and 1870's when the early attempts at large-scale mining were begun. By 1882 there were 50,000 Chinese miners in Larut. This immigration continued in the years that followed and also extended to Johore, and to a lesser extent Kedah, when plantations were started there. By 1907 it was estimated that in the Federated Malay States there were 229,778 Chinese engaged in the tin-mining industry alone. This was the time of peak employment for tin labourers because not long afterwards the introduction of the dredge and other machinery caused the numbers to decrease to 144,000 by 1918. But generally speaking the Chinese, except in Johore, did not provide labour for the large plantations unless the plantations were Chinese-owned. The estates established with European capital employed Indian workers, and it was as this labour force that the Indian immigrants came to the Malay states in the early years of the twentieth century.

It was said earlier that the first European planters in Malaysia came from Ceylon. When they arrived they made some attempts to interest the Malay population in working on coffee plantations. Usually the Malays saw no sense in doing such work when they could exist perfectly well without it. They were not interested in such regulated employment. In these circumstances labour was difficult to obtain, and it was quite natural that the estate managers should turn to the same workers whom they had employed in Ceylon rather than to the Chinese already in Malaysia whose language they did not understand. These workers were Tamils from south India who even today are an important minority in Ceylon. They were first brought to the Peninsula for the coffee plantations, but their numbers increased most rapidly with the development of rubber estates. In the early days labourers were so scarce that they had to be recruited in India and encouraged to come to work. In the early years of this century the supply of Indian workers could not keep pace with demand, for although approximately 20,000 Tamils arrived in Penang annually, they did little more than replace those who returned to India. Even later, when the numbers of Indian immigrants increased considerably, the Indian population still remained largely transitory. The majority of the workers stayed in Malaysia for a number of years and then returned to India. For example in 1908, 54,000 Indians arrived in West Malaysia and 31,000 returned; in 1912, 107,000 entered the country and 63,000 went back to India.

Many of those who came from India were indentured labourers, that is they were recruited in India to work on a specific estate and brought to the Peninsula by their employers or by persons who had contracted to hire workers. Indentured labourers were often unsatisfactory workers; many were not physically fit for the work they had to do and had been engaged by unscrupulous contractors. Also because they were tied to particular estates they were sometimes subject to abuses by bad employers. Free labourers were much more satisfactory, and the Straits Settlements authorities provided a certain number of free passages to encourage them to come to work not only on estates but also for the Public Works Department.

The idea of assistance and supervision was later strengthened in 1907 with the establishment of a Malayan government agent in Madras to supervise the recruitment of workers, and 1908 with the setting up of an Indian Immigration Fund. In future all employers of Tamil labourers had to pay their share of the cost of bringing them to the country. It was hoped that this assistance would prevent the cost of passages being deducted from the labourers' wages, better workers would be attracted, and malpractices by recruiters would be prevented.

In 1912 the revenue collected by the Fund amounted to $1,189,308 and expenditure was almost $900,000. It is interesting to note that the government was the largest contributor to the Fund in order to obtain the workers it needed for the Railway, Public Works and other departments.

By 1914 the number of free labourers had so increased that the recruitment of indentured labour was forbidden by law. It was no longer necessary, for there was now a plentiful supply of labour for government and for estates. The number of Indian immigrants in 1908 was approximately 49,000 while in 1913 the number had risen to 118,000. The total Indian population increased from 270,000 in 1911 to 470,000 in 1921.

The economic development of West Malaysia in the twentieth century up to the First World War had been extremely rapid and had involved not only the existing population of the country but to an even greater extent foreign capital and foreign labour. The possibilities in the Malay Peninsula for the development of tin mining and rubber planting were so great that even if the Malay population had wished to participate in these industries there would not have been enough of them to provide all the labour needed. Therefore the Chinese mining entrepreneurs had brought into the Malay States large numbers of their fellow countrymen to work in the mines and also on some estates. The Indians were brought to work for the government and on the coffee and rubber estates; the rubber industry also employed about 12,000 Javanese workers (1913). We have seen in Chapter 9 how Malaysia's plural society had its beginnings in the mid-nineteenth century. By 1920 the present-day population pattern was largely established and was to change very little in the years that followed. In 1921, the total population of West Malaysia, including Singapore, was 3,328,000 composed of the following groups:

Malays	1,630,000	48.9%
Chinese	1,180,000	35.5%
Indians	472,000	14.2%
Others	46,000	1.4%

Malaysia's plural society was now a reality.

It is an interesting sidelight on the rapid growth of population in the Straits Settlements and the Malay States that at the same time the East Malaysian territories remained extremely short of labour. This was partly because opportunities for advancement were so much better in the western areas and because conditions were still fairly primitive and unhealthy in Borneo. Attempts to recruit Indians for Sabah between 1887 and 1926 were completely unsuccessful and until 1927 the passages of Chinese from Hong Kong had to be paid. The Chinese population of both Sabah and Sarawak was not large until after the Second World War. In 1921 in Sabah 33 per cent. of the labour force was Javanese.

EXERCISES

1 Write an account of the development of the tin industry in West Malaysia up to 1918.

2 Write an account of the development of rubber planting in Malaysia up to 1918.

3 What advantages and disadvantages did Malaysia derive from the tin and rubber industries established in the nineteenth century?

4 Describe the population changes in Malaysia as a result of the tin and rubber industries.

5 Write short notes on:
tin dredging, H. N. Ridley, Dr. Malcolm Watson, the Indian Immigration Fund, Raffles College.

15
SINGAPORE AS A COLONY
1870-1941

ONE of the most immediate effects of the transfer of the Straits Settlements from the Indian Government to the Colonial Office was the setting up of a Straits Settlements Civil Service, recruited specifically for the Settlements and whose members would spend their careers there. This meant that in Singapore, for example, officials began to learn the dialects of the Chinese language and as a result began to understand more about the people whom they were administering. And the most obvious result of this increased knowledge was the formation of the Chinese Protectorate in 1877. Once the Straits Settlements administration was in charge of its own house it could deal with its own problems based on its own list of priorities. First and foremost was the need to control the secret societies which had subverted the government's administration of a large part of the population.

After the transfer from the Indian Office and as soon as the Straits Settlements had become a Crown Colony the Government obtained increased powers to regulate Chinese immigration; perhaps the most important of these was the power to deport criminal elements without them having the right of appeal. As a result of the Penang riots in 1867 the Government passed a Registration Ordinance in 1869—this was an attempt to bring the societies into the open by registering them. But in effect it gave official recognition to the societies and resulted in a great deal of criticism in Singapore. By 1872 all the secret societies had been registered but none had been suppressed. And it was estimated that at least 60 per cent of the Chinese population were willing, or unwilling, members.

THE CHINESE PROTECTORATE

In 1877 the Government set up a special department headed by W. A. Pickering who had played an important part in the negotiations leading up to the Pangkor Engagement. This department was to act as the link between the administration and the Chinese population. It was hoped that this link would be able to undermine, and eventually take the place of, the great influence which the secret societies had over the Chinese people. The new department was called the Chinese Protectorate and it was soon involved in all aspects of Chinese social problems—immigration, the kidnapping of labourers, terms of employment for new arrivals, traffic in women and prostitution. The initial impetus for the establishment of this new department was the lack of control over immigration from China. A Commission of Enquiry noted in 1872 that large numbers of immigrants landed in Singapore without the Government knowing anything about it—and without them knowing anything about the Government. The numbers entering Singapore were enormous; in 1878, 34,000 Chinese were known to have landed in Singapore, in 1888 the number had increased to 103,000. Under Pickering, who became something of a legend in Singapore, the Protectorate established itself as the means by which the Chinese residents and the British administration came into contact.

Secret societies had already been suppressed in China, as they had been in the Dutch and Spanish colonies and also in Hong Kong. Only in the Straits Settlements were they tolerated. Pickering himself was initially a supporter of the registration of the secret societies. He believed in indirect rule by the government through societies which had been weakened in influence. He thought that this was better than driving them underground. But many others in Singapore felt that the policy of Society Registration had proved to be unsuccessful as it did nothing to curtail their activities. And Pickering himself eventually saw that registration was a mistake. As has been said the societies had already been suppressed in Hong Kong and in 1889 the Governor, Clementi Smith who had previously served in Hong Kong, decided that the same should be done in the Straits Settlements. The Societies Ordinance of 1890 made societies illegal until they had been approved and Government took powers to banish members of societies who were not British subjects. Of course this Ordinance did not remove secret societies and it did drive them underground but at least they now had to defend themselves against persistent police pressure and the fact that they were on the defensive cut down their influence.

THE SYSTEM OF GOVERNMENT

While Government was imposing considerably more control over the majority of its population through the Chinese Protectorate and through the fact that more civil servants spoke a dialect of Chinese, the city and port continued to grow in size and prosperity. Immigrants continued to arrive and the population increased as the following figures show:

53,000 in 1850	420,000 in 1931
82,000 in 1860	770,000 in 1941

The commercial and later the strategic importance of Singapore increased as the years went by—though as far as the majority of the population was concerned the former was by far the more important. We have seen in Chapter 9 how the merchants in Singapore were the main instigators of the agitation supporting the British forward movement in the Malay Peninsula. It was they who wanted the opening up of new trading opportunities in the Malay States. At the time the commercial community was extremely influential and as the nineteenth century drew to a close this community began to obtain more influence over many decisions affecting the Colony. Demands for a greater share in official decision-making to begin with, came mainly from the European elements in the population and although they did not produce fruitful results until much later they were instrumental in encouraging significant changes in the working of the constitution.

Although Singapore (and the Straits Settlements) had the traditional Crown Colony type of government with its official majority throughout this period, considerable attention was always paid to the views of the more influential unofficial members of the population. Few controversial laws were made without the leading European merchants and the prominent members of the Chinese community being consulted beforehand.

Nevertheless the organization of the government was traditionally Colonial and autocratic. At the top was the Governor of the Straits Settlements who resided in Singapore and who was usually appointed from outside the Malayan Civil Service, though Swettenham and Clifford were exceptions to this general rule. The Governor was also the High Commissioner to the Malay States. Administration in the Straits Settlements was controlled by the Colonial Secretary who was head of the Civil Service and who also lived in Singapore. The Governor as the executive head of the Government was advised by an Executive Council and he was expected to ask for its advice. The power to make laws and enact bills lay with the Legislative Council.

Membership of the Executive Council consisted (in the period between the two World Wars) of the General Officer commanding the British troops, the Colonial Secretary, the Resident Councillors of Penang and Malacca, the Attorney-General, the Treasurer (later called Financial Secretary), two other officials and three unofficials. It will be seen that any advice given would be essentially the advice of other officials. The Council examined all official business and it was seldom that a Governor acted against its advice. If he did so he had to report the matter to the Secretary of State for the Colonies in Britain.

The Legislative Council also had a majority of official members. For example, between the wars the Council had 26 members plus the Governor. There were 13 official members and 13 unofficials. At that time the unofficial members were represented by seven Europeans, three Chinese and one Malay, one Indian and one Eurasian. The main intention of this kind of representation was to ensure that all major communities were represented but it also gave a somewhat loaded representation to the European community.

The unofficial members of the Legislative Council were selected by their own community organizations such as Chambers of Commerce—they were essentially upper and middle class people and it was noticeable that there was no representation from the trade unions or from the workers they would have as members.

It must be said that in the early part of the twentieth century there was neither a demand for the right to vote nor for the institution of an unofficial majority in the Legislative Council. The general feeling was that if there was to be any introduction of the vote it should be confined to those who were British subjects (Straits born) and this group was itself in a minority. There was little demand for an increase in the number of unofficials even from the largest community, the Chinese; there was even less demand from the minority groups.

Political interest among the Chinese and Indians was largely confined to events in China and India. The Revolution in China (1911) and its aftermath resulted in the setting up of branches of both Kuomintang and Communist Parties in Singapore and Penang, and the growth of nationalism in India stimulated Indian interest in the activities of the Congress Party. But with official majorities in the Councils of government it was unlikely that much public interest would be aroused in the speeches made in the

Legislative Council. In this type of Crown Colony government appointed officials are in charge of most departments and the man in the street is not likely to be very involved in its affairs until he has some say in the selection of those who are members of the Legislative Council. This was not to happen in Singapore until after 1945 and meanwhile the politically conscious residents had to make do with excitements in China and elsewhere.

COMMERCE

By the beginning of the twentieth century Singapore had obtained for itself a significant place in the then dominant British Empire—an empire which was primarily maintained through the control of the world's shipping routes. A glance at the map will soon bring home the importance of this control. Between Europe and China and Australia the key points on the shipping routes were Gibraltar, Malta, the Suez Canal, Aden, Colombo (or the Cape of Good Hope if via South Africa), Singapore and Hong Hong. All these were controlled by Britain and Singapore was a very important link in the chain.

But many of these places were more than strategic centres, military or naval bases. Some had developed into flourishing ports not only because of the facilities which they provided for passing ships but also because of the trade which had grown up with their hinterland or with surrounding countries. Singapore was pre-emminently one of these. As was mentioned in Chapter 9 the opening of the Suez Canal provided a great stimulus to the growth of the port of Singapore. At the time that the Canal was opened roughly five hundred ships called at the port, yet within ten years this number had increased four times. This increase was naturally helped by the growing use which was made of steamships as opposed to sailing ships. They were able to use the Suez Canal throughout the whole year and were not dependent on the seasonal monsoon winds.

In fact it was largely as a trading port that Singapore grew in importance—it was also used as a naval base but it only became one of great strategic importance after the First World War.

Singapore was a commercial centre from which trading connexions spread throughout South-East Asia. After the growth of the rubber and tin industries in Malaya in the last years of the nineteenth century the Straits Settlements ports of Singapore and Penang became the places of shipment for all this produce. They provided, and Singapore especially so, the know-how and techniques of international trade. It is also true to say that many of the mining and plantation companies building up their trade with Malaya were financed and controlled from Singapore—and this applied to Chinese as well as European companies. The hinterland of Singapore, as far as commerce was concerned, was the Malay Peninsula and the connexions between the two were extremely strong, although curiously enough in the early twentieth century the majority of the inhabitants of the Straits Settlements showed an unusual lack of interest in the affairs of the Malay States. This coincided rather strongly with a suspicion on the part of the States of anything which seemed likely to emphasise the economic and political domination of Singapore (see Chapter 16).

At the same time it must be stated that a large part of Singapore's prosperity was based on trade from outside Malaya especially from the Dutch East Indies. Therefore the suggestions for a Customs Union between the Straits Settlements, the Federated Malay States and the Unfederated Malay States which came to the surface periodically in the years between the Wars never received much support in either Singapore or Penang. Neither Settlement wished to lose its free-port status.

SOCIAL CONDITIONS

Singapore presented a picture of a society free from the majority of government restraints, with the administration interfering as little as possible in the day-to-day affairs of its residents. The essential thing to remember is that the great majority of the population of Singapore was composed of immigrants, whether they were the sons of the founders of companies like Bousteads and Henry Waugh or whether they were *singke's* from Kwangtung or labourers from Madras, all had come to Singapore to make money, preferably in the fastest way possible so that they could return to their own countries, Scotland, China or India. The greater part of the population until about the time of the first World War was essentially transient with everyone hoping to make enough money to retire home before he died. Of course not all immigrants became rich and, although many did make their fortune, very many more existed at a subsistence level as employers always kept wages as low as possible. For a coolie the margin between life and starvation was small.

However, as the years passed the decreasing chances of making a fortune forced many of the immigrants to give up the idea of returning rich and famous to their homes. Instead they became permanent residents of the Straits Settlements. Once this percentage of the population became substantial the administration was forced to concern itself more directly in curtailing social evils and at the same time to take a more active part in assisting in the advancement of the welfare of its subjects.

A free port presupposes few taxes on imports and exports, thus precluding the main source of most goverments' revenue; and Singapore did in fact have few alternative ways of raising money. It must be conceded that until almost 1930 the largest single revenue producing item (about half the total) was the opium monopoly with the result that the Government tended to be unenthusiastic about pressure to abolish the smoking of opium.

However, it was realized early in the twentieth century that the effects of opium could be nothing but harmful and the report of an Investigating Commission published in 1908, while noting that most opium smokers in the Straits were moderate rather than excessive users, nevertheless recommended stricter control. The report did not however recommend the prohibition of opium sales.

The most important innovation at the end of 1909 was the abolition of the practice of farming out the opium revenue; this resulted in the taking over of the selling of opium by the Government. After the first World War more restrictions were placed on the sale and smoking of opium. In 1929 all opium smokers had to register and soon afterwards users were rationed regarding the amount they could purchase. Then in 1934 no new opium smokers were allowed to be registered and these measures caused a significant fall in the consumption of opium—a fall from 1,300,000 tahils in 1928 to 506,000 tahils in 1938. There is little doubt that control was tightening and the problem was diminishing before the outbreak of war in 1941. Finally the sale of opium was prohibited by the British Government during the war (1943), and after the Japanese surrender the legal opium shops were never allowed to reopen.

STRATEGIC IMPORTANCE

Singapore was always important as a base for British troops and British ships but in the nineteenth century the island's strategic importance was largely over-shadowed by its commercial significance. Also during this period Britain's wars in Asia were either in India or in China, and if the latter case the base used was Hong Kong.

However the twentieth century saw a change in the world balance of power and the increase in great power rivalry which resulted in the World War of 1914-18. Singapore and the Malay Peninsula were not greatly affected by the fighting during these years, for despite its name, the war was in fact largely confined to Europe and the Middle East. Furthermore during the war Britain was allied with both the main powers in East Asia—Japan and Russia. Any fighting which did take place in the Far East was as a result of Britain and her allies taking over control of Germany's colonies.

The main excitement of the war was caused by the activities of the German cruiser *Emden* which left its base in China at the outbreak of war and caused considerable losses by attacking allied shipping in South-East Asia and the Indian Ocean. The *Emden* also shelled Madras and then Penang in October 1914 before she was finally cornered at the Cocos and Keeling islands and sunk by the Australian cruiser *Sydney*.

Indirectly the prisoners from the *Emden* assisted in the other dangerous event of the war as far as Singapore was concerned, this being the mutiny of some Indian troops in Singapore in 1915. The majority of the garrison troops in Singapore were Indian soldiers and their dissatisfaction was evidently encouraged by the German prisoners whom they were guarding.

One of the first things the mutineers did was to release these German prisoners. The mutiny itself, which happened on Chinese New Year's Day, could have been serious but in the event the mutineers had no leaders and they were soon put down with the help of loyal troops, the Singapore Volunteers and some soldiers from Johore. But there is no doubt that if the Mutiny had been better led it could have caused a great deal more inconvenience.

Although the strategic value of Singapore had not been put to much use between 1914-8, its significance increased considerably in the 1920s. This was mainly because of the Washington Naval Treaties of 1922. These treaties were signed by all the major powers, except Russia which had interests in the Far East, and wanted to try to preserve peace by limiting the building up of armaments by the Great Powers. As a result of the 1914-8 War Japan had emerged as the strongest Asian country and the Washington Conference was in reality an attempt by Britain, the United States, China and France and other countries to prevent the continued growth of Japanese naval strength.

The main treaty limited the building of battleships by Britain, the United States and Japan to a ratio of 5:5:3. Although on paper this ratio appeared unequal Japan in fact was able to concentrate her attention on the Far East whereas Britain and the United States had ships throughout the world. As part of the agreement Britain agreed not to construct a naval base in Hong Kong or anywhere east of 110° longitude; the Americans said that they would construct a base no nearer to Japan than Pearl Harbour in Hawaii; and the Japanese agreed not to build bases on any of the former German colonies. Singapore being outside the area of limitation could house a naval base and it was therefore decided to begin the construction of the main British Far Eastern base there as soon as possible after the Washington decisions. The first sums of money were allocated in 1923.

The site of the Naval Base was given by the Singapore Government but the expenditure for construction was provided by Britain. The base was to be complete in the facilities it was to offer and it was many years before it was finished. Labour Governments in Britain were not keen on spending the money needed but after Japan became more obviously aggressive against China in the 1930s and after she refused to renew the Washington Treaties in 1936 work was pushed along to completion. The base was finally finished not long before the outbreak of the Second World War and by that time $500,000,000 had been spent on it. But as we shall see on p. 220 below, when the time came to use the base Britain, already fully committed to a war in Europe, did not have the ships to put in it.

EXERCISES

1 Describe the secret society threat in the Straits Settlements and the steps which were taken to defeat it.

2 Write an account of Singapore's importance to the British Empire up to 1941.

3 Describe the system of Crown Colony government as practised in Singapore.

4 Write short notes on:
   W. A. Pickering, opium revenue, the *Emden,* the Singapore Mutiny of 1915, the Washington Treaties.

16

MALAYSIA BETWEEN THE WARS:
1918-41

CENTRALIZATION VERSUS RIGHTS OF THE STATES

ONE of the most important trends which runs through the history of the Federated Malay States is the conflict between the position of the Sultans and the centralization of administration which came with economic progress. The British had come to act as advisers to the rulers but, especially in the years following Federation, advice had given way to direct administration, and the legal position as laid down in the treaties between Britain and the Malay states had been lost sight of in a wave of economic and material development. Administration became more and more centralized, and the British officials slowly began to realize that both the Sultans and the Malay community as a whole had been overlooked in the concentration on tin and rubber. As the High Commissioner, Sir Lawrence Guillemard, said in 1925, 'the Federated Malay States of today are not a Federation but an amalgamation'.

During the economic boom years before the First World War little attention had been paid to political and constitutional matters. They had seemed unimportant when the rapid growth of Malaysia's wealth had turned everyone's attention in other directions. The great prosperity had caused even those few who worried about political matters to accept centralization as a system of administration which boosted such progress. However the years after 1920 saw the first slump in economic development due to the over-production of tin and rubber. Many began to question whether the federal administration was so successful after all, and once the working of the federal organization began to be investigated, many other trends began to be questioned by British officials and, more important, by the Malay rulers.

The Sultans realized that they had exchanged political influence for economic prosperity, and when revenue began to fall in the early 1920's, they wondered whether they had made a very profitable exchange. Their position became even less acceptable when they compared it to that of the rulers in the Unfederated States who seemed to have much more initiative in the government of their states. Before 1920, when the Federated States were rich and comparatively developed and the Unfederated States were not, the Sultans of the former were pleased with their position. But the Unfederated States were gradually becoming richer and their rulers still retained a great deal more power. The Sultans of the Federated States decided that they had given up too much. These feelings were also shared by many British officials and were supported by the report of a Retrenchment Committee in 1923 which said that over-centralization had proved expensive. The Chief Secretary, Sir George Maxwell, considered that the trend towards over-centralization should be reversed; a committee which he set up to investigate the whole problem recommended, in 1924, that decentralization was necessary, for otherwise the tendency of the government would be contrary to the whole spirit of the Federation Treaty. As a result of these recommendations, the powers of the Residents were increased in relation to those of the Chief Secretary, as the Resident-General had been renamed in 1909, and the Federal heads of departments; and it was suggested that in future the control of some departments, for example Agriculture and Forestry, might be transferred to the state governments.

But this did nothing to help the position of the Sultans themselves. Therefore the High Commissioner in 1925 set out fairly detailed proposals for decentralization, proposals which would increase the powers of the state governments and their rulers. He suggested that there should be a gradual handing over of the Chief Secretary's powers to State Councils and Residents. States would obtain control of certain departments, and the rulers would deal directly with the High Commissioner instead of through the Chief Secretary, whose post was to be abolished.

The Sultans supported these proposals as a necessary first step, but opposition came from the European and Chinese business communities. They feared two things: firstly, that the proposed changes would harm their prosperity by weakening federal control, and secondly that a weaker Federation would be more likely to come under the control of Singapore, and Federation interests would probably be subordinated to those of the Colony. As the High Commissioner lived in Singapore there were others who maintained that the important post of Chief Secretary was necessary if the Federated States were to exercise any influence on him.

The outcome was a compromise, as is often the case with the

British, and only a limited instalment of decentralization was introduced by granting the state governments control over some sources
of revenue and greater freedom in the allocation of the revenue
grant received from the Federal authority. But these measures really
only touched the problem. All real control and power still remained
in Kuala Lumpur, for the Federal Council could pass laws affecting
all the four States. In line with these changes the Sultans in 1927
withdrew from the Federal Council; taking part in debates had
added nothing to their dignity. Henceforth they were to discuss the
agenda with their Residents and were to sign every law that was
passed in the Council. There was also to be an annual Rulers' Conference. Unfortunately the intentions behind these proposals did
not bear fruit, for the withdrawal of the Sultans from the Federal
Council meant that they no longer took part in legislation, in
making laws, but merely had the suggested laws presented to them
afterwards for signature. This particular move therefore did nothing
to increase the Sultans' influence.

It was fairly obvious to the visiting Under Secretary of State for
the Colonies in 1928 that the efforts so far made towards decentralization were extremely inadequate. Very little had been accomplished. It was also realized that to accomplish a great deal would
be difficult (because much government administration was not
limited by state boundaries), and would arouse considerable opposition. Nevertheless in his report the Under Secretary of State
pointed out how practice had fallen short of promise:

> Our position in every state rests on solemn treaty obligations
> ... (the States) were, are and must remain 'Malay' States and
> the primary object of our share in the administration of these
> countries must always be the progress of the indigenous Malay
> inhabitants.... To me the maintenance of the position, author-
> ity and prestige of the Malay rulers is a cardinal point of policy.

Clementi's Proposals

Despite these protestations about the necessity to do something
to restore the correct balance in the Federated Malay States' constitutional organization, another four years went by before the
problem was examined again. In 1931 the new High Commissioner,
Sir Cecil Clementi, who had been Governor of Hong Kong until
1930, revived the question of decentralization at the annual Rulers'
Conference. By this time the question of administrative decentralization was complicated by other problems which in the opinion of
Clementi made action immediately desirable.

Clementi realized the growing necessity of some kind of co-operation and eventual association between the Federated and Un-federated Malay States. He hoped that later the Straits Settlements and British Borneo would also be included. As individual units they were all too small to survive independently in the twentieth century. The Malay Peninsula was too small a country to have so many independent governments, and unnecessary duplication, he considered, was both expensive and inefficient. Clementi also main-tained that it was becoming more and more essential for the Malay rulers to agree to certain principles of policy, especially with regard to the immigrant races. The preliminary figures for the 1931 census proved something of a shock; for the first time the Malay population was clearly outnumbered by the non-Malay population: 1,930,000 to 2,330,000. It was essential that all states should have a common policy on immigration, for more and more Chinese were becoming permanent residents in west Malaysia and the Straits Settlements. Clementi himself with his experience of Hong Kong wished the government to exercise much stricter control over those Chinese who were settled in the country, especially more control over educa-tion as well as over the political and secret societies.

Essentially, however, Clementi's proposals, when they were made public, were designed to make the Federated States as similar as possible to the Unfederated States, so that the latter would have no objection to closer association. The rulers of the Unfederated States had no intention of giving up the powers which they possessed at that time in order to become as restricted as the Sultans of the Federated States. Clementi hoped to overcome this important objection by increasing the powers of the rulers of the Federated States so that they were no longer merely figureheads. It was pro-posed that, while federal control was to be retained for central services like customs policy, immigration and railways, all other departments would be transferred to the states whose Councils would be enlarged, strengthened, and given some legislative powers. The states were to receive two-fifths of the available revenue, and the post of Chief Secretary was to be renamed Federal Secretary and made subordinate to the four Residents, who, it was hoped, would become more like the Advisers in the Unfederated States.

Opposition to Clementi's Proposals

The proposals outlined by the High Commissioner were opposed strongly by the same business interests that had objected in 1925 and for largely the same reasons. Those who had invested money were afraid that the stability of the country, and as a result their profits, would suffer if the powers of the central government were reduced. Clementi's plans were vigorously opposed by the Chinese who had by this time become a much more settled community. The High Commissioner had realized that the existence of a permanent Chinese community brought many problems. Fewer Chinese were now returning to China; more were finding permanent homes in Malaysia. In so doing the Chinese had established many schools which were entirely outside government control and after 1930 were subsidized directly or indirectly by the Chinese government. The authorities now proposed to bring these schools under supervision. Also important was the growing strength of the Chinese political parties amongst the immigrant Chinese, many of whom had become revenue collectors for either the Nationalist (Kuomintang) or Communist organizations. The Chinese feared that as federal control weakened, they would come to be more under the control of the Malay-dominated state governments. Hence their opposition to proposals for decentralization.

It is ironic that opposition also came from groups in the Unfederated States of Johore and Kedah who viewed with suspicion any moves by the British which seemed designed to bring them into the same position as the states of the Federation. These states were quite content to have British assistance but not control. Thus Clementi's suggestions were attacked from both sides in the Malay states, while in Singapore there was much opposition to his suggestion of a Customs Union as the first step towards closer association. The idea of a Customs Union seemed to be a threat to the free-port status of the Colony. Finally, the suggestions and criticisms were examined in Great Britain, and in 1932 the Colonial Under-Secretary, Sir Samuel Wilson, came out to investigate. He said that centralization was probably best, economically, for the country but that, politically, decentralization was essential. The principle of of indirect rule should be safeguarded in order to prevent the Malays being submerged by Western ideas and by the immigrant communities. It was again stressed that the maintenance of the position of the Malay rulers and their authority and prestige must be cardinal points of British policy—points, he also added, which had often been lost sight of. The final recommendations made to the British Government were somewhat changed by the opposition which had been aroused and were a compromise between the ideas of Clementi and those of his critics.

DECENTRALIZATION BEGINS

Decentralization, however, was agreed on, though the whole process was to be gradual. The first steps were to be introduced over a period of four years and would consist of the transfer of a number of government departments to state control. These included amongst others, Agriculture, Education, Forestry, Medical, Mining and Public Works. State governments were not to collect their own revenues but were to receive an annual block grant from the Federal authorities. Thus the states were given less financial independence than was originally proposed, and although the post of Chief Secretary was in fact abolished in 1935, the process of change was to be much slower than had been visualized by Sir Cecil Clementi.

One important resultant change was the strengthening and enlarging of the State Councils. These Councils now had greater powers, and they needed capable men to be members if the powers were to be properly exercised. For example, in 1927, the Perak State Council consisted of the Sultan and the Malay chiefs plus the Resident, his secretary and two Chinese. In 1937 it had twenty-six members, of whom twelve were Malays, seven were officials and seven were unofficials. By this time a greater percentage of the members had experience in administration and commerce, and the Councils often exercised considerable influence in the administration.

In line with his major constitutional proposals which aimed at returning, if possible, to the older ideals of indirect rule, Clementi extended the programme of employment of Malayans in government service. A Malay Administrative Service had existed since 1910 in order that Malays could take part in government service with eventual promotion to the Malayan Civil Service, and for almost the same length of time Malays had been in the higher grades of the police. Sultan Iskandar Shah of Perak had been a high-ranking police officer before becoming ruler. While the new proposals increased the number of Malays appointed to the Malayan Civil Service, Clementi also established a separate Straits Settlement Civil Service. For some time Chinese in the Settlements had been asking for employment in the civil service, but as long as the service members were interchangeable between the Colony and the Malay states such appointments were not considered. No sultan would have agreed to the employment of Chinese administrative officers. For this reason a separate service was established.

By the time war seemed imminent in 1939-40, almost all the first stages of decentralization had been carried out. State governments had full control over the Medical and Public Works Departments and partial control over the other departments. State Councils had also acquired the power to legislate on certain subjects and had much more initiative in spending revenue. It is interesting to note that the whole emphasis on gradual change away from over-centralization which was carried out prior to 1940 was abruptly and ironically altered after the Japanese occupation by the introduction of a Malayan Union which did not recognize states' rights. The situation is even more ironic when one considers Sir Samuel Wilson's words in 1932: 'His Majesty's Government have no intention of requiring the Ruler of any Unfederated State to enter, against his will, into any kind of Malayan League or Union.'

Nevertheless before the outbreak of war, decentralization had increased the influence of the sultans in the Federated States, for they were certainly consulted more often. This factor together with the increase in the number of educated Malays and the number of Malays in the civil service was part of a rather belated effort to reinforce the position of the Malay community in relation to the immigrant communities who had now settled in west Malaysia. Throughout most of the period between 1860 and 1920 the Chinese and Indians had been looked upon as temporary residents by both the Malays and the British. They had been accepted as much-needed labour but had not been considered as permanent inhabitants on any large scale. That the whole position had changed was suddenly realized after the 1921 census, and the 1931 census showed that the Chinese and Indian communities had become the majority in the country.

When war broke out in Malaysia in 1941 the constitutional problems of the Peninsula had by no means been solved. Unity appeared to be as far distant as ever and the country was still divided into the four Federated States, the five Unfederated States and the Straits Settlements. The prevailing opinion was that unity between the Malay states could only be brought about by breaking up the type of federation established in 1896, making all the units, federated and unfederated, as similar to each other as possible, and then devising some means to bring about closer association. The Unfederated States were generally not in favour of any of these proposals, for as things stood they obtained the best of both worlds. While retaining their independent identity, they could also obtain British officials and advice when required. Not unnaturally they were in no hurry to give up such advantages. The slow movement towards the distant goal of complete decentralization in the Federated Malay States was rudely interrupted by the Japanese invasion in December 1941, and all constitutional change was shelved until 1946.

ADMINISTRATIVE CHANGE IN EAST MALAYSIA

While the arguments swayed back and forth in the Malay Peninsula between the advocates of centralization and decentralization, the main problems facing the territories of East Malaysia concerned the extension of actual administration. Fortunately for the future association of the east and west parts of Malaysia the Borneo states took many of their methods of administration and law from the experience of the Malay States or the Straits Settlements. For example Sabah continued for many years to recruit officers from the Malayan Civil Service and it was not until 1936 that the Company appointed as governor an official who had previously served in Africa rather than the East. As it happened this change resulted in the introduction of some interesting new ideas especially in the field of local government. The new governor, Jardine, attempted to bring about a greater domestic involvement in local affairs. He revived the annual conference of chiefs which had been begun in 1897 but had not met since 1917; and he renamed it the Native Chiefs Advisory Council. Jardine also introduced control over finance to some of the local government authorities and this was perhaps his most important innovation, for it was the first time in Malaysia that local councils had been given some financial responsibility. But even Jardine had to concede that the spread of local government authorities was hindered by the scattered presence of Chinese who, in Sabah as elsewhere in Malaysia at this time, were not regarded as permanent residents. It would have been difficult to fit them into the authority of councils controlled by the indigenous peoples.

In the 1920's the numbers of Chinese immigrants to Sabah had shown a significant increase, so much so that from 1927 the immigrants began to pay their own passages and assisted immigration was no longer necessary. By 1937 the average number of new arrivals had reached 8,000 a year and for the first time restrictions were imposed. The economic development of the state had been greatly helped by the building of the railway on the west coast and the establishment of rubber plantations in the area through which the railway ran. A further result was the growth of the towns of Jesselton, Beaufort and Weston. Before the Second World War rubber was by far the most valuable export; in 1940, for example, rubber exports were worth $14 million while timber exports were worth only $2 million.

In Sarawak the main trend in the 1920's and 1930's was towards a more professional administration. The third Raja, Vyner Brooke, was less of an autocrat than his father whom he succeeded in 1918. After the First World War he also came under a certain amount of pressure from the British Government to make his administration less personal and less amateur. The state of Sarawak was now almost completely pacified, particularly after the great reconciliation ceremony in 1921 between the Sea Dyaks of the Rejang and the Kayans and Kenyahs who lived across the border in Dutch Borneo. The feud between these peoples had been in existance for a long time and was finally brought to an end through the efforts of Penghulu Koh who was, as a result, appointed Penghulu Temenggong, the senior Dyak chief.

As far as modernizing the administration was concerned the most important innovations were to bring about decentralization. Some examples of this were the creation of the post of Chief Secretary in 1923, the promulgation of the Sarawak Penal Code, based on the Indian Penal Code, in 1924, the institution of the position of Secretary for Chinese Affairs in 1929 and the appointment of Sarawak's first Chief Justice in 1930. These were very necessary changes if the government, advised by the Council Negri, was to be able to deal with an administration which was becoming more and more complex. The Raja could no longer hope to supervise a system of personal rule and personal justice. More attention was also paid to the provision of what today would be called social services—the building of more schools, hospitals and roads. However Sarawak, like Sabah, never had much money to spend on these items; her resources were sufficient for normal expenditure, but because she relied entirely on her own sources of revenue there was never enough available for large-scale capital works. Sarawak felt the effects of the fall in the price of rubber in the 1930's but she was fortunate that the revenue which was lost on rubber was made up by that obtained from oil which was produced at Miri.

The centenary of Brooke rule in Sarawak was celebrated in 1941 and to mark the occasion the Raja gave the state a new constitution, which was intended to increase local responsibility in government. The main change affected the Council Negri. In the past the Council had only been able to advise the Raja who alone had made the laws; in future the Council Negri would approve all legislation and expenditure and it would meet twice a year instead of once every two years. However the members of the Council were not elected, they were still nominated by the Raja to represent all the indigenous peoples, but not the Chinese. Thus this change in the constitution did not introduce any measure of self-government. Raja Brooke had also agreed to accept from the British Government the appointment of an Adviser whose task was to make sure that Brooke's methods did not differ too much from those of other British possessions and to keep a watch on foreign policy. The new constitution of 1941 was bitterly criticized by Anthony Brooke, the Raja's heir apparent, because of the possibility that the succession could now be changed. As a result he was dismissed from the service of the Sarawak government and this quarrel with his nephew—all the Brookes quarrelled with their successors—may have helped the third Raja to decide in 1946 to transfer possession of Sarawak to the British government. But the new constitution had little chance to come into effect before the Japanese invasion brought all administrative experiments to an abrupt end.

ECONOMIC PROBLEMS

The period between the Wars was one of economic uncertainty for Malaysia; this uncertainty illustrated the danger of relying for prosperity on primary products. During the First World War, Allied demand for both tin and rubber had been responsible for maintaining the income which Malaya received while the high prices which could be obtained for tin and rubber encouraged increased production. It was economically attractive to prospect for tin-bearing areas and to invest money for their development. More mines were opened, and the production of tin continued to increase.

The same process applied to rubber, although in this case the profits were not obtained so quickly. Unlike tin which can be removed from the ground fairly easily, rubber takes seven years to produce profits from the time of planting to the time of tapping. Thus money invested in a rubber estate in 1914 would not bring any return until 1921. As a result of the great boom in rubber in 1910-12 and due to demand during the war, the acreage given over to rubber estates continued to increase. Investment in rubber was something of a gamble; nevertheless individuals were attracted towards rubber planting by the high prices ruling in 1912 (high prices which were a result of the demand for rubber being much greater than the available supply), and many felt that investment in rubber would be profitable. As a result, new estates were established, trees were planted, and by 1919 they were ready for tapping. Increased acreage had thus caused increased production, the supply of rubber was able to meet the demand, and because rubber no longer had the same scarcity value its price began to fall.

In Malaysia it was doubly unfortunate that the period of increased production of rubber, 1919-20, coincided with a considerable fall in American demand for the material. Over-production by itself or under-demand by itself would have caused a lowering of rubber prices, but the two happening together caused a catastrophic fall in prices (a 'slump'). This happened in Malaysia in 1921-2. Until 1920 the price of rubber had never been below about eighty-five cents a pound; in June 1922 it had fallen to a little over twenty cents a pound. This price was, of course, much lower than the cost of production, and many estates were threatened with bankruptcy.

To understand these violent fluctuations in prices, it is important to realize that the price of anything is governed by its *value*. An article is valued because it is desired by many people or because it is in short supply. Not many things have any intrinsic price or value; for example, diamonds are considered valuable because they are in short supply, and not everyone can have diamonds. In fact the companies which produce diamonds make sure that the price stays high by only allowing a limited number on to the market. If all the diamonds which are produced were set out for sale, they would be no more valuable than glass.

Price is governed by *supply* and *demand*. If demand is greater than supply, then the article has a scarcity value and people may be willing to pay a high price for the article. This situation may be called a 'seller's market' for the seller is in a position to do well. On the other hand supply may exceed demand, people may not want the article and will have to be encouraged to buy. This can be done by lowering prices, and this situation is called a 'buyer's market' because it is the purchaser who benefits. In most trading transactions the aim is to try to cut down the differences between supply and demand, between seller and buyer so that both are satisfied. Thus the price that we pay for a new bicycle is composed of the cost of production *plus* whatever the manufacturer considers we will be willing to pay for his bicycle. This *plus* factor or *profit* must not be too high otherwise no one will buy the article concerned; it also must not be so low that the manufacturer makes no profit.

In Malaysia's economy both rubber and tin have been subjected to violent fluctuation of price because it has not always been possible to settle the differences between seller and buyer. In the early days before the First World War the demand for rubber was much in excess of supply, so prices went up and up as buyers competed with each other for the available supplies. By 1921-2 demand for rubber had decreased, the production of rubber had gone up, and thus supply exceeded demand; the rubber could only be sold by producers competing with each other by lowering prices. Thus we have the difference in prices between five dollars a pound in 1912 and twenty cents a pound in 1922. In the rush to take part in the boom and to share in the high financial returns, so much rubber had been produced that the rubber industry had almost destroyed itself.

The Great Depression

The same problem was to affect the tin industry at the time of the Great Depression—1929-32—a period when the rubber industry was again badly hit by falling prices. Tin had not been so adversely affected after the First World War, demand had stayed reasonably high, and the mines remained prosperous. In fact tin had reached its peak price of $2,414 per ton in 1926. It continued to remain reasonably profitable until 1929. The Great Depression caused economic disaster all over the world and had very adverse effects on all primary industries like tin and rubber. The depression or slump began in the United States in 1929 with the collapse of the stock market (that is, people were no longer willing to buy stocks and shares). The prices of these shares went down so far that they became almost valueless, and thousands of investors became bankrupt almost overnight. The whole effect of a slump in an integrated economy is cumulative: that is, a shortage of money causes people to purchase, for example, fewer motor cars; the car manufacturers decrease production thus decreasing the demand for steel and rubber; quickly the workers in the motor car, steel, and rubber industries face the prospect of unemployment with less money to spend; in this way fewer radios are sold, less food, and so on. Very soon the whole country is affected. In the case of the 1929 depression, the effect was world-wide; all over the globe there were slumps and unemployment. The demand for tin fell so much that the price in 1931 was $1,020 per ton while the demand for rubber almost disappeared. In 1932 the price was nine cents per pound.

In Malaysia the result was large-scale unemployment on mines and estates, for in most cases it was not worth continuing production. Costs and wages were higher than the price that could be obtained when the product was sold, and so tapping stopped on many estates. Everyone connected with the tin and rubber industries was immediately affected. So also were all the secondary industries— shops, entertainment—which catered for those employed on mines and estates. The government was also badly hit for its revenue almost disappeared. The administration depended almost entirely on the export tax on tin and rubber, but when there were no exports there was also no income. Government was also forced into a policy of retrenchment; wages of government employees were cut and almost all capital expenditure had to stop. Great hardship resulted amongst all sections of the population, not only mine and estate workers but also shopkeepers, government employees, and many in other trades.

How did the administration react to these difficulties and how did it attempt to solve the underlying problems? There was the short-term solution which tried to steady the Malayan economy by attempting to raise the price of tin and rubber. There was also the long-term solution which aimed at lessening Malaya's dependence on tin and rubber by diversifying the economy.

We have seen that price is governed by the relationship between supply and demand. We have seen that a falling off in demand coupled with over-production was the basic cause of lower prices in the tin and rubber industries. It was obvious that nothing could be done to increase demand, so prices could only be raised by limiting supply, that is, by making the two products less easily available. This is known as *restriction* of production, and it was first suggested by the Stevenson Committee in 1922. This committee was set up to try to solve the difficulties of the rubber industry, and it proposed that Malaysia, Ceylon and the Dutch East Indies should limit production, cut down supply, and so raise the price. The Dutch authorities, however, refused to agree to this proposal; they felt that their estates were more scientifically advanced than those in Malaysia and Ceylon and would be able to overcome the crisis. Malaysia and Ceylon, both within the British sphere of influence, decided to go ahead on their own for they accounted for over 70 per cent. of world production.

This percentage was not enough for restriction to be effective, for, although limitation of production did cause an immediate rise in price, once the price did rise production in the Dutch East Indies increased. Restriction of production in Malaysia and Ceylon did bring about a small rise in price (in 1928 the price was thirty-five to forty cents a pound), but the main beneficiaries were the small holders and plantations in the Dutch East Indies who increased their production to take advantage of the better prices. As a result, between 1922 and 1928 the Dutch share of world production increased from 25 per cent. to over 40 per cent. while the share of Malaysia and Ceylon fell from 70 per cent. to 52 per cent. Restriction which left out major producers was not successful, and so restriction in Malaysia ended in 1928.

The Great Depression of 1929 caused an even greater fall in prices. As all producing countries were adversely affected agreement between them was now vital. Nevertheless negotiations between the major rubber-producing countries took a long time even after the disastrous price drop to nine cents a pound in 1932. But in 1934 an agreement was made between all rubber-producing countries by which they would impose restriction of production for four years in the first instance. There was to be no expansion of existing acreage, and a fixed quota of exports was given to each country— Malaysia, Ceylon, the Dutch East Indies, Indo-China and Siam. A percentage of the quota was allocated by each government to each producer and in Malaysia was divided between plantations and small holders in the proportion of 60 per cent. and 40 per cent. This restriction did lead to an increase in price; in 1935 it was twenty cents and in 1937 forty-three cents a pound. The price also remained more stable, and fluctuations became less extreme. However, although restriction by producers helped to raise prices, it was still true that the price depended on the rise and fall of the demand in the United States, a matter over which the producers had no control.

The same type of restriction was introduced with regard to the tin industry in order to defeat the effects of the depression. In 1931 the four major producers, Malaysia, Bolivia, the Dutch East Indies and Nigeria, agreed on restriction of production. At that time the price had fallen to $1,020 per ton. In the beginning the agreement was not successful because it left out too many smaller producers like Siam, who took advantage of restriction to increase their own production. These other producers were induced to join by being given a favourable quota in the total production allowed, and from 1932 the price of tin did rise, reaching $1,815 a ton in 1935. Thereafter it remained at an economically reasonable price until the outbreak of war, the restriction scheme being renewed in 1934 and 1937. Under the quota system, Malaysia's allowed production was between 70,000 and 80,000 tons per year; her potential output was in the region of 100,000 tons per year.

The short-term solution, therefore, after much trial and error had brought some stabilization to prices, though the gradual increase in United States demand had also had much to do with the attainment of higher prices. The depression also induced people to think in terms of long-term solutions, one of which was mentioned above: the diversification of the economy. However, before the War little was done to encourage this on a large scale. Palm-oil plantations provided another source of revenue, as did the scientific production of pineapples. Both these industries were mainly in Johore. But little was done to revive and modernize agriculture and fishing, and little was done to make Malaysia more self-supporting in her basic food, rice.

Results of the Depression

However the depression did produce much thinking in the tin and rubber industries about how they could cut production costs and make their products more economically attractive to the consumer.

The slump of 1929 exposed the inefficiency of the tin mines and the rubber estates. The situation in the rubber industry had been first illustrated in 1922, but the Great Depression brought home very clearly that both industries needed drastic reorganization. In tin mining it was obvious that more mechanization (resulting in less labour) was needed in order to cut down the costs. The good old days of high prices had resulted in little attention being paid to administrative efficiency; too many supervisors and managerial staff had been employed. More dredges were now introduced and profits were obtained from working land which was otherwise of no profitable use. All energies were turned towards a lowering of the costs of production which would make the metal cheaper and easier to sell.

The rubber industry was also administratively 'top-heavy'. Little attention had been paid to the scientific side of rubber planting, and research designed to obtain higher yields from trees had not gone far in Malaysia. Higher yields meant that more rubber could be obtained from the same number of trees with the same amount of effort, thus reducing costs. The idea of improving the rubber trees by budgrafting had been successfuly introduced by the Dutch in Java in 1917. The depression showed up this weakness in British plantations in Malaysia and resulted in much greater attention being paid to scientific research. Rubber had to make itself competitive in order to continue as a major industry, and for this to happen estates had to be run in a much more efficient way.

Thus one important positive result of the depression was that the tin and rubber industries were forced to bring about very necessary reforms in their own methods of production. These reforms were intended to make them more competitive and therefore better able to survive. Today we are continually told that natural rubber must lower its costs if it is to compete with synthetic rubber; the absolute necessity of this became apparent as long ago as the 1930's.

SOCIAL CHANGES

Social changes were in many cases closely related to political problems, for they were connected with the establishment of a plural society. The development of permanent communities of the Chinese and Indians would obviously complicate the social structure of the country; the Chinese especially, because of their greater numbers, brought to the country extra problems and difficulties connected with their own way of life.

In the early years of Chinese settlement, that is in the late nineteenth and early twentieth centuries, the majority of the immigrants had not remained in the country permanently. Many had as their main aim in life the prospect of retiring to their village or town in China. To that end few brought their families to Malaysia even if they were married Rather, they supported their relatives by remitting money from Malaysia to China. The majority therefore considered themselves as temporary residents and were looked upon as such by the government and the Malay population in general. The government began its relations with the Chinese communities by leaving them almost entirely to themselves and maintaining contact with them through their headmen, the *Capitans China*. Left to themselves, the Chinese had perforce to do most things for themselves. They lived in close-knit groups, the Cantonese for example having little to do with the Hokkien or the Hokkien with the Hakka. They had little contact with the Malay inhabitants of the Peninsula, with the other immigrants, the Indians, or with the British officials in the administration. They made little attempt to assimilate; to do so would have been extremely difficult, for the two peoples, Chinese and Malays, are very dissimilar in religion and social habits.

Rather than assimilate, the Chinese tried to preserve their cultural identity and were determined, even though they were 'overseas', to preserve their language and their customs. Chinese immigration began with these attitudes and Chinese settlement continued to be guided by them. Even though by the First World War many

Chinese had become permanent residents, the administration still continued to regard them as temporary. This was especially notice-able in education which the Chinese provided for themselves by building and staffing their own schools. Gradually by the 1920's the government saw that such education completely outside official control would lead to many dangers especially when it became closely tied to China's own politics.

Chinese Secret Societies

Perhaps the most important aspect of the Chinese way of life introduced into Malaysia with the first immigrants to the Straits Settlements was the Chinese secret society. Today, just as much as in the 1860's, these societies play an important part in the life of the Chinese community.

Today we hear of the secret society as an illegal organization of criminals, who control sections of the underworld in Singapore and in the larger towns of the Peninsula, and who extort, assault, or murder for a price. Today the secret societies operate on a big scale, forcing protection on shopkeepers and controlling gambling, pros-titution, and drugs in their own areas. They have become a vicious menace, but they have not always been as bad as they are today.

For the origins of these societies, which have had such a consider-able influence in the country, we must turn to China itself. Such societies have a long history in China, existing in simple form as early as A.D. 300, but these early societies were generally of local importance only.

The secret society which later was to have most influence and become the root from which all the others have grown, was establish-ed in China in the seventeenth century in opposition to the rule of the foreign Manchu (or Ching) dynasty. This was the Triad Society, also called the Hung League. It was established by the remnants of a group of monks of the Shao Lin monastery in Fukien who were falsely accused of plotting rebellion. This happened during the reign of the third Manchu Emperor (1723-36). The Emperor ordered this monastery to be burned down; most of the monks perished, only five managing to escape. These five, on their flight, came to a stream and found a white porcelain bowl floating in the water; inscribed on it was 'overthrow the Ching, restore the Ming' which meant 'remove the foreign dynasty and bring back the native Chinese Ming dynasty'. The monks then swore the oath of blood brotherhood and set about forming a society which would become the core of resist-ance to the foreign dynasty. Open rebellion could not be successful, and they were forced to scatter to evade pursuit. But wherever they went they set up lodges of their society, waiting for the opportunity to begin an open and successful rebellion. Thus the original aim of the society was to overthrow the Manchu rulers of China. The society was called the Triad Society because of its sign of an equilateral triangle representing Heaven, Earth, and Man united together.

Throughout the eighteenth and early nineteenth centuries, the Society in China was not particularly successful in stimulating rebellion, though it was responsible for minor local revolts especially in the southern provinces. In fact the southern provinces of Kwangtung and Fukien were the centres of the society's activities. But the Triads were very much involved in the mid-nineteenth century Taiping Rebellion which came very close to overthrowing the Manchu dynasty. Hung Hsiu Chuan, the leader of the Taipings, was often involved with the Triads, and he made considerable use of their well-established organization. Naturally enough in the waves of emigration in the nineteenth century, the emigrants took with them the traditions and organization of the societies they had joined in China. The Triad Society, in fact, had many branches overseas.

However the societies which were first established in the Straits Settlements and later in the gold mines at Bau and in the tin-mining areas of the Peninsula were not entirely political organization aiming to overthrow the Ching dynasty in China. Although this political element ideally continued to exist, among the early settlers the societies were more like trade unions, freemasons or mutual benefit clubs. The societies, still secret, concentrated on looking after the welfare of the newly-arrived settlers, fitting them into the existing political and social structure. It often gave them loans when times were bad and put the newly-arrived immigrants in touch with prospective employers. Of course, not all the new settlers and immigrants joined the same society; they came from different parts of China, spoke different languages, and had different customs. As a result rival groups of the original Triad Society began to develop, gradually becoming entirely rival societies.

Nearly all immigrants were forced to join one or other of the societies and as a result, the leaders had considerable power. In the early days of the Straits Settlements they helped to preserve peace, and the leaders of the societies were appointed *Capitans China* by the government, so that until about 1880 the Chinese community was largely governed through these societies. Members owed more allegiance to the society than to the laws of the country. Gradually the various societies began to compete for power, and the mutual aid aspect of the organizations began to be replaced by aims that became more and more criminal. The fact that members of the various societies came from different parts of China and often brought traditional rivalry with them only added to the animosity evident in the Straits Settlements. There were two main groups, the Ghee Hin and the Hai San societies, the former mainly Cantonese, and the latter largely Hakka. As Singapore (and also Penang) became more prosperous, so the societies came into conflict over who should control the legal and illegal prosperity. Quarrels broke out over the delimitation of districts within which a society could extort protection-blackmail money from shopkeepers or could control the gambling houses and brothels. In 1824 and 1846 the quarrels in Singapore became fights and riots. In 1851 the societies attacked and killed over five hundred Chinese Catholics who, as a group, had remained aloof from society activities. In 1854 in Singapore the societies' quarrels among themselves led to a riot which lasted over a week and caused four hundred deaths. In 1857 they were responsible for the destruction of Kuching and nearly brought about the overthrow of the Brooke government. Again in 1863 there was a week-long riot in Singapore and in 1867 a ten-day riot in Penang. Behind all these troubles were the societies, now far from benevolent and rapidly becoming criminal. Rivalry between the Ghee Hin and Hai San had also spread to the tin mines of Larut and Selangor where the two societies were trying to obtain sole control of the wealth from tin. This rivalry was so great that it in fact caused civil wars in Perak and Selangor which went on for many years and, as we have seen, indirectly led to British intervention in Malaya.

In an attempt to bring the societies under some kind of supervision in the Straits Settlements the government registered them in 1869. But this did not improve control over their activities, and by an ordinance passed in 1889 the societies were declared illegal; henceforth they operated as underground organizations. They also came to be more and more controlled by criminals and gangsters and they also split into many smaller groups. Later, members of some of these societies became interested in politics and supported the local branch of the Kuomintang Party or the local cell of the Communist Party.

CHINESE POLITICAL PARTIES

Political feelings among the Chinese in Malaya became important at the time of the revolution in China in 1911. We have seen in an earlier chapter that many of those who had left China in the nineteenth century had been disaffected towards the Manchu Government. When Dr. Sun Yat Sen began his revolutionary movement outside China it was from many of the exiled Chinese that he received financial support. Branches of his party were established in Malaysia for fund-raising purposes, and the money obtained materially helped the successful establishment of Sun Yat Sen's Government in Canton after 1911. Few Chinese in Malaya had been supporters of the old dynasty, and they generally agreed with the ideals of the Kuomintang Party which was formed in 1912. Sun Yat Sen himself personified the emergence of Chinese nationalism, and his success was a source of pride to the Overseas Chinese.

The Government of China had always maintained that no Chinese could ever lose his Chinese citizenship. Even if he lived overseas he always remained a Chinese citizen. The Kuomintang or Nationalist Party in China took this same stand; as far as they were concerned the Chinese in Malaysia, even those born in Malaysia, were considered Chinese citizens. This outlook, if seriously adopted by the Malaysian Chinese, was bound to have important repercussions in the Straits Settlements, and more especially in the Malay states.

During the 1920's Kuomintang propaganda in Malaya became openly anti-British and was communicated through Chinese schools and political parties aimed at stimulating Chinese nationalism. As a result, in 1930 the Kuomintang Party was banned as a subversive society; many Chinese educational classes were suppressed, and the importing of textbooks from China was controlled. The political groups were not, of course, completely suppressed but were driven underground. Nevertheless two events brought about a lessening of Chinese Nationalist propaganda in Malaya. The first, in 1927, was the split in China between the Communists and the Kuomintang Parties; the second was the Japanese threat to China in 1931.

The split between the Kuomintang and the Communists in China brought an element of competition to the political activities of the Chinese in Malaya. The two parties began to compete for support, and thus both, for a time, were less effective than the old Kuomintang by itself. Chinese political parties remained underground organizations, and after the Kuomintang under Chiang Kai-Shek became the legitimate Government of China, Malaya continued to refuse to allow branches of a foreign political party to operate freely in the country.

The development of Communism in Malaya will be discussed again in a later chapter; but its beginnings were seen in the later years of the 1920's when it became a rival of and infiltrated into the

Kuomintang. By 1936 the Communists were influential enough within the trade unions to be able to organize strikes.

However the stress on Chinese nationalism was played down by the Kuomintang and later by the Communists as the Japanese threat to China increased in the 1930's. China wanted allies, and anti-British propaganda in Malaya was not going to enable her to obtain help from Britain. After the Sino-Japanese War broke out in 1937, Chinese nationalist fervour was directed almost entirely against the Japanese, with the organizing of boycotts of Japanese goods and the discontinuing of trade with Japan. It may be said, therefore, that Chinese political activity in Malaya reached a climax in the 1920's and died away in the 1930's because of events in China itself. However the activities of Chinese political groups had been sufficiently widespread to arouse apprehension among the Sultans and the administration, with the result that it was decided to exercise stricter control over Chinese education and also over immigration. In 1930 an Immigration Ordinance was enacted for the Federated Malay States, following a similar one which had been passed for the Straits Settlements two years earlier. The depression of 1929 had caused much unemployment in Malaya, and this made even more necessary some control over immigration. A quota for immigrants was applied to the Straits Settlements, while entry to the Malay states virtually stopped completely. At the height of the slump in 1932 almost nine times as many Chinese left Malaya as arrived (282,779 to 32,925). Those immigrants who came to Malaya in the middle 1930's were mainly families of Chinese already in the country, a movement which was quickly accelerated by the Japanese invasion of China. Families naturally made the Chinese communities less temporary and more desirous of owning land.

This desire for land, permanent title for which was difficult to obtain, led to the problem of squatters. Many immigrants just moved into remote unsettled areas, cleared the land, and became farmers. All this was done without title or permission. Many of these squatters lived on their isolated holdings throughout the Japanese occupation and were not discovered until after the outbreak of the Emergency in 1948.

These, then, were the extra problems which a plural society brought to Malaysia: Chinese nationalism, secret and political societies, multi-lingual education, and the illegal acquisition of land. All seemed formidable threats to the special position of the Malays. By treaty the Malays had a special position, and by treaty the safeguarding of this position was the responsibility of the British. In the 1930's the educated Malays began to realize that the Malays had not done enough to help themselves in the fiercely competitive environment which Malaysia now had become. They also felt that the administration had not done enough to protect their interests.

It was true that the 1913 Malay Reservation Enactment prevented the alienation of large areas of land to foreigners, but because so little was done to develop the rural areas, much land was lost by the Malays because it was pledged to money-lenders. A 1933 enactment stopped that being done. These were however essentially negative measures.

It was also true that in government employment there was a three to one ratio in favour of the Malays but little had been done to educate very many Malays to take advantage of this ratio. The schools giving modern education were in the towns, and there were only limited hostel facilities to enable rural people to share in this education.

MALAY NATIONALIST MOVEMENTS AND POLITICAL PARTIES

The impact of Chinese secret societies and their political movements, and what was thought to be the failure of British protection stimulated the growth of Malay nationalist ideals and political movements.

When discussing Malay nationalism in Malaysia we cannot forget the part played by Islam, since Malay nationalism actually began with the reform movement in the Islamic religion and the rise of the Young Turks under Mustaffa Kemal Ataturk (1880-1938). The reform movement in the Islamic religion was started under the leadership of Mohammad Abduh (1859-1905) and the Al-Manar Group in Cairo. This movement came to Malaysia when Sheikh Mohd. Tahir and Sheikh Al-Hadi, the followers of Sheikh Mohammad Abduh, returned to Malaya from Egypt in 1904 and started the publication of Al-Imam, the first Malay newspaper, in 1906.

From 1906 to 1926 Malay political attitudes were governed by religious concepts, and it was the reformation in the Islamic religion that sowed the seeds of political consciousness in the Malays. The reformers, known as Kaum Muda, wanted to modernize Islam so that it could meet the social and economic challenges of modern society. Kaum Muda was an urban rather than a rural movement and its leaders were mainly Arabs and Jawi Pekan. Religious schools were set up, and many religious writings began to be published in newspapers such as Neracha, Warta Malaya, Al-Ikhwan and Saudara, apart from Al-Imam. Although these papers published writings on the Islamic religion, at times they also published political material. Political matters and nationalism were discussed more freely in periodicals such as *Seruan Azhar* and *Pilihan Timur* which were published in Cairo in a joint venture of Malay and Indonesian students. Malay students in the Middle East, though they were few in number at this time, saw for themselves the development of Arab nationalism in the Middle East, particularly after the collapse of the Ottoman Empire. They channelled the political ideals which influenced them to the Malay public through periodicals which they published in foreign countries. These Malay students in the Middle East hoped that Malaysia and Indonesia would amalgamate.

In 1926 the first Malay political party, the *Kesatuan Melayu Singapura*, was set up. This party was organized by Eunos bin Abdullah with the help of Tengku Abdul Kadir, and Embok Suloh. At the time this party was set up Eunos had already been appointed Member of the Legislative Council for the Straits Settlements, the first Malay to receive such an honour. In point of fact, the Kesatuan was only set up because there was a prevailing feeling that the voice of Eunos would not be of much value unless supported by the Malay public. The Kesatuan aimed at encouraging the economic interests of the Malays; stimulating the interest of the Malays on matters of politics and administration; urging Malays to improve themselves in social and economic fields; putting forward the views of the Malays to the government and fostering Malay interest in higher education among Malay students.

In the State Councils of the Federated Malay States there arose a group of young English-educated Malays who were later to be well-known. Among them were Raja (later Sir) Chulan of Perak, the Undang of Rembau and the Raja Muda of Perak. Another was Onn (later Dato' Sir Onn) bin Ja'afar who was appointed to the Johore State Council. He accepted the appointment only after he had been assured that he would be given freedom in speech and in action. Dato' Onn made full use of this freedom and his name became well known on the national level, being the main force behind the establishment of UMNO in 1946.

The war between China and Japan and the boycott of Japanese goods launched by the Chinese resulted in making the Malays more politically conscious. Malay leaders realized the need for increased Malay political consciousness to counter Chinese economic strength. Therefore, between 1937 and 1939 there grew up a number of associations throughout the whole of the Peninsula. In 1937 branches of the *Kesatuan Melayu Singapura* were set up in Malacca and Penang. Two years later Malay associations had been set up in Pahang, Selangor, Negri Sembilan and in Province Wellesley. A much more radical party, the *Kesatuan Melayu Muda* (KMM), was formed in 1938.

The early efforts of Malay nationalism came to fruition on 6 August 1939 when the Conference of Pan-Malayan Malay Associations was held in Kuala Lumpur. This conference was a step in the direction of national solidarity. The second conference was held in Singapore on Christmas Day of the following year (1940) and another was planned, but cancelled when the Pacific War broke out.

By this time the Malays had divided into two political groups. The first leaned to the right and was the main sponsor of the Conference of Pan-Malayan Malay Associations. The ideology of this group was based on the principle of 'Malaya for Malays' and the group was led by the upper class of the Malays who were English educated and this is often referred to as the Malay College group. The others leaned towards the left and were more interested in association with Indonesian nationalism. They were generally Malay educated and often graduates of Sultan Idris Training College.

The leftist group was led by Ibrahim bin Haji Yaakob. Ibrahim was born in Kertau in the district of Temerloh, Pahang, in 1911. In 1929 he joined the Sultan Idris Training College, Tanjong Malim, and it was while there that he became associated with Indonesian political leaders who had fled from Indonesia after the failure of the 1926-7 Communist-led revolution. Among the Indonesian leaders were Tan Malaka, the Comintern representative for South-East Asia, Alimin, Musso and Sutan Djenain, the latter an active member of the Malayan Communist Party. After his meeting with Sutan Djenain, Ibrahim became very interested in politics and was on the whole anti-colonial in his political outlook.

In 1938 Ibrahim and his companion, Ishak Haji Mohammad, together with a pro-Indonesia group, formed the *Kesatuan Melayu Muda*. Many members of the *Kesatuan* were journalists and also students at the College of Agriculture, Serdang, and the Technical College, Kuala Lumpur. The aim of this *Kesatuan* was independence for Malaya but within the framework of Greater Indonesia. Their attitude was 'non-cooperation' with the government particularly after the outbreak of war in 1939. The British government in Malaya realized that the aims of the *Kesatuan Melayu Muda* threatened their position and interests. So, in 1940, the leaders of the *Kesatuan Melayu Muda* were arrested. Among them were

Ibrahim Yaakob, Ishak Haji Mohammad, Ahmad Boestamam and Sutan Djenain. At first the British intended to fly Ibrahim Yaakob to India and intern him there, but the sudden fall of Singapore caused this to be cancelled and Ibrahim, together with his companions, was released instead.

As soon as they were released Ibrahim re-organized the *Kesatuan Melayu Muda* and continued to pursue his aims. He co-operated with the Japanese in order to shield those who were working underground. But the Japanese realized the danger of those underground movements. Therefore they banned the *Kesatuan Melayu Muda.* But the ban did not destroy the leadership of the organization; the *Kesatuan Melayu Muda* only ceased to exist as an official body. When the *Kesatuan Melayu Muda* came to an end, a Malay army known as the *Gyu Gun* was formed. The formation of this army was directly initiated by the Japanese and Ibrahim Yaakob was appointed as its commander with the rank of Lieutenant Colonel. Other Malays however formed an underground movement called *Wataniah* to fight against the Japanese.

A plan for the joint independence of Malaysia and Indonesia was made by the *Kesatuan Melayu Muda,* which at this time took a new name, the *Kesatuan Rakyat Indonesia Semenanjung* (KRIS), led by Dr. Burhanuddin, Ibrahim Yaakob, Onan Haji Siraj and others. On 8 August 1945 an Indonesian delegation led by Dr. Sukarno and Dr. Hatta arrived in Singapore en route to Saigon in order to hold discussions regarding independence for Indonesia with the leaders of the Japanese Regional Command for South-East Asia in Saigon. A section of this delegation remained in Singapore to have discussions with leaders of the KRIS who were at that time planning to hold a Congress in Kuala Lumpur, while Sukarno and Hatta continued their journey to Saigon. During their return trip from Saigon Sukarno and Hatta managed to meet the leaders of KRIS at Taiping.

The programme for the joint independence of Indonesia and Malaysia including the amalgamation of Malaysia with Indonesia fell to pieces when Japan suddenly surrendered three days later. Even the KRIS went ahead with its scheduled Congress on the 16 and 17 August in Kuala Lumpur although Ibrahim Yaakob flew to Jakarta on 19 August. Although the ultimate aim of joint independence with Indonesia had failed, this aim was continually pursued by the successor of KRIS, the Malay Nationalist Party (MNP), which became active in the political field as soon as the Second World War ended. The aim of the MNP was clearly to be 'Indonesia-Malaya is one'. MNP was led by Mokhtarruddin, then by Dr. Burhanuddin and Ishak Haji Mohammad. Its youth organization, the *Angkatan Pemuda Insaf* (API) was led by Ahmad Boestamam, and its women's section, the *Angkatan Wanita Sedar* (AWAS) was led by Shamsiah Sutan Fakeh. When API was banned a new organization was formed to take its place, the *Pembela Tanah Air* (PETA).

All these left-wing Malay political parties, including the *Gerakan Angkatan Muda* (GERAM), which joined the *Pusat Tenaga Rakyat* (PUTERA) under the leadership of Ishak Haji Mohammad, were banned by the British Government soon after 1948 when the Emergency Regulations were announced, crippling all left-wing movements in the Malay Peninsula. With the banning of all left-wing Malay political organizations, Malay nationalist leadership was consolidated in the hands of the more moderate elements who in UMNO determined to gain independence by more constitutional means. UMNO (United Malays National Organization) together with MCA (Malayan-Chinese Association) and MIC (Malayan Indian Congress), was able to achieve independence for Malaya from the British government in 1957.

A SUMMING UP

By 1941 the Chinese realized that they were permanent residents with future prospects in Malaya, and the Malays knew that something drastic was necessary to preserve Malaya as their country. But both these realizations were lost sight of at the beginning of the Second World War in 1939, and were to be faced later in an entirely changed world.

We can close this survey of Malaysia between the wars by outlining the problems which faced the country at the time when war broke out in Europe in 1939. (War had already been in progress in China since 1937.) The following problems were awaiting solutions:

(a) Unity in the Peninsula: this was non-existent in 1939. There was as yet no national consciousness; people felt they came from states, not from a nation, Malaysia. This consciousness, which might be called nationalism, could only develop out of administrative unity. It was necessary that the three Settlements, the four Federated States, and the five Unfederated States should come together in some form of closer association. It seemed in 1939 that the only way to do this was to break up the existing example of unity, the Federated Malay States, and then start all over again.

(b) The serious imbalance of the economy: while it was necessary to do something to increase the efficiency of Malaya's two main industries, tin and rubber, it was also necessary to ensure that less reliance was placed on them. A greater range of products had to be encouraged, but though the necessity for this was realized, little had been done before 1939.

(c) Closely connected with the constitutional issue of administrative unity was the problem of a racially mixed society: the Chinese and Indians had become permanent residents in Malaya and were beginning to look for security as well as the rights which they considered went with residence. These demands highlighted the precarious position of the Malay community and their rulers, those with whom the British had signed the original treaties at the time of intervention. It was absolutely necessary to work out a formula by which the immigrant communities could be given status in Malaya without at the same time infringing the rights of the Malays.

(d) The economic development of the Borneo states: in Sabah and Sarawak the administrations had barely enough money to balance their budgets, there was little left over for capital expenditure which was so badly needed if progress was to be made. The States were not able to raise enough money from their own resources and not being colonies they could not look to Britain for financial assistance. Those responsible for the two States had not seriously considered any way out of this stalemate before the war but its effects took the situation out of their hands.

No solutions to any of these problems were apparent in 1939; in fact it can be said that no serious attempt had been made to produce concrete solutions. The motto of the various administrations was perhaps 'Make haste slowly'. The events of the War directed attention in Malaysia away from these problems so that eventually a political solution was produced in Britain.

EXERCISES

1 What were the arguments for the against the decentralization proposals discussed during the 1920s and 1930s?

2 Describe the different constituent elements making up Malaysia at the time war broke out in 1941.

3 What effect did the Great Depression have on the economy of Malaya?

4 Describe the measures taken by the tin and rubber industries to counter the effects of the depression in the 1930s.

5 Write an account of the nationalism which had developed in Malaysia and Singapore before the Second World War.

6 Write short notes on: Vyner Brooke, the Stevenson Rubber Restriction Scheme, *Kesatuan Melayu Muda*, the Kuomintang.

17

THE SECOND WORLD WAR IN ASIA

WAR came to Malaysia at the same time as it came to Pearl Harbour—in December 1941. It began with Japanese air attacks on Singapore and with Japanese troops landing in Kelantan. It came to a country that had not prepared for a war to be fought against an army advancing from the north. For the mass of the population it came suddenly and brutally, and as it happened, it was also over unexpectedly quickly. To see how Malaysia became involved in this war we must examine the background to Asian politics, for only by so doing can we discover the reasons for this Japanese attack. Malaysia had not been involved in in the First World War, but she was most disastrously involved in the Second. Why was this so?

The Second World War is generally considered to have started in Europe in September 1939, with Germany's attack on Poland. But as far as Asia was directly concerned, an event of more importance was the beginning of the Japanese campaign against China in 1937. It was as a result of the Sino-Japanese War as much as the European War that Malaysia became involved. The Japanese attack on China had come after a long series of incidents, incidents which the Japanese had provoked in order to take advantage of China's weakness.

JAPANESE DESIGNS IN CHINA

As a result of rapid modernization in the latter part of the nineteenth century, Japan had become a strong and powerful nation with a rapidly expanding population. Japan had also become more and more dependent on imports of raw materials needed for its industrialization programme. In contrast, China at the beginning of the twentieth century was at the nadir of her power. Divided up into spheres of influence by the major powers, China was governed in an out-of-date and inefficient manner. This situation provoked the Chinese Revolution in 1911, but even then there was little growth of unity. First the Kuomintang Party found itself fighting with disruptive local war-lords and then with the Communists who broke away from the Kuomintang Party in 1927. China was still weak and Japan took advantage of this weakness to obtain special privileges in China itself.

At the end of the nineteenth century, the main rivals for power in the Far East had been Russia and Japan. The area of competition was Manchuria and Korea, both nominally subject to China who, however, was too weak to exert much influence. It had been to prevent Russian expansion into Korea that Japan had gone to war with China in 1895; it had been to prevent Russian expansion into Manchuria that Japan had gone to war with Russia herself in 1904. Japan had been successful in both these conflicts, gaining the island of Taiwan (Formosa) in the first, and Korea and the dominant influence in Manchuria in the second. Manchuria had many attractions for the Japanese. It could supply two important raw materials, coal and iron; and it could be used as an area of settlement for Japan's excess population. Thus the Japanese treated it as their sphere of influence, obtaining many special privileges. But in 1927-8 it seemed that China would be unified under Chiang Kai-Shek and once unified would turn to ejecting the Japanese. Already the Chinese Government had encouraged the emigration of Chinese into Manchuria. To forestall such moves, the Japanese decided to act first.

An incident occurred at Mukden in 1931 between the Japanese in Manchuria and Chinese officials. This led to fighting and with this excuse the Japanese rapidly occupied Manchuria, expelling the Chinese administration and setting up a puppet government in Manchuria which they now called Manchukuo. The Chinese Government of Chiang Kai-Shek was not strong enough to offer any effective resistance, for its attention was distracted by its quarrel with the Communists. The Kuomintang had attempted to suppress the Communists within China but had only been able to force them into isolation in Hunan province in the south-eastern part of the country. Here the Communists led by Mao Tse-tung had established a government of their own and were a continual thorn in the side of the Kuomintang. Chiang Kai-Shek at first decided to try to eliminate this internal opposition before trying to halt Japanese aggression which had brought about the annexation of Manchuria. In 1934 the Kuomintang launched an attack on the Communists in Hunan. They were unable to defeat completely the Communists who were however driven northwards on what came to be called the 'Long March'. Eventually Mao Tse-tung and his followers reached Yenan where they established another centre of govern-ment which the Kuomintang was unable to capture. However, in 1937 the two rival Chinese political factions came to an agreement to establish a 'united front' against the external Japanese aggressor. Meanwhile the strength of the Chinese Nationalist Government was slowly being built up, a process which the Japanese viewed with concern. It was in order to forestall retaliatory action by the Chinese that the Japanese decided to move first by invading China. War began in 1937 with Japanese attacks on Peking and Shanghai. The coastal areas were quickly over-run, forcing the Kuomintang Gov-ernment into the interior, where they eventually established a new capital at Chungking, a position which the Japanese found difficult to attack but which was also not easily accessible to supply routes from outside. World opinion generally was on the side of the Chinese, but the major European powers were more concerned with the Germans (with whom the Japanese had made a treaty in 1936), the Italian invasion of Abyssinia and the Spanish Civil War, all events of more direct concern in Europe. After the Kuomintang was cut off from Hong Kong, American and British supplies had to be sent overland from Burma which necessitated the building of the famous Burma Road. In this way the Kuomintang was able to continue fighting while the Japanese naturally resented this foreign aid being given to China.

By 1939 the Japanese were making slow progress in their conquest of the inland areas of China and were finding that it was becoming more difficult to obtain supplies of essential raw materials like oil, rubber, tin and iron because of restrictions which had been placed on the supply of these goods by the producing countries who sym-pathized with China. Then in September 1939, as we have mention-ed, a war broke out in Europe with the German invasion of Poland. In May of the following year, the Germans, having already protect-ed their eastern border by making a treaty with Russia, attacked Britain and France. The Germans were immediately successful, and within a matter of weeks France was occupied and Britain was facing invasion. This invasion threat was averted by the lack of success of the German air attacks on Britain during the summer and autumn of 1940 and the winter of 1940-1.

Frustrated in his attempts to invade Britain, Hitler, like Napoleon, turned against Russia and attacked the country which had recently been his partner in the partition of Poland. By the summer of 1941, Russia was desperately fighting for her existence.

Japan was now ready to move. France had been conquered by

the Germans, and the Japanese moved into French Indo-China. The Germans had also over-run Holland and therefore little could be done to protect the Dutch East Indies which produced rubber, oil and tin. Britain was heavily committed to defending herself from blockade by German U-boats and to defending the Suez Canal from capture by the German and Italian armies in North Africa. She was not able to do much to protect Malaysia and Burma. Russia was the country Japan probably feared most for previously they had been bitter rivals in Manchuria. The Japanese had defeated the Russians in 1904-5 but they had always feared Russian revenge especially when their own attention was directed southwards. This had been Japan's main reason for signing the German-Japanese anti-Communist Pact of 1936. But in late 1941, Russia presented no threat to Japanese ambitions, being wholly concerned with defending herself against the Germans. Only one potential threat to Japan remained: the United States.

JAPANESE ATTACKS ON THE UNITED STATES AND MALAYSIA

The United States had an important naval base at Pearl Harbour in Honolulu and military establishments in the Philippines. They lay within striking range of Japanese supply routes to armies fighting in South-East Asia. The Americans presented a real threat to Japanese plans for, although they were still neutral, they were more interested in Asia than in Europe. The Japanese knew the Americans could be dangerous for they were becoming more hostile to Japanese intentions and had always been critical of Japan's invasion of China. The Japanese had to obtain control of the areas in South-East Asia which produced strategic raw materials if they were to bring the campaign in China to a successful conclusion. And Japan had to obtain this control before the United States could intervene to stop her.

Thus the Japanese, without warning or declaration of war—in fact while their Ambassador was still negotiating in Washington— launched an air attack on the American Pacific fleet in Pearl Harbour on December 7th, 1941. The fleet was almost entirely eliminated, and so the main threat to the Japanese lines of communication was removed. With almost the same startling suddenness the war came to Malaysia, with air attacks on Singapore and Japanese landings on the beaches of Kelantan. From their jumping-off points in French Indo-China, the Japanese had short lines of communication, and after they had imposed an alliance on the Government of Siam, they had no fear of attack from the rear. The landings on the east coast of the Malay Peninsula were made very easily, in fact almost without opposition.

The Malay Peninsula was not prepared for this kind of war at this time because it had always been assumed by the British that any attack on the great naval base of Singapore would come from the sea, that no invader would fight his way down the Peninsula. The Singapore Naval Base was the major defence commitment in Malaysia, and it was thought that an enemy would naturally wish to eliminate such a base first. In any case, that an enemy such as Japan would value Malaysia's tin and rubber so highly was not thought to be so vital as Japan's desire to capture the naval base. However it would be to overstate the case to say that Japan attacked merely to obtain tin and rubber. These products were incidental to the main Japanese strategic plan which aimed at nothing less than the German-Japanese domination of Eurasia. Because Britain was, in 1941, the main obstacle to this ambition, Britain and her possessions and protectorates were certain to be attacked. Britain had to be weakened at all points.

But the guns of Singapore were pointing out to sea, and the troops who were in the Peninsula and who were intended to prevent the Japanese reaching Singapore were ill-trained in jungle warfare. Of even greater importance was the fact that the Japanese had command of the air from the outset of the campaign, and after the sinking of the battle-ships, the *Prince of Wales* and the *Repulse,* off Kuantan, they also had command of the sea. There was therefore no reason to expect that the Japanese would fight an orthodox campaign down the main roads. The defending troops were bombed and machine-gunned from the air, the Japanese sailed down the coast and landed behind them, and others cycled down forest paths led by Japanese who had earlier lived and worked in Malaya.

Attempts by defending troops—British, Indian, Australian, as well as the Malay Regiment and the Malayan Volunteers—to hold fixed defensive positions proved fruitless. The Japanese infiltrated and outflanked these defensive positions and unit after unit found that it had to retreat southwards to avoid being surrounded. Stands were made at Jitra in Kedah, Slim River in Perak and again in north Johore, but they only delayed the seemingly inevitable Japanese advance. By 31 January 1942, the defending forces were bottled up in Singapore with little chance of being able to prevent its capture. There was no air defence, the Japanese had command of the sea, and Singapore depended on Johore for much of its water supply.

THE SECOND WORLD WAR AND AFTER

A common means of transport for Japanese troops during their occupation
of Malaya

Japanese troops landing in Kota Bharu

The atomic cloud after the bomb was dropped on Nagasaki

General Percival on his way to surrender to the Japanese Commander

Japanese surrendering to Admiral Mountbatten

Sandakan before the war, 1940.

Sandakan after the war, 1945.

JABATAN PENERANGAN, MALAYSIA

Sir Edward Gent

Lieutenant-General Sir Harold Briggs

A Malay Regiment patrol in the jungles in Kedah. They were constantly a menace to the Malayan Communist Party guerillas

JABATAN PENERANGAN, MALAYSIA

Sir Henry Gurney speaking to Malay Kampong Guards

General Sir Gerald Templer speaking to Chinese in a new village

JABATAN PENERANGAN, MALAYSIA

JABATAN PENERANGAN, MALAYSIA

The Baling Talks, 1955

Communist delegates being escorted to the jungle after the Baling Talks

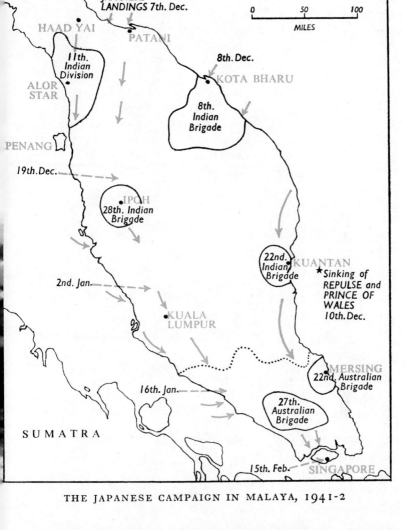

JAPANESE
LANDINGS 7th. Dec.

HAAD YAI

PATANI

0   50   100

MILES

11th.
Indian
Division

8th. Dec.

KOTA BHARU

ALOR
STAR

8th.
Indian
Brigade

PENANG

19th. Dec.

IPOH
28th. Indian
Brigade

22nd.
Indian
Brigade

KUANTAN

★ Sinking of
REPULSE and
PRINCE OF
WALES
10th. Dec.

2nd. Jan.

KUALA
LUMPUR

MERSING
22nd. Australian
Brigade

16th. Jan.

27th.
Australian
Brigade

SUMATRA

15th. Feb.

SINGAPORE

THE JAPANESE CAMPAIGN IN MALAYA, 1941-2

Events moved equally rapidly in North Borneo and Sarawak
where the troops available for defence were hopelessly outnumbered
by the Japanese. In Sarawak there was only a small garrison of
Indian troops in Kuching to try to repel the 10,000 Japanese who
arrived off the coast at Miri on 26 December. Neither territory was
prepared for war and no plans had been made to organize any real
defence. To make matters worse, in Sarawak there was no readily
available leadership as the Raja was in Australia and his probable

THE JAPANESE ADVANCE IN SARAWAK, 1941-2

Forces moved rapidly in North Borneo and Sarawak, where the troops available for defence were hopelessly outnumbered by the Japanese. In Sarawak, there was only a small garrison of Indian troops in Kuching to try to repel the 10,000 Japanese who arrived off the coast at Miri on 16 December. Neither territory was prepared for war and no plans had been made to organize any real defence. To make matters worse, in Sarawak there was no readily available leadership as the Raja was in Australia and his probable caused the Japanese a certain amount of trouble in hit-and-run raids, and their continued existence was a reminder that the occupation authorities could not suppress them. However their main purpose was not to stir up rebellion against the Japanese but to train and organize in preparation for the eventual Allied landings when they would be expected to carry out acts of sabotage. In 1943 they were joined by 'Force 136' officers who came from India by air or by submarine to co-ordinate the activities of the resistance groups.

But one attempt at rebellion against the Japanese did take place in Borneo despite the fact that the state was controlled by an occupation force of 25,000 men. The Japanese had set up their administrative headquarters inland at Ranau and Pensiangan and the resistance forces decided to try to capture a town on the coast. As elsewhere in Malaysia it was the Chinese who had to suffer the worst of the Japanese atrocities and it was they who also provided a large part of the anti-Japanese resistance forces. In Borneo these groups were in contact with the United States supported guerillas in the Philippines. With this encouragement and because the Japanese were about to conscript 3,000 young men and girls it was decided to make an attempt to capture Jesselton on 10 October (the Double Tenth) 1943. A combined force of Chinese and Bajaus led by Albert Kwok took the Japanese by surprise and occupied Jesselton for some hours but were in the end forced to surrender. Japanese retribution was swift, 175 of those captured were decapitated and a further 131 died in captivity in Labuan. But these stern measures did not deter the planning of another rising for 1944; unfortunately the Japanese discovered the plans and, during the mass executions which followed, the west coast suffered the loss of 16 per cent. of its population through illtreatment or excution. But generally speaking Borneo lay outside the main theatres of the war and there were only limited attempts to stir up resistance movements. In Sarawak it was possible to utilize the revival of headhunting against the Japanese so that the occupation troops were discouraged from venturing outside the towns.

THE DECLINE OF JAPANESE POWER

The war itself passed on from Malaysia with the Japanese conquest of the Dutch East Indies and the invasion and capture of Burma. These however were to be the limits of Japanese success. By the middle of 1943 the Japanese had been halted on the frontier of India; they had become involved in a very bitter campaign in New

Guinea as they were held back from Australia. Of great importance was the battle of the Coral Sea in May 1942, when the growing Japanese sea power was halted for the first time by the United States, and Australia was saved from possible invasion. The Americans also defeated the Japanese sea forces again at the battle of Midway Island in July 1942. Once American industrial organization was turned over to full war-production the initial defeat at Pearl Harbour and the loss of the Philippines could soon be avenged. In Burma the British and Indian armies gradually mastered the technique of jungle warfare and having stopped the Japanese thrust into India, began to push the invaders south again.

But the defeat of the Japanese took time, for the British and Americans had agreed that they would first of all concentrate on the defeat of Germany in Europe and not weaken their forces by dividing them. Full force would be turned first on Germany and only afterwards on Japan.

In 1942 the main campaigns in Europe were in Russia and in North Africa. Perhaps the two turning points in the war were the Russian defence of Stalingrad and the British victory over the Germans at Alamein, both in the autumn of 1942. Thereafter, though very slowly at first, the tide began to turn. In November 1942 came the American and British invasion of Morocco and the defeat of the Germans in Africa; in late 1943 the Western Allies landed in Italy, and the Russians began to push the Germans westwards. After the successful landings in Normandy in June 1944, the American and British in the west and the Russians in the east forced the Germans rapidly back to their own borders. The war in Europe ended with Germany's surrender and the suicide of the German dictator, Hitler, in May 1945. All attention was then to be concentrated on Japan.

However the campaigns in Asia had not been at a standstill. The Japanese after a series of naval defeats had lost command of the sea. The Americans had control of the air and were beginning to bomb the home islands of Japan. By the time the war ended in Europe the Japanese had been driven out of Burma, and by means of the island hopping campaign in the Pacific the Americans were within striking distance of Japan itself. They had moved across the Pacific using sea and air superiority and captured island after island usually after very bitter fighting. In all cases the Japanese had defended desperately. The Americans were now poised for the invasion of Japan itself, while the British were preparing the liberation of Malaysia and the East Indies. Australian troops had landed on the island of Labuan on 10 June 1945 and this was to be the stepping-off point for the liberation of Borneo. The towns of Jesselton and Sandakan had already been heavily damaged by allied bombing raids in preparation for the landings. The Japanese forces had put up fierce resistance and the allies anticipated that this was the kind of fighting to be expected in the Malay Peninsula when the time came.

THE END OF THE WAR

Then on 6 August 1945, an atomic bomb was dropped on the Japanese city of Hiroshima. A few days later, on 9 August another was dropped on the naval base of Nagasaki. This was an entirely new weapon equivalent to thousands of tons of the high explosive previously used. A complete city was wiped out at one blow, and in a few days the Japanese surrendered. The War was over. It had ended without the invasion of Japan and without the necessity for more fighting in the Malay Peninsula.

In fact the Japanese surrender came so unexpectedly that the Allies were unprepared to take over from the Japanese. There was a period of weeks between the Japanese capitulation and the return of the Allied armies. The gap was filled in many places by the members of the MPAJA who came out of the jungle and attempted in some places to take over the administration. Many of the guerillas took advantage of this period to pay off old scores by killing those whom they considered had collaborated with the Japanese. The collapse of administration and law and order gave ample opportunity for revenge.

In September 1945, British forces landed in the Peninsula and took over from the Japanese to begin the period of the British Military Administration (or the BMA). A similar type of government was set up in the Borneo states where it lasted until April 1946. A military administration was not the most welcome type of government to establish in country which had just been through three and a half years of occupation, but it was the only type of government available. It had been thought that the Allies would only return to Malaysia by defeating the Japanese in battle, as had happened in Burma, and a military administration was all that could be immediately set up in Burma. In the rapid change of events after the dropping of the atomic bomb there had been no time to gather together a civil government, and as a result the BMA was installed as originally planned.

Although it can be argued that a military administration tends to establish a government similar to that in an occupied country and also that the officers of the British Military Administration generally had little knowledge of Malaysia and its problems, it must also be conceded that the military by rather rough and ready methods did re-establish a peacetime government again.

Meanwhile the planners in the Colonial Office had not been idle, and, within a few months of the end of the war, they had produced the plan for an entirely new Malayan constitution, (this was the ill-fated Malayan Union), introduced in 1946, as well as entirely new constitutional arrangements for Sarawak and North Borneo.

EXERCISES

1 Give the reasons for the Japanese attack on Malaysia and Singapore in 1941 and account for its success.

2 What resistance was there in Malaysia and Singapore to the Japanese occupation?

3 Describe both the short term and long term effects of the Japanese occupation.

4 Write short notes on:
Pearl Harbour, the Malayan Campaign 1941-2, the MPAJA, Hiroshima.

would prevent the formation of a united front against them. However the return of Kedah, Perlis, Kelantan, and Trengganu to the rule of Siam in October 1943 did not gain for them the support of the Malays. Nevertheless, the bad feeling which they stirred up between the two communities caused Sino-Malay antagonism which erupted into fighting in the period between the surrender of the Japanese and the return of the British. Attempts by the predominantly Chinese guerilla groups to exact revenge caused clashes in Negri Sembilan and along the Perak River. These events complicated the already existing administrative problems. It was into this situation that the proposals for Malayan Union were introduced.

CONSTITUTIONAL CHANGES

Malayan Union, prepared in Britain during the War by the Colonial Office Planning Unit and put forward by the newly elected Labour Government, had been decided upon without any consultation with the Malay rulers; in fact, consultation with anyone in Malaya had been impossible because of the Japanese occupation. The term 'Malayan Union' referred to the new constitution that was proposed. These proposals were a complete reversal of the trend in British policy as pursued before the outbreak of the Second World War. We have seen in a previous chapter that before the war British inclinations had been towards decentralization with the long-term aim of bringing all the Malay states into closer association with each other. This policy was now radically altered.

Malayan Union proposed a 'union', not a federal association. There was to be complete centralization, with the Sultans losing practically all their powers. The state governments were to become entirely subordinate to the central government. Laws were to be passed by the Central Legislative Council and the assent of the Rulers was no longer required; they became merely advisers. The separate governments which had previously had quite considerable powers in the Peninsula were to be virtually eliminated, and they were now all to be fused together. Included in this new Union were the Federated Malay States of Perak, Selangor, Negri Sembilan and Pahang, the Unfederated States of Johore, Kedah, Kelantan, Trengganu and Perlis and also the Straits Settlements of Malacca and Penang. The Colony of Singapore was not included, not only because of its strategic importance, but also because the addition of its overwhelming Chinese population would make the Chinese the largest single community in Malaysia, and at this time such a situation would have added greatly to political problems.

There undoubtedly existed a case for greater unity in the Malay Peninsula, but the proposals for Malayan Union and the methods of implementation were not the best way of gaining the necessary support. The elimination of states' rights and the transfer of jurisdiction from the Rulers to the King of England had turned the former protectorates into a colony. This was bad enough for the Malay population; what was worse were the proposals with regard to citizenship. A Malayan Union citizenship was created which gave equal rights to members of all races who had been born in Malaya or who had lived in the country for ten out of the preceeding fifteen years. In this way the special political status of the Malays was destroyed, and it seemed that the British Government no longer considered the states to be 'Malay' states. The Malays were clearly in danger of being swamped by the three million Chinese and Indians whose loyalty at that time was, to say the least, dubious.

The proposals contained in the Malayan Union of 1946 were intended to change completely the political and constitutional organization in the Peninsula, and they had been carried through without consulting those whose position was to be so radically altered. Matters were made worse by the way in which the British Government obtained the agreement of the Rulers to the loss of their powers. Sir Harold MacMichael was sent to the Malay States to examine the behaviour of the Rulers during the Japanese occupation, preparatory to their recognition by the British Government. They were also asked to agree to Malayan Union, and there is little doubt that in some cases MacMichael made sure that agreement to Malayan Union came before recognition. The Rulers were forced into agreeing to the abdication of their powers.

THE BORNEO STATES BECOME COLONIES

Equally radical changes were announced in the same year (1946) for the Borneo States of Sarawak and Sabah. The war had caused much damage in these territories, particularly in Sabah, and neither the Brooke administration nor the North Borneo Company felt that it possessed sufficient capital resources to ensure that the two states regained their pre-war level of prosperity. Another important point was that government by a private family and by a chartered company had become out of date in the middle of the twentieth century. This was certainly felt by the British Government which encouraged the proposals suggested by the directors of the Company and by Raja Brooke. These proposals were that the two states should be taken over by Britain and become Crown Colonies.

In Sabah th
cause it broug
territory had l
before the war
same. The bi
British Govern
the other han
for the British
policy of slowi
Vyner Brooke
to revive Sara
Brooke agreed
influenced by
successor, Ant
state.

Opposition t
Brooke and
would be affect
of the posts in
tion, the Raja s
Malays to sup
interests of th
used over-pers
ed that they h
papers which
Parliament tl
opinion in Sar
in the interests
what was inv
transfer.

Despite this
was introduced
by 18 votes to
12 against. 'I
Sarawak becar
Brooke constit
considerable I
opposition to
service and t
culminated in r
by a Malay sch
the opponents

Anthony Brooke told his supporters to accept cession and in 1951 he formally abandoned his claim to Sarawak. Opposition gradually came to an end and the new constitutional position was accepted.

OPPOSITION TO MALAYAN UNION

Meanwhile the publication of the details of Malayan Union provoked a storm of protest amongst the Malays and also among many British officials. Sir Frank Swettenham, who was still alive in England, supported these protests, and others like Sir Roland Braddell became advisers to the newly formed United Malays National Organization (UMNO) founded in March 1946 by Dato' Onn bin Ja'afar, the Mentri Besar of Johore. The Malay community went into symbolic mourning and boycotted the installation of the first Governor of the new Union, Sir Edward Gent. For the first time the Malay community throughout the country set about organizing itself to safeguard its own interests. Protest meetings were held throughout the country; there was a large one in Kuala Kangsar which the Rulers themselves attended. These events, as well as the fact that the new constitution was harshly attacked in the British Parliament, forced the British Government to realize that a mistake had been made.

It was therefore agreed that a conference would be called to review the whole constitutional position. A working committee was set up including the representatives of both the sultans and UMNO. It was presided over by Mr. Malcolm MacDonald, the Commissioner-General for South-East Asia. This committee eventually agreed to the constitution which was embodied in the Federation of Malaya Agreement of 1948 and which is the basis of Malaysia's Constitution today.

A NEW CONSTITUTION

The most important difference between the new 1948 plan and the Malayan Union was that the Malay Peninsula was to be a federation rather than a union; the states and their Rulers were to retain certain definite powers. However it was accepted that there should be one over-all government for the nine states and two Settlements (Singapore was still excluded) and thus the pre-war disunity was at last ended. Nevertheless it was still emphasized that the Malay community had special rights, and though there was to be a common form of citizenship, its method of acquisition was to be tightened up. The residence qualification was increased to fifteen years (out of the previous twenty-five). The applicant also had to make a declaration of permanent settlement and be able to speak Malay or English. The Malays felt reasonably satisfied with the changes, especially as the agreement provided for 'the means and prospects of development in the direction of ultimate self-government'. In that sentence lay the importance of the new Constitution.

The proposals for Malayan Union had aroused the nationalism of the Malays. Although the British had been welcomed back to Malaya in 1945, it was obvious that they had been unable during the War to fulfil their promise of protection. This lessening in prestige was accelerated by the 1946 proposals which to the Malays gave the impression that the British had lost interest in them. They had to do something for themselves. The attack on their rights roused their political consciousness and began their interest in politics on a wide scale. There had been Malay nationalists before 1946, but because of their association with left-wing elements in the Dutch East Indies, they had made little impression on the Malay ruling classes. But after 1946, the lead, even in the UMNO, was taken by this same ruling class. Politics became the affair of the whole community. By stirring up Malay nationalism, Malayan Union was perhaps unintentionally the first step towards independence. This was a great change, for Malay national feeling before the War had been largely Indonesian-inspired and was supported by an Islamic reaction against the West. It had affected a limited number of the Malay intelligentsia who looked towards a union with the Dutch East Indies in an independent *Indonesia Raya* (Greater Indonesia). The events of 1946 for the first time focussed attention on Malaya itself and involved all classes of the community.

The Federation of Malaya Agreement of February 1948 also included provision for an enlarged Legislative Council with a majority of unofficial members and a Federal Executive Council with seven unofficial members. These unofficial members were not elected but were nominated by the government. However, this was the first important post-war step towards an elected Federal Council. In 1951 the 'Member System' was introduced into the Council. This was intended to make the unofficial members of the Council spokesmen for particular departments. They were like ministers but, being nominated rather than elected, they were responsible to the High Commissioner, not the electorate. The Member for Home Affairs was Dato' Onn, the Member for Education was Dato' Thuraisingham and the Member for Health was Tun H. S. Lee.

The first important elections in Malaya were the Kuala Lumpur

Municipal Elections in December 1951. These elections are memorable because they witnessed the first appearance of the 'Alliance' (between a Malay and Chinese political party) which was later to be responsible for obtaining independence for Malaya. At these elections the newly formed Alliance Party won its first political victory, defeating the Independence of Malaya Party led by Dato' Onn, who had in August 1951 resigned from UMNO. Dato' Onn had made the rather radical suggestion at this time that membership in UMNO should be opened to all races in an attempt to make it a national party. His proposal was not accepted by the Party, Dato' Onn resigned, and his place as leader of UMNO was taken by Tengku Abdul Rahman, at that time a lawyer and the brother of the Sultan of Kedah. It was he who saw that while his Party was not yet ready to accept other races as full members of UMNO, the best way to bring about some closer association was by a political alliance. Such an alliance did develop between UMNO and the MCA (Malayan Chinese Association) which had been set up in 1949 largely as an anti-Communist organization. These two Parties were later joined by the Malayan Indian Congress (MIC); thus was formed the Alliance Party which was to win the first general elections in Malaya in 1955 and in 1959.

THE EMERGENCY

Before continuing the story of how Malaya became independent in 1957, we must examine the events which have been called the 'Emergency', for the Emergency both slowed down and in some ways speeded up the achievement of *Merdeka*, or independence.

Malaysia is one of the few countries in the world to have met and successfully defeated a Communist attempt to take over the government by force. Communism has come to power in many countries since 1945, but in no country has it been chosen by means of free elections. It has always gained control by force and very few countries have been able to defeat this force; therefore the methods that were used in Malaysia are now copied by other countries which have to face the same threat.

How did the Emergency start?

The Emergency was a rebellion begun by Communist forces against the Government of Malaya in June 1948. These forces had been preparing for such a rebellion since the period of the Japanese occupation, but the actual origin of Communism in Malaysia occurred in the 1920's.

Communism entered Malaysia in the late 1920's under the patronage of the branches of the Chinese Kuomintang Party which had been set up in the country. We have seen in an earlier chapter that in China prior to 1927 there had been an alliance between the Kuomintang and the Communists. Until 1925 the Kuomintang was a legal organization in Malaysia, and under its cover Communist agents entered the country where they soon gained influence in schools and small trade unions. In 1926 they were able to organize the Nanyang General Labour Union which, though established in Singapore, was in fact controlled by the Chinese Communist Party. Then in 1927 Chiang Kai-shek dissolved the alliance in China between the Kuomintang and the Communists, and the latter could no longer make use of the Kuomintang branches in Malaysia which still remained in existence, though illegally. As a result, the Chinese Communists had to establish their own organization in South-East Asia. This was the Nanyang Communist Party, and it was responsible for supervising all Communist activity in the region.

This organization achieved only limited success, and in 1930 the international Communist organization decided that a Malayan Communist Party should be set up in Singapore controlled not by the Chinese Communist Party but by the international Communist supervisory body known as the Comintern which had its regional headquarters in Hong Kong.[1] During the 1930's the Malayan Communist Party concentrated on infiltrating into trade unions and youth organizations. In these activities it was quite successful; in 1936 and 1937 there were many strikes and many unionists were arrested. As a result of these arrests, Communist popularity and influence declined. Its influence among the Chinese community only began to increase again when the Party began to play a leading part in the encouragement of anti-Japanese feeling in Malaysia. This was particularly so after the outbreak of war between China and Japan in 1937. Thus by emphasizing Chinese nationalism in the years between 1937 and 1940, the Malayan Communist Party was able to regain its influence among the Chinese community, but as it was a Chinese-dominated party its influence among the Malay and Indian communities was very limited. Between 1936 and 1940 the Communists in Malaysia were influential in the trade-union movement, and their influence resulted in many strikes during those years. However, despite these labour troubles, it is estimated that by 1939 there were not more than 37,000 Communists in Malaysia

[1] The representative of Russia in this regional branch of the Comintern was Ho Chi-Minh, now the President of North Vietnam.

igh proportion
re in jail for
nvasion, even
e Communists

ups of Chinese
owns and went
hese men were
hunted down
rs were secret-
n the groups.
ased all Com-
they would 'go
ities. The Com-
osition to the
icially allied to
nists. It was to
e attached.[1]

ize resistance
Var the Com-
for the time
n the British.
of the British
rder to obtain
real intentions
n Communist
nt of a Peoples
ist leadership
secret units of
hidden from
to be hidden

bout eight so-
Actually, as a
never employ-
ish forces did
surrender, the
as those who
g revenge on
ly after some
hinese Communist

difficulty that the British persuaded the MPAJA to disband and hand in its arms. It took part and even had a place of honour in the Victory Parade in Kuala Lumpur on September 12th, 1945. Not all the arms which had been acquired during the War were handed in to the government; many were kept to be added to those already hidden for future use. It is fair to say that in all the discussions dealing with the disbanding of the MPAJA the Communists were treated very leniently.

This leniency was probably due to the general climate of opinion after the War in which Russia had been an important ally. Generally people were pro-Russian, willing to give them the benefit of many doubts and hopeful that Communists and non-Communists could live together peacefully. Perhaps, as Russia said, Communism was only another form of democracy. In Malaya the Malayan Communist Party was not illegal and had branches in all the main towns. And in the years immediately after the War, there was plenty of opportunity for creating trouble. It took many months for living conditions to improve, for machinery to be repaired, and for full employment to return. Food—especially rice—was scarce, and prices were much higher than before the War. Order was restored slowly. In the first flush of enthusiasm of the newly elected Labour Party in Britain, trade unions were established without adequate preparation. They were quickly taken over by Communists. The General Labour Union, set up in Singapore in October 1945, quickly came to be Communist-controlled while the New Democratic Youth League was formed by the Communist Party in December; strikes began in 1946, strikes which were aimed at disrupting the economy. The number of strikes increased in 1947 to over three hundred major strikes, mostly on estates. Thus rehabilitation in Malaya was seriously obstructed. However, further Communist success in 1947 was weakened by internal conflicts within the Party. It was discovered that the Secretary-General, Loi Tak, had betrayed Party members to the Japanese during the War and many had been killed by the Japanese at Batu Caves in September 1942. He had also possibly worked for the British and in 1947 he absconded with the Party funds. In his place, Chin Peng was elected Secretary-General of the Party, and its reorganization began.

In February 1948 a South-East Asian Youth Conference was held in Calcutta, sponsored by the Soviet controlled World Federation of Democratic Youth. All countries in South-East Asia sent delegates and there were two from the Malayan Communist Party. In the months following the conference a series of Communist-led uprisings occurred in Burma, Indonesia, Indo-China and Malaya. Although it is doubtful whether any specific instructions for rebellion were issued by the Russians at the Calcutta conference, there was certainly discussion of the need for armed risings. The conference speeded up the tempo of revolutionary movements in South-East Asia and particularly encouraged the Malayan Communists who were also urged on to more aggresive action by the Australian Communist, Sharkey, who visited Singapore in February. Thus at the meetings of the Malayan Communist Party in March and May 1948 it was decided to move towards rebellion.

At first the government was reluctant to concede that the growing lawlessness was Communist inspired. Strikes, started in Singapore in April and May, soon spread to the Federation resulting in restrictions being placed on Communist activity in the trade unions. In June 1948 there were sixty-seven murders and attempted murders carried out by the secret societies of the old MPAJA. Eventually, however, the police produced evidence that there was a co-ordinating authority behind these attacks on estates and mines, but the leaders fled into the jungle before they could be arrested. The Malayan Communist Party now moved towards open rebellion, though it is believed that this occurred rather earlier than they had planned. A co-ordinated assault had been prepared for August or September 1948, but increased police activity and the impatience of some Communist groups caused widespread terrorist attacks to begin a few months earlier. In June 1948, after increased violence throughout the country, three European planters were murdered near Sungei Siput in Perak. A state of emergency was declared in Perak, and as murders took place elsewhere, very soon this emergency was extended to the whole Federation.

The declaration of a state of emergency enabled the government to have wider powers than are normal in peace-time conditions for the arrest and detention of persons suspected of taking part in subversive activities. These were embodied in the Emergency Regulations which gave increased authority to the police. The most important of these powers was the ability to detain people who were suspected of engaging in terrorist activity or of assisting the terrorists, as the Communists in the jungle came to be called. In time of peace the police cannot detain a person without bringing him to trial, but under the Emergency Regulations this became possible.

At first the initiative lay with the Communists who concentrated their attacks on rubber estates and tin mines in an attempt to disrupt the economy. Managers, foremen, and workers were attacked and murdered as the Communists tried to prevent the mines and estates from continuing production. If they had been successful in doing this, the Malayan economy would have collapsed, and the Communists would have been able to take full advantage of the resulting chaos. In June 1948, the number of troops in the country was small—only about eight full-strength active battalions— while the police force was still being reorganized after the Japanese occupation. The defence forces therefore faced a very difficult task, for terrorist attacks were taking place all over the country. The government decided that first priority must be given to the defence of estates and mines so that the country would still be able to obtain the revenue necessary for combating the rebellion. The task of the security forces was at first mainly defensive. Small units of troops were scattered about on estates, and the police protected the railways, police stations, and other vulnerable points of attack. The first essential was to bring the police force up to strength and at the same time to recruit men to become permanent guards on estates and mines. These latter were the special constables who numbered 24,000 by September 1948. They were mainly Malays who left their *kampongs* to join the defence forces though later there was also formed the Chinese Kinta Valley Home Guard for the defence of the mines in the Ipoh area. For almost a year the security forces had to concentrate on defence, to make sure that the Communists were not able to gain control of any part of the country or force the closing down of rubber and tin production. The security forces were not always static; attempts were made to seek out the terrorists in the jungle, but there was not much co-ordination between the various groups in the security forces until the appointment of Lieutenant-General Sir Harold Briggs as Director of Operations in 1949.

A state of emergency is not a war, and at no time were the military authorities in control of the anti-terrorist operations. The army supported the civil power, and the civil government always had final control over policy. The Malayan campaign against the Communists was never a full-scale war, in the first place it was difficult to find the enemy or even know who was the enemy. A person might be a rubber tapper by day and a terrorist by night. Because the security forces were not capable of defending every individual, many people, especially the squatters who lived away from the town and villages on the edge of the jungle, were terrorized into helping the Communists. We have noted in an earlier chapter that this squatting had begun even before the War. The occupation had increased the numbers as many Chinese fled from the towns and as workers on mines and estates became unemployed. By 1945 there were probably 400,000 squatters.

General Briggs is remembered in Malaya for the Briggs Plan which began the resettlement of these squatters in 'new villages'. Not only the squatters but all those whom government could not protect because of the remoteness of the areas in which they lived were involved in this scheme. Resettlement is probably one of the most important long-term results of the Emergency, for it brought large numbers of Chinese into contact with the government for the first time. For the first time also about 500,000 people lived in settled communities and were introduced to a semi-urban way of life. The settlers were gathered into new villages which were surrounded by wire fences and protected by police posts. The aim of this operation was twofold: to give protection to those who had been forced into assisting the terrorists because of fear, and to prevent the settlers giving supplies to the Communists. During the Japanese occupation the guerillas in the jungle had built up a supply organization called the *Min Yuen*[1] composed of helpers, both willing and unwilling, who supplied food, medicine, money and information. The *Min Yuen* was taken over by the Communists and became their supply line during the Emergency. The main aim of resettlement was to weaken this supply line; this would cause shortages for the terrorists who would be driven into the open to look for supplies. Then they could be captured by the security forces. Altogether, under the Briggs Plan, five hundred new villages were established, mainly in the west-coast states. The success of this plan was a major factor in the eventual defeat of the Communists as inhabitants who were most vulnerable to threats and force were withdrawn from the Communist 'sphere of terror'.

The second innovation of General Briggs as Director of Operations was the introduction of War Executive Committees at federal, state and district levels. These Committees were composed of civil, police and military representatives and were formed to bring about co-ordination between all those who were involved in planning emergency operations. At state level the chairman of the committee was the Mentri Besar and at district level it was the District Officer, illustrating the fact that the civil authorities retained final control. This co-ordination was most important if there was to be full liaison between food control, police information and military operations. While the organization for dealing with terrorist activities was

[1] Literally means 'Masses Movement'.

being streamlined, the initiative still lay with the Communists. Throughout 1949, 1950, and 1951, attacks continued on planters, miners and innocent civilians, culminating in the assassination of the High Commissioner himself, Sir Henry Gurney,[1] in 1951 as he was on his way up to Fraser's Hill. This was probably the low point in public morale, and the fact that the Communists were not more successful was due to their inability to bring about a collapse of the economy. Even though it was often extremely dangerous the ordinary man still continued to go to work. The death of the High Commissioner convinced the British and Malayan Governments that the Emergency could not be ended by half measures. The new High Commissioner was a soldier, General Sir Gerald Templer, who was also the Director of Operations. He was therefore the head of both the civil and military power and by combining the two offices could operate more rapidly. General Templer himself concentrated on the military side of his duties, and he had a Deputy High Commissioner, Sir Donald MacGillivray, to deal with the civil side.

The impact of General Templer, who was a very forthright man, was immediate. He set about restoring morale by concentrating on achieving military successes and at the same time ruthlessly punishing those who had no excuse for not co-operating with the government. He was helped in his first objective by the provision of more troops for Malaya, not only from Britain but from other parts of the Commonwealth. The expanded Malay Regiment of seven battalions was joined by a Gurkha Brigade and battalions of troops from Britain, Fiji, East Africa, Australia and New Zealand. The campaign to bring the Emergency to an end thus became a joint Commonwealth exercise.

General Templer himself travelled throughout the country exhorting and investigating. Without warning he would descend on a 'black area' (an area of much terrorist activity) to punish the guilty and raise the morale of the innocent. He seemed to breathe a new fire into the anti-terrorist operations. At the same time the Malayan Communist Party leaders realized that their initial rebellion had been unsuccessful largely because they had been unable to gain popular support. It was little use claiming to be the spearhead of a Malayan national rebellion if the majority of the population was against them. Their tactics of terrorizing the people had provoked antagonism as much as fear, and the Communist lack of success was due to the steadfastness of all those who

[1] Sir Henry Gurney had replaced Sir Edward Gent who was killed in a plane crash on his way back to England soon after the Emergency had begun.

worked on mines and estates, manned isolated police posts or lived in remote *kampongs*. The Communists therefore stopped their indiscriminate attacks and withdrew into deeper jungle to reorganize their tactics. The Communists realized that the 'military solution' had failed. Their show of strength had been defeated; they had lost support, not increased it. The Communist leadership therefore decided that policy must be changed to win the sympathy of even the middle classes and that indiscriminate attacks should cease. This rethinking coincided with increased pressure from the security forces, and from 1953 onwards the Communists lost the initiative which they were never able to regain.

Military and police operations became more aggressive and more mobile. Large-scale operations were launched to clear specific areas of terrorist activity. The security forces now concentrated on jungle operations to seek out and destroy the terrorists and their hiding places. Forts were built in the deep jungle to act as forward bases and to give protection to the aborigines who had been forced to act as informants by the Communists. Use was made of parachute troops and helicopters to overcome the difficulties of the jungle terrain. Troops and police were able to stay for long periods on patrol, for they were now supplied by air. Both the planning and execution of anti-terrorist operations were much improved with the result that the Communist casualties very soon exceeded those of the security forces and civilians. As the terrorists were forced deeper and deeper into the jungle, so the number of 'incidents' decreased.

General Templer also began the policy of creating what were called 'white areas'. These were regions where terrorists had been eliminated and where it was considered possible to relax both the restrictions on food and other emergency regulations. It was intended that these relaxations would act as an incentive for the people to give more information about the terrorists; this would enable them to be eliminated, thus allowing another area to become 'white'. The first 'white area' was declared in Malacca in September 1952 and this was to be the first step towards making the whole of the Peninsula 'white'. The process, however, was to be a slow one, for although after 1954 the number of terrorist surrenders began to increase, the hard core of the Communists refused to give up the struggle. In 1955 at Baling in Kedah, the newly elected Chief Minister, Tengku Abdul Rahman, met the Communist leader, Chin Peng, to try to bring about the end of the wasteful struggle which had been going on for seven years. The Communists would not agree to his terms and went back into the jungle. However the surrender rate of terrorists increased, and by 1960 the whole country was 'white' except for areas near the Siamese border. From their refuge in south Thailand (as Siam is now called) the Communists still continued what by that time had became a hopeless struggle. Nevertheless, when Malaya became independent in 1957 the Emergency had still not been brought to an end.

The Emergency had ceased to be a threat to Malaya after 1954, though it still remained an extremely expensive 'nuisance'. It is estimated that between 1948 and 1955 the Emergency cost the Malayan Government between $150 and $200 million per year while the British contribution (largely for troops and military equipment) was $550 million per year. These large sums of money, which would have been so useful for the building of hospitals and schools, had to be used to defeat an armed rebellion by a maximum of ten thousand men. The Emergency was extremely expensive for Malaya though the country was fortunate that the Korean War of 1951 resulted in boom prices for tin and rubber and these prices greatly increased government revenue.

There were also some indirect benefits, not only in the form of new villages but also for the aborigines and others living in the rural areas. For the first time the government took notice of them. While those who were resettled in the new villages obtained such amenities as water, electricity, schools, and dispensaries, it was also necessary to extend the same facilities to the kampong people who had not needed to be resettled. The latter considered it rather unfair that those who had been suspected of aiding the terrorists obtained more benefits than those who had remained loyal to the government. Thus more roads were built in the rural areas, travelling dispensaries and clinics were sent out to the kampongs, and the kampong people received benefits from increased government attention. General Templer had said that the way to beat Communism was not so much by military victories but by winning the hearts and minds of the people. It was essential that the people should be on the side of the government, not sitting on the fence waiting to see the outcome of the struggle. To win the people to its side the government had to show a real interest in their welfare and at the same time encourage them to do things for themselves.

The government's plans did not merely involve providing the people with protection and social amenities; it was also necessary that the people should take part in the campaign themselves. Home-guard units were established in kampongs and new villages, first of all to aid the police but later to be entirely responsible for their own defence. Village councils were established, elections were held for them and for larger and more important councils, even while the Emergency was at its height. The High Commissioner realized that political progress was necessary alongside the military defeat of terrorism if the Communist threat was to be really ended.

In the Borneo states the years during which the Malay Peninsula was struggling against communist subversion were years of progress towards greater prosperity and economic development. Both Sarawak and Sabah were fortunate in not being directly involved in this struggle though Sarawak did provide assistance to the Commonwealth forces in Malaya by sending Dyak scouts who later in 1953 were formed into the revived Sarawak Rangers.

Attention in the two states was focussed on social and economic matters—more hospitals, schools and roads—rather than on political affairs. It was not until 1956-7 that the first elections by secret ballot, to the Kuching Municipal Council, were held and at the same time the Council Negri gained an unofficial majority. In Sabah political developments were even slower and it was not until 1962 that there was an unofficial majority in the Legislative Council. However there had been economic progress. Between 1881 and 1954 three hundred miles of roads had been built in Sabah; in the three years 1954-7 six hundred miles were constructed. This helped to bring about a great increase in agricultural development. After the war harbours were reconstructed and enlarged and the tonnage handled increased from 500,000 tons in 1951 to 2½ million in 1963. But the product which made the most spectacular progress in the years after the war was timber, now Sabah's main source of wealth and revenue. Timber exports have leapt forward owing to the discovery of new markets in Japan which now takes 80 per cent. of Sabah's production and production has risen from 9 million cu. ft. in 1954 to 82 million cu. ft. in 1963. Timber exports were worth $150 million in 1963. The other two main revenue producers in Sabah are rubber and copra while in Sarawak they are rubber and pepper.

With more revenue available to the administrations the social services have improved in both territories, the birth rate has gone up and the death rate from disease has gone down. Thus one of the most important developments in the Borneo states has been the steady rise in the population. In Sabah the population has increased from 334,141 in 1951 to 454,421 in 1960, an increase of 36 per cent. in contrast to a rise of only 20 per cent. between 1931 and 1951. In Sarawak the population had grown to 744,529 by 1960. In both states the indigenous peoples comprised 67 per cent. of the population and the Chinese numbered 31 per cent. in Sarawak and 23 per cent. in Sabah. A plural society was now well established in the Borneo states.

In view of what was to come later perhaps one of the most important trends in the post-war years in the Borneo territories was the movement towards closer association between Sarawak, Sabah and Brunei. The British Government felt that co-operation between the three would be valuable particularly in the fields of communications, legal organization, defence and other matters of common interest. In view of the tremendous financial resources necessary for development it would obviously be less wasteful to co-operate. Thus in 1951 the higher courts of Sarawak, Sabah and Brunei were unified so that there was one High Court and one Court of Appeal for the three states. In 1953 there was an inter-territorial conference to consider administrative co-operation.

In the early 1950's closer co-operation was considered to be administratively sensible but later there developed suggestions of closer political association. By 1958 there was open discussion of the possibilities of a federation between Sabah, Sarawak and Brunei. Malaya had recently become independent, there were now very few colonies remaining in Asia, but at the same time it would be difficult for the three Borneo states to exist as separate independent units. However in some form of association they would have much more chance of success. There were reservations about the suggestion in all three territories but interest was shown in both Sabah and Sarawak. However the Sultan of Brunei was not at all enthusiastic. Brunei hinted that its ties were much closer with the Malay states of the Peninsula rather than with its neighbours Sabah and Sarawak. The proposals were not pursued any further, since a Borneo federation would not be financially strong without some contribution from Brunei's wealth from oil. It is an interesting point that five years later it was Sabah and Sarawak and not Brunei which joined with the Malay Peninsula.

INDEPENDENCE

We must now return to the developments leading to the attainment of Malaya's independence. The progress towards self-government had of course been interrupted by the events of the Emergency, for the growth of self-governing institutions was at first subordinated to the suppression of Communism. But the final goal of independence was never forgotten even in the directive given to General Templer when he was appointed High Commissioner in 1952. This stated:

> The policy of His Majesty's Government in the United Kingdom is that Malaya should in due course become a fully self-governing nation. His Majesty's Government confidently hopes that that nation will be within the Commonwealth....
> Communist terrorism is retarding the political advancement and economic development of the country and the welfare of its peoples. Your primary task in Malaya must, therefore, be the restoration of law and order, so that this barrier to progress may be removed.

The new High Commissioner realized that the two objectives must develop side by side and that the best way of defeating the terrorists was by encouraging the development of Malayan nationalism which would mobilize public feeling against the Communists. Therefore although the suppression of terrorism had to be given priority, in a way the Emergency stimulated the growth of national feeling and speeded up the participation of Malayans in the work of government. We have seen how Malay feeling had been aroused in 1946 and how the formation of UMNO had produced a political party which had popular Malay support. This had been specially a Malay feeling aroused to defend what the Malay community considered were its special rights. The development of a Malayan nationalism came later and was certainly stimulated by the Emergency. The terrorists took no notice of race or community in their ambushes and murders; all were victims and all groups began to realize that it was in the common interest for them to co-operate in the suppression of Communist activity. From this it was only a small step before they also began to co-operate politically. We have mentioned how the MCA, formed originally to do welfare work in the new villages, came to represent many sections of the Chinese community and in 1951 formed an 'alliance' with the Malay party, UMNO, in order to take part in the Kuala Lumpur Municipal Elections. The alliance was so successful that this political co-operation was continued for other elections at municipal, state and eventually federal level. The Malayan Indian Congress later became the third member of the Alliance party which then represented large sections of the three major communities.

1951 saw the introduction of the Member System in the Federal Government and the first series of local elections. The gradual improvement in the Emergency situation in 1953 encouraged the Alliance to demand elections to the Federal Legislative Council. In the negotiations with the British which followed this demand, the Alliance maintained that there should be a majority of elected members in the Council. It was eventually agreed that fifty-two of the ninety-eight members would be elected; the first national elections, in which the electorate numbered 1,280,000, were held in July 1955. The Alliance Party was opposed by Party Negara led by Dato' Onn and by the Pan-Malayan Islamic Party both of which were rather more conservative than the combined Party led by Tengku Abdul Rahman. The latter won a sweeping victory (fifty-one of the fifty-two seats and with approximately 80 per cent. of the votes cast), and Tengku Abdul Rahman became Malaya's first Chief Minister. He was Chief Minister of a government which was composed of both elected ministers and also official civil servants, but it was a government in which for the first time Malayans had real influence. It was this government which offered an amnesty to the terrorists in 1955 in an attempt to end the Emergency, and it was Tengku Abdul Rahman, with Tun Tan Cheng Lock and Mr. David Marshall (at that time Chief Minister of Singapore), who met the Communist leader, Chin Peng, at Baling in Kedah to try to bring about the terrorist surrender. However, the meeting was unsuccessful, and the Emergency continued even after attainment of independence in 1957, only coming to an end officially in 1960.

One of the most important problems facing the newly elected government was the forging of national unity in Malaya, which was shortly to become independent. It has already been said that the Alliance Party, which had won these first elections, was essentially a combination of three parties who represented the three main communities in the country. In many ways the Alliance personified the country as a whole and this association of the three communities was an essential step towards gaining independence, but the ultimate aim was the development of a united Malayan nation.

Two aspects of disunity had to be tackled. Firstly there was the economic imbalance between the two largest communities, the Malays and Chinese, in that the Malays had a disproportionally small share (as farmers and agriculturalists) of the national wealth. One community with such an economic grievance would hinder the growth of national unity. Secondly there was the need to hasten the assimilation of the Malayan Chinese and Indians by setting out a national policy of education which would emphasize Malayan unity.

The Government first turned to the second problem with the formation in 1956 of a special education committee under the chairmanship of Dato' (later Tun) Abdul Razak, the first Minister of

Education. This committee decided on, for the first time, a national programme of education with a common syllabus for all schools whatever their language of instruction. It was intended that Malay and English would become the two media of instruction with provision for the teaching of the Chinese and Indian languages. As far as possible all schools would be absorbed into the government system and those schools which did not wish to conform would not receive financial assistance from the Government.

The main aim behind these proposals, which were introduced in 1957, was to have a policy which, because it was common to all schools, would unify the younger generation. Great emphasis was placed on the building of new schools so that in the first instance all children would be able to have six years of primary education.

The economic position of the Malay community had been a source of grave concern to Malay leaders even before the Second World War. However not much had been done to obtain Government intervention until the formation of UMNO in 1946, and little of lasting value was achieved before the appointment of Dato' Onn as Member for Home Affairs in 1951. Dato' Onn also became Chairman of the Rural and Industrial Development Authority (RIDA)[1] which was set up to provide economic assistance, by means of training and loans, for the rural Malay community. RIDA was a first step to encourage the rural people to raise their standard of living but the full scale attack on rural poverty was only made after Independence and the ending of the Emergency when Rural Development became a major aspect of Government policy and was once again placed under the control of Tun Abdul Razak, the Deputy Prime Minister.

The demands for independence increased throughout the Emergency period. In 1955, the Alliance had asked for self-government in two years and complete independence in four. It was soon realized that with the Emergency definitely under control, such a timetable was too slow. Thus in 1956 a Malayan delegation, composed of representatives of the Rulers and the Alliance Ministers, went to London to negotiate for independence in 1957. In Britain they met with little opposition to their demands. The British Government had no intention of delaying independence in the Federation with the risk of provoking the breakdown of all the co-operation which had been achieved to end the Emergency. There was almost no argument about the grant of independence; the negotiations were mainly concerned with the type of constitution for an independent Malaya.

[1] Now called Majlis Amanah Ra'ayat (MARA).

This was not a straight-forward problem for which an easy solution could be produced. There were many complications, the most important being Malaya's plural society; also requiring much debate were the position of the rulers and the question of citizenship.

The Alliance Party suggested that a Commonwealth Commission should be responsible for drawing up a constitution. The Commission's proposals would then be put before the rulers, and the Malayan and British Governments. The Commission, whose Chairman was Lord Reid, had members from Britain, India, Australia, and Pakistan. It eventually produced a draft constitution in March 1957, which was largely based on the memorandum submitted by the Alliance Party. With minor changes this became the Malayan Constitution and later the Malaysian Constitution of today.

The Malayan Constitution which came into force with the proclamation of independence was a Federal Constitution. It was modelled on the Federation of Malaya Agreement of 1948 in so far as the states and their rulers were to retain certain rights and powers while at the same time the central government would have the supreme power in all important matters. In other words Malaya's Constitution was to be a 'strong' federation in which the main powers and the residual powers were to lie with the Federal Government. The states were only to have limited authority and only limited sources of revenue. Unlike the American Constitution which lays great emphasis on 'states rights' and limits the authority of the Federal Government, in Malaya the powers of the Federal Government were practically unlimited.

In the first place, therefore, Malaya was to be a highly centralized Federation, though the various states were to retain their individuality, as in the case of Kelantan, for example, keeping its own civil service, Johore its own military forces, and all the Unfederated States their own Thursday-Friday week-end holiday. Secondly, the basic structure of government was to be Constitutional Monarchy; that is, there was to be a king who would rule through Parliament. As it was virtually impossible to choose a permanent monarch from among the nine ruling families, it was decided that the nine Rulers would themselves select one of their number to be the Paramount Ruler, or *Yang di-Pertuan Agong*, for a period of five years. The first Supreme Ruler of an independent Malaya was the Yang di-Pertuan Besar of Negri Sembilan, Tuanku Abdul Rahman ibni Al-Marhum Tuanku Muhammad.

Parliament was to be composed of two Houses, a House of Representatives of 104 directly elected members and a Senate of 38 members both nominated and indirectly elected. Most powers would lie with the elected Dewan Ra'ayat, and the Dewan Negara only had the power to delay legislation, except on measures like the Budget, for one year.

In the Senate, sixteen members were to be nominated to represent special interests, for example, the *orang asli*, the tin and rubber industries; while two members were to be elected by each State Assembly.

As the Malayan Constitution was federal, each state retained its own government and they were joined by the former Settlements of Penang and Malacca which were to have the same status. The Queen of England gave up all sovereignty over the Settlements, and they were given a type of government similar to the other states but with a Governor as head of the state instead of a Sultan. Each state was to have its own fully elected State Assembly, and its government would be chosen from the party which had a majority of elected members in the Assembly. The maximum life of a State Assembly would be four years, after which an election had to be held. This was one year less than the Federal Parliament itself for the latter's maximum length of life was to be five years.

Other important points concerned the special position of the Malays, citizenship and the national language. It was agreed that special privileges should be given to the Malays for a period of ten years after independence to enable them to improve their economic position in the country. This involved, for example, a favourable ratio in civil-service employment and in the awarding of scholarships. Citizenship was to become the right of all those born in Malaya after independence, while some of the qualifications for acquiring citizenship for those already living in Malaya were to be relaxed for a limited period after *Merdeka*. The national language of independent Malaya would eventually be Malay, but until 1967 both Malay and English were to be official languages.

On 5 August 1957, the Federation of Malaya Agreement, by which Malaya was to become an independent nation, was signed in Kuala Lumpur by the rulers of the Malay States and the High Commissioner, Sir Donald MacGillivray, who signed on behalf of Queen Elizabeth II. All was now prepared for the proclamation of independence itself. As midnight struck on 30 August 1957, huge crowds gathered on the padang in Kuala Lumpur and saw the Union Jack lowered for the last time. The next day the Duke of Gloucester, who had come to Malaya as the representative of the Queen, handed over to the Prime Minister, Tengku Abdul Rahman, the formal instrument of independence. This ceremony took place in the Stadium Merdeka before a large crowd which included the Rulers and the newly elected Yang di-Pertuan Agong who was formally installed as Malaya's first Head of State on September 2nd. With these ceremonies and the inauguration of the new Constitution, the nine states and two Settlements had become the independent nation of Persekutuan Tanah Melayu.

EXERCISES

1 Assess the main differences between Malayan Union 1946 and the Federation of Malaya 1948.

2 Describe the constitutional changes which took place in Borneo after the Second World War.

3 Write an account of the reasons for the outbreak of the Emergency in 1948.

4 What were the main reasons for the defeat of the Communist rebellion in Malaya?

5 Trace the post-war steps by which Malaya achieved Independence in 1957.

6 Describe the Constitution adopted by Malaya when it became independent.

7 Write short notes on:
   Dato Onn bin Jaafar, General Templer, the Briggs Plan, Chin Peng, the Alliance.

19

SINGAPORE — FROM COLONY TO CITY STATE

THE population of Singapore particularly the Chinese population had suffered severely during the Japanese Occupation. Many Chinese were arrested without reason and shot without being tried —the Japanese excuse was they were determined to remove all the Communists in particular but they also wanted to eliminate all 'subversive' elements. Thousands of Singaporeans were picked out at identification parades, they were interrogated and tortured and about 50,000 people were killed. The Japanese also had the habit of leaving heads on poles in the streets in order 'to encourage the others' in the population. The new Japanese name for Singapore was Syonan meaning 'Light of the South'—a name that must have seemed ironic to the majority of the population.

It was with considerable relief therefore that Singapore heard of the surrender of the Japanese in August 1945—especially as it forestalled the probable destruction of a great deal of the city if the Allied armies had had to recapture it from the Japanese. We have noted on p. 228 the constitutional arrangements which the Planning Unit in the Colonial Office in London had devised for post-war Malaysia. As far as Singapore was concerned the Malayan Union Constitution of 1946 brought about an end of the Straits Settlements as such by joining Penang and Malacca to the new Malayan state and leaving Singapore as a separate Crown Colony. During the remainder of 1945 and 1946 the British Military Administration administered Singapore as a separate entity in anticipation of this new arrangement.

CROWN COLONY GOVERNMENT

The separation of Singapore from the Malay Peninsula was made for two main reasons—firstly the importance of the Singapore military base and the political problems this might bring about; and secondly, Singapore's overwhelming Chinese population would upset the racial balance in the Malay Peninsula. However the possibility of the two units later rejoining was not ruled out (see p. 261 below).

Constitutionally the most important innovation in the new arrangements for Crown Colony government was the introduction of an unofficial majority into the Legislative Council. The Council was to be composed of 13 unofficial and 10 official members—and of the former 6 were to be elected directly and three by the Chambers of Commerce. All British subjects over the age of 21 were to be given the right to vote. British policy still considered that constitutional progress would consist of the gradual transfer of power to the English educated Straits-born British subjects. However this approach disregarded the effect of the war and events elsewhere in Asia, especially in China. The younger generation in Singapore, particularly those educated in Chinese medium high schools, were intensely interested in the struggle going on in China between the Communists and the Kuomintang and they were greatly affected by the resurgence of Chinese nationalism.

Perhaps the key to the immediate post-war history of Singapore has been to understand the essential division which existed on the island between those influenced by China and those who wished to be considered Singaporean. The policy of the British Government, with the transfer of limited powers to the latter group only, was bound to cause friction and conflict, as indeed it did. The solution to this divisiveness could only come when a political group, which had its roots in the China-orientated Chinese elements of the population, began to absorb some of the Singaporean outlook of the other part. This has really been the reason for the success of the Peoples Action Party, which came to power on the votes of the former group but later felt sufficiently successful and popular to remove the more extremist pro-China elements.

However constitutional progress in Singapore proceeded at a slower pace than that of the Federation. This was not entirely because of the Emergency as there had been little terrorist activity on the island. Although the Communists had been very active in infiltrating the trade unions and extending their influence among the pupils of some of the Chinese middle schools, police action had driven the MCP leaders underground. Nevertheless this basis of Communist influence, together with the importance of the military bases in Singapore, caused the British reluctance to consider self-government.

Singapore's first elections were held in March 1948, with a total

RADIO TIMES

Members of the Federation of Malaya Constitutional Conference held in London, January 1956

Tuanku Abdul Rahman ibni Al-Marhum Tuanku Muhammad, the first Yang di-Pertuan Agong.

JABATAN PENERANGAN, MALAYSIA

b.

c.

d.

e.

a. Tun Abdul Razak; *b.* Lee Kuan Yew;

c. Tun Tan Cheng Lock; *d.* Lim Yew Hock;

e. David Marshall

Sir Donald MacGillivray signing the Declaration of Independence for the Federation of Malaya on 5th August 1957.

JABATAN PENERANGAN, MALAYSIA

Tengku Abdul Rahman proclaims Merdeka

The Victory Parade celebrating the end of the Emergency, 1960

Singapore's first National Day parade in 1966. The picture shows a school contingent marching past the saluting dais. Representative groups from all school uniformed groups were represented in the parade.

President Yusof bin Ishak.

The Prime Minister proclaiming Malaysia in the presence of the Third Yang di-Pertuan Agong, Tuanku Syed Putra Jamalullail

Azahari

Tun Abdul Razak and Adam Malik shaking hands at the conclusion of peace talks in Bangkok

Jesselton 1911 and 1960

Tunnelling in the Cameron Highlands Hydro-Electric Scheme. The scheme when completed will meet the needs of expanding industrial works all over the country

The viaduct in Kuala Lumpur, one of the many improvements in road transport which will lead to greater progress

New blocks of flats in Queenstown, Singapore built to house the increasing population of the island

SINGAPORE MINISTRY OF CULTURE PHOTO

A view of the docks. The port of Singapore is now the fourth busiest in the world.

SINGAPORE MINISTRY OF CULTURE PHOTO

A view of the Jurong Industrial Estate, the largest of its kind in South-East Asia. This estate represents a major part of Singapore's efforts to industrialize and at last count some 200 factories were in production.

JABATAN PENERANGAN. MALAYSIA

Graduates of the University of Malaya after Convocation ready to play their part in the development of their country

Schools in Malaysia and Singapore are providing training in Science to meet the needs of the two independent countries

SINGAPORE MINISTRY OF CULTURE PHOTO

Singapore, the old and the new. Note the impressive buildings clustered at Raffles Place (centre, left), Singapore's business heart and the old shophouses (foreground) which are soon to make way for Urban Renewal projects.

SINGAPORE MINISTRY OF CULTURE PHOTO

Air view of the University of Singapore. It has a student population of 5,000, 3 halls of residence and 5 research centres.

electorate of 22,385. Only six members of the new Legislative Council were elected by territorial constituencies and of these three were from the Progressive Party. The elected members were not only a minority in the Council but they themselves represented only a small minority of the population. Before the next election in 1951 (elections were to be held every three years) the number of elected members had been increased by three and the British authorities had agreed to an unofficial Deputy Council President being appointed. Nevertheless the officially appointed members and the nominated members were still in a majority and the electorate had only grown to 48,155. Two thirds of the population were not eligible to vote, either because they were not British subjects or because they were under age. The result of the election again saw a majority from the Progressive Party (six seats) with the new Labour Party winning two seats, plus another in a by-election later. It was also announced that two elected members would be members of the Governor's Executive Council. The next step would, by increasing the number of elected members, bring about the ending of official control in the Legislative Council and was therefore of vital importance for the future. A Commission was set up in 1953 with Sir George Rendel as Chairman, to make recommendations for a new constitution for Singapore.

THE RENDAL CONSTITUTION

The Report of the Rendal Commission 1954 became the basis of the Constitution which came into force in the following year. Its most important recommendations concerned the size of the electorate and the constitution of the two Councils. Firstly there should be a considerable increase in the number of voters by means of automatic registration (previously registration had been voluntary as it is in most Commonwealth countries). This increased the electorate from 75,000 to 300,000 though the basic qualification was still British citizenship.

Secondly, the Rendal commission recommended a Legislative Assembly of 32 members — 25 elected, 3 ex-officio (the Chief Secretary, the Financial Secretary and the Attorney-General) together with 4 nominated by the Governor who would also nominate the Speaker. Thirdly, there would be a Council of Ministers composed of the same three ex-officio members and six from the majority party in the Assembly. The latter would have charge of particular government departments and the Council would be res-

ponsible to the Assembly. This Constitution was a form of dyarchy.
New parties were formed for the elections which followed—from
the more moderate left-wing groups and the trade unions came
the Labour Front and on a platform of socialism and anti-
colonialism was built the Peoples Action Party (PAP). These presented the most serious challenge to the centre party, the Progres-
sives. However the election itself resulted in a multiplicity of parties
winning seats, as follows:

Labour Front	10	Progressive Party	4
PAP	3	Democratic Party (backed by Chinese Chamber of Commerce)	2
Independents	3	Alliance (with the same constituent elements as in the Federation)	3

No one party had a overall majority but the Labour Front leader
David Marshall as head of the party with the most seats was asked
to form a government and he became the first Chief Minister of
Singapore, forming a coalition with the Alliance and two Labour
Front members nominated by the Governor. The first Speaker was
Sir George Oehlers.

However this administration of divided responsibility soon ran
into trouble and within four months there was a dispute over the
relative powers of the Chief Minister and the Governor, Sir Robert
Black, over Mr. Marshall's wish to appoint four Assistant Ministers. Persuaded by the Chief Minister the Assembly demanded
immediate internal self government and the dispute had to be
referred to Britain. Constitutional talks between Singapore and
Britain were arranged for 1956 but the explosiveness of the situation was shown when an airport demonstration turned into a riot.
In fact the whole period saw a revival of militant trade unionism
and the formation of a large number of mass organizations; all of
which made the task of goverment more difficult.

Although there was a fair measure of agreement between the two
sides in the talks which were held in 1956 (Singapore to have
internal self government while Britain retained control of external
affairs and defence) the British side refused to give up its responsibilities for internal security. As a result of this failure to reach
agreement David Marshall resigned. He was succeeded by Lim
Yew Hock from the same party who was immediately faced with

a wave of strikes from trade-unionists, and sit-ins from the pupils of many Chinese middle schools. Police attempts to control demonstrations by extremists resulted in widespread rioting in October-November, 1956. These demonstrations were firmly suppressed by the Lim Yew Hock government and many of the leaders were arrested and detained. These disturbances illustrate the climax of the conflict between the largely English educated middle classes and the Chinese educated workers and students, the latter considerably influenced by Communist and nationalist feelings. This was not the ideal background for the granting of self-government.

NEGOTIATIONS FOR SELF GOVERNMENT

In 1957 an All-Party delegation left Singapore for further talks in London—talks aimed at removing the obstacles to fresh constitutional advances. Although not all British hesitations were overcome the most important advance was the agreement to establish an Internal Security Council with equal representation from Singapore and Britain (three members each) and with one member from Malaya who would have the casting and decisive vote. This overcame Singapore's objections to Britain having a continued say in the internal security of the island—which would in future be known as the State of Singapore.

While the basic constitutional discussions were proceeding throughout 1957 and 1958, important legislation was being passed by the Assembly. This legislation was to have an important effect on the way the state would develop after self-government for it dealt with three very basic matters—the civil service, citizenship and education. As far as the leaders of Singapore's political parties were concerned the most important task was to ensure that all the residents of Singapore who wanted to accept Singapore as their home felt that they were being fairly and equally treated. The localization of the Civil Service in Singapore was encouraged by the establishment of a Public Service Commission which speeded up the appointment of local officers. The electorate was greatly extended through the Citizenship Bill which instituted a new Singapore citizenship for those born in Singapore and also for those who had eight years residence. This Bill created 325,000 new citizens and also resulted in the Chinese educated becoming a majority of the electorate. Finally the Education Bill of November 1957 ended the division between the Chinese medium schools and the others and for the first time envisaged a national system of education as the most important basis for national unity.

Another important educational event during this period was the campaign for the establishment of Nanyang University. This too fitted into the general policy of giving greater recognition to students educated in the Chinese medium. As matters stood they had no hope of achieving higher education in Singapore as the University of Malaya (now University of Singapore) only gave instruction in English. Pupils from the Chinese high schools were therefore forced to go either to China or Taiwan (or perhaps to the United States) if they wished to go to the university. The campaign to collect money for the building of Nanyang University had been going on for some time and it had become a vital issue amongst all sections of the Chinese community, with donations being received from both millionaires and hawkers. The University was opened in March 1958 and though it had its initial troubles, due to lack of governmental supervision, it has recently made a significant contribution to educational progress in Singapore.

Another important step also took place at the end of 1957—the coming into being of the first fully elected City Council. This was dominated by the PAP which won 13 seats out of 30, the remainder being divided amongst four other parties and two Independents. Mr. Ong Eng Guan, the Treasurer of the PAP became a controversial first Mayor of Singapore (the first and last as it happened). Although he often came into conflict with the civil service and the middle classes he did show a new concern for the poorer members of the community. But the importance of this election was that it showed the way political trends were moving in Singapore and was an indication of the successful organisation and growing strength of the PAP.

Throughout 1958, with negotiations over the new constitution still in progress, the various political parties began gathering their resources for the forthcoming elections. There was little doubt that the PAP was the best organized, in fact it was the only party whose organization was anything like as efficient as that of the Communists. Its leaders seemed to realise that this was the only way to overcome the Communist challenge. The other parties, the Labour Front, the Workers Party and the Liberal Socialists, still retained their essentially middle class base and less professional outlook. The new Constitution for Singapore finally became law in November, 1958.

SELF-GOVERNMENT

This Constitution was to give Singapore full internal self government—that meant complete control of her internal affairs (subject only to the voting in the Internal Security Council) and also control of external trade and commerce. Britain still remained responsible for foreign relations and for the defence of Singapore, but it meant that actually power over the general day-to-day administration of the island would with the fully elected Assembly.

This Assembly was to have 51 members who would be chosen by an electorate of 555,655. This was a great increase over the 300,000 eligible to vote in 1955. Through the efforts of Mr. Lee Kuan Yew, the Secretary-General of the PAP, voting was made compulsory and this inevitably helped to prevent the election being dominated by activists and extremists.

The election campaign went smoothly and without incident and 90 per cent of the electorate voted. The PAP scored a handsome victory winning 43 of the 51 seats and Mr. Lee Kuan Yew was asked by the Governor to form a government. This he only agreed to do after the political detainees (some imprisoned since the riots of 1956 and others in 1957) had been freed. Many of these were subversives but it was felt that a gesture of this kind was needed at the time. Ironically many of these same people, like Lim Chin Siong, were to be re-detained later by the PAP government.

The first action of the new government was the abolition of the City Council, something which the PAP had promised to do if elected. The functions of the Council were transferred either to the Public Utilities Board or to departments of the state government. It was probably true that in a state the size of Singapore there was not enough room for two elected authorities which might have conflicting policies and conflicting representation.

The final episodes in the formal establishment of the new constitution were the installation of the first Malayan born head of state, the Yang di-Pertuan Negara, Inche Yusof bin Ishak, in December 1959 together with the flying of the new Singapore flag and the singing of the new National Anthem, *Majullah Singapura*. Mr. Lee Kuan Yew became the Chief Minister of what was the smallest state in South-East Asia.

SOCIAL AND ECONOMIC PROGRESS

The most important phenomenon in post-war Singapore was the fact that the population ceased to have a large number of people whose main desire was to save enough money to run to China or to India. The war had prevented any movement between China and Singapore for four years, perhaps longer; people became more settled and there had been no new immigration. Another factor was that a greater and growing proportion of the population had been born in Singapore, did not want to return to either China or India and thought of Singapore as its home. The important change in outlook that resulted had repercussions, as we have seen, on the direction of political change. But there was also a different outlook toward the multi-racial society and its problems with emphasis being placed on unity and equality of opportunity. Examples of this are multi-lingualism in the legislature, equal treatment for all media of education, the fostering of trade unions to safeguard the rights of workers and much later the emphasis on equality in the 'rugged society'.

But post-war Singapore also saw vital changes in the welfare of the people—the expansion of medical and health services, the provision of more schools and perhaps most important of all the building of modern housing in order to replace the slum dwellings in which so many people lived. In this latter development the activity of the Housing and Development Board (HDB) was of great importance. The new blocks of flats, as in Queenstown and elsewhere, not only provided adequate housing for large numbers of people but indicated the determination of the administraion to improve living conditions.

And at the same time Singapore retained its importance as a port and trading centre. Much of its trade was connected with the rubber and tin industries of the Malay Peninsula and Singapore had a vital part to play in the exports and imports of the Malaysian region. Important also were its trading links with Indonesia and Borneo and much of the commerce with these areas was financed from Singapore. The numbers of ships using the facilities of the port increased and Singapore flourished as the world's fifth largest port in respect of tonnage (today it is fourth).

Yet at the same time the administration of Singapore realized that the future progress and prosperity of its increasing population could not entirely depend on trade. There has therefore been a determined effort to diversify the economy by introducing new industries, as at Jurong, which will provide additional employment for school leavers. Every encouragement has been given to foreign investors to establish new industries in Singapore, and many companies have done so. The government has realized that dependence on trade makes a state too dependent on other countries—the growth of industry provides an important alternative source of prosperity.

EXERCISES

1 What was the importance of the Rendel Commission in the constitutional history of Singapore?

2 Describe the more important internal reasons which delayed Singapore's achievement of independence.

3 Write an account of the development of political parties in Singapore.

4 Outline the more important aspects of social and political progress which have taken place in Singapore since 1956-7.

5 Account for the success of the Peoples' Action Party in the election of 1959.

6 Write short notes on:
David Marshall, the Internal Security Council, the Citizenship Bill 1957, Nanyang University.

20

MALAYSIA AND CONFRONTATION

INDEPENDENCE ushered in a new era of vitality and change for Malaya and everyone living in the country in the years since 1957 has been impressed by the progress which has been made. On the material side this has been best shown by the programme for rural development and the beginnings of a planned policy of industrialization. These measures have aimed at bringing greater prosperity to the countryside and more employment to those who leave the rural areas to join their fellow citizens in the towns. With the official end of the Emergency in 1960 the government had more money to spend on road and bridge building, irrigation projects and power schemes, agricultural improvement and rural education. The efforts of the government and its officials were directed towards broadening the base of the country's wealth.

But the years since 1957 have not only shown change in a material sense; at the same time there has developed a new spirit, a new pride in the country, a feeling of confidence and a desire among the younger generation to introduce measures of social change and reform. To some extent the new architecture of Kuala Lumpur illustrates this spirit, particularly the prestige buildings which people are proud to see. It is also shown by the interest in art exhibitions, the growth of literature, success in international sport and the part which Malaya played in the affairs of the United Nations Organization.

Politically the years immediately after 1957 were years of unspectacular and steady progress as the democratic system became adjusted to the temper of Malayan life and culture. The Alliance Party which had negotiated Independence was re-elected to power in the national elections of 1959 with 74 seats in Parliament out of a possible 104. However this election saw the emergence of other national parties, the main ones being the Pan-Malayan Islamic Party (PMIP) with 13 seats, the Socialist Front with 8 and the

People's Progressive Party with 4. In the State elections the Alliance was successful in all the states except Kelantan and Trengganu where the PMIP gained majorities. This growth of an opposition was a healthy sign in the development of Parliamentary government though at this time none of the opposition parties presented any real challenge to the Alliance lead by Tengku Abdul Rahman.

In foreign affairs the government pursued a middle of the road policy favoured by the majority of the Afro-Asian countries. Malaya did not join the Western-sponsored treaty organization, SEATO; she took the lead in the condemnation of the South African policy of apartheid and she was largely instrumental in the formation of the Association of South-East Asia composed of Malaysia, Thailand and the Philippines (ASA). But being a small country she relied on her links with the Commonwealth for help in defence and protection against the possible renewal of Communist terrorism.

PRELUDE TO MERGER

It was, however, events in Singapore, which had had internal self-government since 1959, that gave added impetus to the Malayan government's feeling that Communist subversion was never very far away. In 1960 the People's Action Party (PAP) government of Mr. Lee Kuan Yew suffered its first set-back with the defection of five left-wing members of Parliament and then in April 1961 the PAP lost the Hong Lim by-election. The PAP successfully overcame this immediate display of Communist sympathies, but it soon became obvious to the less extreme elements in Singapore that Britain would be unwilling to grant full independence with this threat in the background, while to the Malayan government the prospect of a Communist dominated Singapore (a South-East Asian Cuba) was not inviting. It was therefore events in Singapore which were largely instrumental in bringing into being the project of a merger of the Federation and Singapore.

The Malay States of the Peninsula had always been cautious of association with Singapore because of the latter's overwhelming Chinese population. It was largely for this reason that the island had been excluded from the Malayan Union of 1946 and the Federation of Malaya of 1948 although an additional reason was that the British wanted to keep full control of the important defence installations in Singapore. Yet by 1961 it had become apparent to the Alliance government that it might no longer be possible to ignore developments across the Causeway. If Communism was successful there the island might become a very dangerous point of entry into

South-East Asia for Communist China. Therefore, instead of having nothing to do with Singapore it might be better for the Malayan government to prevent the spread of Communism by associating with her. (Tanganyika was to do a somewhat similar thing with the island of Zanzibar in 1964 to form the state of Tanzania.) But this change of policy would mean absorbing the one and a quarter million Chinese in Singapore, and the Malay leaders in the Alliance were obviously going to find it difficult to persuade some of their followers to agree, particularly those who thought that too many concessions had already been made to the Chinese in the Federation.

THE PLANNING OF MALAYSIA

Even to-day there has been no official outline of the sequence of events, of proposal and counter-proposal which led up to the formation of the state of Malaysia. Much discussion must have taken place before Tengku Abdul Rahman first mentioned the project in a speech in Singapore in May 1961. During consultations with the British government the Malayan Prime Minister is likely to have pointed out the dangers of the Communists dominating a Singapore which would have to be given independence in the not too distant future; and, because independence could not be delayed forever due to Malayan fears, Britain may well have suggested that a merger between Malaya and Singapore would be the best way to safeguard Malayan anxieties.

Malaya's objections to absorbing so many Chinese were long-standing and not easily overcome, but the proposal that the British territories in Borneo (Sarawak, North Borneo and the protectorate of Brunei) should be included in the new state provided an additional 1,340,000 people to balance the Chinese in Singapore. Sarawak had a population of 780,000, North Borneo 475,000 and Brunei 85,000 though it should be remembered the 25 per cent. of the people of the Borneo territories were in fact Chinese. These states were Britain's last colonial responsibilities in South-East Asia and because of their small populations would find difficulty in becoming independent by themselves. As far as administrative procedures, law, education and currency were concerned they already had much in common with Malaya and Singapore and association with the more politically advanced states would bring independence to the Borneo territories more quickly.

Interest was immediately aroused after Tengku Abdul Rahman's Singapore speech, discussion began in all the areas involved but most of all perhaps in Singapore, for the proposal seemed a solution to so many of her difficulties. As things turned out it may be true to say that the concept of Malaysia tried to be a solution to too many problems at the same time. But in 1961 it seemed a way of coping with firstly, Malaya's fear of Communism in Singapore together with the PAP government's fear of Communism in Singapore; secondly, Singapore's desire for independence, seeing merger with Malaya as the best means of obtaining it; and finally, Britain's wish to work out a future for her Borneo colonies which would enable her to withdraw from the area.

At first all went well and the international difficuties, which appeared later, were not apparent. Representatives of all the parties involved became members of a Malaysian Consultative Committee which met in Jesselton in August 1961. Reaction varied; in Singapore there was considerable enthusiasm, though not from the left wing of the PAP who feared Federal control of internal security. As a result eight Assembly members left the Party to join the five who had resigned earlier in 1960 and together more extreme elements formed the Barisan Socialis Party. Enthusiasm for the project grew in both Sarawak and Sabah but not in Brunei, for the latter was not enthusiastic about others spending her oil revenues.

Discussions between the governments of Malaya and Singapore and between the governments of Malaya and Britain resulted in their official approval for the idea in November 1961. It was agreed to set up a Commission to find out the views of the peoples of the Borneo territories where elections had not yet been held. The Commission, composed of Malayan and British members, and with Lord Cobbold as chairman, visited Sarawak and Sabah between February and April 1962. The Commission interviewed over 4,000 people in thirty-five different places, as well as receiving many written memoranda. The members therefore obtained a very good cross-section of opinion. The Commission eventually reported that one third of the people favoured entering Malaysia immediately; one third was willing to enter Malaysia but wanted safeguards for the indigenous inhabitants, while the final third (mainly Sarawak Chinese) wanted independence first, and until then the retention of British rule. There were certainly more in favour than were against and as a result of the Cobbold Report the Malayan and British governments agreed in July 1962 that the new state of Malaysia would come into being on 31 August 1963.

In Singapore the government pushed ahead with its plans for merger despite opposition from the Barisan Socialis and in September 1962 a referendum was held on the type of association which was to be arranged with Malaya—the fact that association was to happen was taken for granted. In the referendum 71 per cent. voted for the PAP proposals while 25 per cent. followed the advice of the Barisan Socialis and returned blank voting slips. All the peoples of the territories which were to be joined with Malaya had now given evidence of their approval and there seemed every hope towards the end of 1962 that Malaysia would come into being on schedule.

Unfortunately these optimistic forecasts had not taken into account the attitudes and policies of Indonesia. . . .

CONFRONTATION

After the Second World War Indonesian-Malayan relations were always rather ambiguous. Before the war many Malays living in the Peninsula had looked upon Indonesia, or the Dutch East Indies as it then was, as a country of inspiration in both literature and politics, for nationalism had always been more developed in Indonesia. There had always existed in Malaya a significant pressure group which was politically attached to the idea of a union between the two countries. On the other hand the Indonesian leaders had been rather condescending towards Malayan leaders, treating them in a somewhat patronizing fashion. This attitude was probably not helped by the fact that the centre of power in Indonesia was in Java while the main connexions of the Peninsular Malays were with Sumatra.

During the 1950's this patronizing attitude seemed to have less and less reason. Malaya made steady progress in suppressing the Communist terrorists and was well on the way to independence and greater prosperity, while during the same period Indonesia plunged from one economic crisis to another, from disorganization to chaos to civil war. Indonesia became to Malaya an example of 'how not to do it' while Malaya became to Indonesia an awkward example of a country which prospered by putting first things first. It was tragic that two countries which culturally and linguistically are so similar should have drifted so far apart; but it was significant that, despite invitations, President Sukarno, an inveterate traveller, should never have made a visit to his nearest neighbour.

From 1958 to 1961 the Indonesian government was fully occupied in suppressing the military rebellion which had broken out in Sumatra and the Celebes; and from December 1961 to August 1962 the attention of the Sukarno administration was wholly taken up with gaining control of West Irian from the Dutch. The western part of the island of New Guinea had not been handed over by the Dutch at the same time as the rest of their East Indian possession to the new Indonesian state in 1949 and President Sukarno had long wanted to make the Dutch withdrawal from the East complete. Using infiltrators and paratroop landings he finally forced the Dutch to the conference table and gained control of West Irian in August 1962. Thus during the first stages of the planning of Malaysia the Indonesian government was fully occupied.

To begin with, an Indonesian spokesman, Dr. Subandrio, welcomed the formation of the new state. In a letter to the *New York Times* in November 1961 he said '... we do not show any objection to this Malayan policy of merger. On the contrary we wish the Malayan government well if it can succeed with this plan'. In the same month while addressing the United Nations General Assembly he also said '... when Malaya told us of its intention to merge with the three British (territories) of Sarawak, Brunei and British North Borneo as one Federation we told them that we had no objections and that we wished them success with this merger so that everyone might live in peace and freedom'.

Fourteen months later however the Indonesians openly admitted that they had changed their minds and Dr. Subandrio stated that 'Indonesia must carry out a policy of confrontation towards Malaya because Malaya is now an accomplice of neo-colonialism and is pursuing a policy of enmity towards the Indonesian people'. The Indonesian government now maintained that the inhabitants of the Borneo territories had not been consulted, that Malaysia with a population of ten million was a threat to Indonesia with a population of one hundred million and that the whole project was a British plot.

This change of face by President Sukarno can be openly dated from the Brunei revolt led by Azahari in December 1962, for many of the members of Azahari's 'army', Tentera Nasional Kalimantan Utara (TNKU), had been trained in Indonesia. This revolt gave the Indonesians a dissident group to support despite the fact that the rising was quickly put down and that Azahari directed it from Manila; and the Indonesians began to use the threat of force to prevent the formation of the new federation. At the same time the Philippines government put forward a claim to the territory of North Borneo on behalf of the descendants of the Sultan of Sulu who had originally ceded the area to the predecessors of the North Borneo Company. The Philippines now maintained that the land had never been ceded for ever and that if Indonesia was going to prevent the implementation of the Malaysia plan then there was a chance of the Philippines picking up one of the pieces.

Indonesian objections can be put down to two causes, pride and jealousy. There was jealousy of Malaya's successful economic progress together with the feeling that Malaya's independence was not 'real' independence because she had not had to fight for it—forgetting that the Emergency had been fought to make sure that eventual independence was not dominated by the Communists and that 3,283 civilians and 1,865 members of the Security Forces had lost their lives in the twelve-year struggle. There was also Indonesian dislike for the sympathy which had existed in Malaya for the Sumatran rebels in 1958-9. Finally the establishment of the enlarged state of Malaysia thwarted Indonesian ambitions to absorb the Borneo territories when the British finally departed and frustrated any plans she had for the setting up of a Greater Indonesia based on nostalgic memories of the empire of Srivijaya.

THE FORMATION OF MALAYSIA

In April 1963 political confrontation changed into armed violence with invasions across the borders of Sarawak and Sabah from Indonesian Kalimantan. However these new threats did not deter the leaders of the territories which were to form Malaysia from going ahead with their arrangements; in fact this opposition probably convinced many waverers that association together was even more necessary. Indirect elections were held in Sabah in December 1962 and in Sarawak in June 1963 and of the candidates returned in Sabah 95 out of 110 supported Malaysia and in Sarawak 313 out of 429. Taken with the result of the referendum in Singapore it was certain that the majority in the three territories wished to associate with the Federation of Malaya.

Malaya's leaders, shocked by Indonesia's growing hostility tried to convince President Sukarno that the Malaysia which they had in mind was no threat to Indonesia. In May 1963 Tengku Abdul Rahman went to Tokyo to meet him and as a result of the talks agreement seemed possible. At the same time negotiations continued between Malaya, Singapore and Britain. The bargaining was long and hard but most of the difficulties were resolved in the agreement signed in London in July. This confirmed the date of 31 August 1963 as the date for the establishment of Malaysia and set out the details of the new constitution. For example, in the new federal Parliament of Malaysia, Malaya would have 104 seats, Sarawak 24, Sabah 16 and Singapore 15 while the last named would retain control over labour and education to compensate for the smaller number of seats in the federal Parliament. It was at this time that Brunei indicated that she would remain outside the new federation; talks had finally broken down over the question of federal taxation of Brunei's oil revenue and the precedence of the Sultan of Brunei in relation to the other Rulers. In July after a further conference in Manila between the Malayan Prime Minister and the Presidents of Indonesia and the Philippines, Malaya stated that she was willing to make further concessions in the hope of preserving peace. She agreed that, despite the opinions in favour of Malaysia already expressed in Sarawak and North Borneo, the Secretary-General of the United Nations should send observers to confirm that the two territories were not being included against their will as had been suggested by both Indonesia and the Philippines. It was also agreed that the date for the establishment of Malaysia would be postponed so that his inquiry could be carried out

In August 1963 a team from the United Nations carried out the investigation of public opinion in Sarawak and North Borneo and they reported back to the Secretary-General that, in their view, the majority of the people were in favour of joining Malaysia. The Indonesian government refused to accept this verdict and intensified its policy of confrontation. This refusal to accept the report of the Secretary-General's committee made the leaders of the four territories all the more certain that Malaysia must come into being on the appointed date despite the objections of Indonesia and the Philippines. It seemed to all of them that Indonesia particularly did not wish to reach agreement. Thus on 16 September 1963, the new state of Malaysia, comprising Malaya, Singapore, Sarawak and Sabah, came into existence. And on that same day the governments of Indonesia and the Philippines broke off diplomatic relations, while the Indonesian campaign to crush Malaysia began in earnest.

WAR AND PEACE

Indonesian confrontation had made the leaders of the four territories all the more resolved to go through with the formation of Malaysia for their own protection; and this resolution was needed in the months which followed as Indonesia stepped up her open attacks on the new state and increased her subversion within. Malaysia herself did not have sufficiently large forces to provide adequate defence against these attacks but she was able to call on Commonwealth assistance in the form of military support from Britain, Australia and New Zealand. Indonesian incursions across the borders of Sabah and Sarawak increased during the remainder of 1963 and the early part of 1964. At the same time Indonesian propaganda aimed at stirring up communal conflict between the Chinese and other races within Malaysia. These latter efforts were particularly directed against Singapore where the PAP government had been strengthened by winning 37 out of the 51 seats in the recent General Election. It was easy for troublemakers to cross the few miles of sea separating Singapore from the Indonesian Riau Islands and this subversive activity bore fruit in the racial riots which occured in Singapore in July and September 1964.

At the same time open attacks took place on the Malay Peninsula where in April a General Election fought on the question of support for the Malaysia idea had resulted in the Alliance Party winning 89 out of the 104 seats and 58 per cent. of the vote. There were landings by sea on the Malayan coast in August and then by air in September; and the timing of these attacks to coincide with the communal unrest in Singapore was not unplanned. The riots in Singapore were extremely dangerous and caused the loss of thirty-five lives but fortunately the leaders of the two communities were able to damp down the racial feelings which had been stirred up. At this time the danger from internal disorder was a greater threat to Malaysia than the attacks by the Indonesian armed forces. The latter received almost no support from the population and were quickly captured or killed by the security forces. Even in eastern Malaysia Indonesian attacks were easily contained and the year 1964 passed without military confrontation being any nearer success. Furthermore Indonesian aggression had been condemned in September by the Security Council; in a vote of nine to two only Russia and Czechoslovakia registered disagreement.

However the differences of approach to political problems by the leaders of Malaya and Singapore had been brought into the open by the communal unrest in Singapore; and possibly because the Indonesian threat had been so negligible it became apparent that it was more and more difficult for the Alliance government of Malaysia and the PAP government in Singapore to exist within the same state. From the viewpoint of Kuala Lumpur it seemed that the Chief Minister of Singapore was pushing too rapidly for what he called 'a Malaysian Malaysia' and the Alliance resented the intervention of the PAP in the 1964 elections in Malaysia. At all events it began to seem to the members of the Federal Government that all the arguments with Singapore were not worth the probability of increased inter-communal tension. After much consideration, in the middle of 1965 the Malaysian Prime Minister suggested that it would be in the interests of both Malaya and Singapore if the latter left the Federation and became an independent state. Pressure was put on Mr. Lee Kuan Yew to agree to this proposal and in August 1965 he rather reluctantly had to do so. The result was that after barely two years Singapore had ceased to be part of Malaysia.

There were many who thought that the separation of Malaysia and Singapore was playing into the hands of Indonesia which would use this division to her own advantage. But fortunately for Malaysia and Singapore, on 30 September 1965, the Communists Party of Indonesia attempted to take over the government by assassinating the leaders of the armed forces. This attempt at a *coup d'état* was unsuccessful but it provoked immediate retaliation from the army and brought the country to the brink of civil war. Therefore, for many months to come the Indonesians were much too occupied with their own affairs to be able to carry out their policy of confrontation with any vigour. Then in 1966 it became apparent that the new army-dominated administration in Indonesia, which had taken over much of President Sukarno's power, was less keen on continuing the policy of confrontation. The army leaders were in fact willing to negotiate to bring the undeclared war to an end. Preliminary talks were held in Bangkok and these led to direct contact between Malaysia and Indonesia. The negotiations which were then begun eventually led to an exchange of visits between the Malaysian Deputy Prime Minister and the Indonesian Foreign Minister and the signing of a peace agreement in Jakarta on 11 August 1966.

The 'war' was now over and the new states of Malaysia and Singapore were free of Indonesian hostility. Confrontation had caused a wasteful misuse of resources, for instead of fiighting each other the countries of South-East Asia should have been concentrating on improving the economic and social conditions of their peoples; for only in this way can the causes of instability be removed. The restoration of peace should now allow this development to take place.

EXERCISES

1 What were the reasons for the establishment of Malaysia in 1963?
2 Why was the formation of Malaysia opposed by Indonesia and the Philippines?
3 Describe the events which led to Singapore leaving the Federation of Malaysia.
4 Write short notes on:
  the Cobbold Commission, Azahari, Confrontation.

SUPPLEMENTARY READING AND REFERENCE MATERIAL

BOOKS

ALLEN, G.C. and DONNITHORNE, A.G. *Western Enterprise in Indonesia and Malaya*. Allen and Unwin, London, 1957.

BAKER, M.H. *Sabah, the first ten years as a Colony, 1946-56.* M.P.H., Singapore, n.d.

BASTIN, J. and ROOLVINK, R. *Malaysian and Indonesian Studies*. Oxford University Press, 1964.

BEGBIE, P.J. *The Malayan Peninsula*. Reprinted, Oxford University Press, 1966.

BIRCH, W. de G. (ed.). *The Commentaries of the Great Alfonso d'Albuquerque*. 4 vols., Hakluyt Society, London, 1875-84.

BIRD, I.L. *The Golden Chersonese and the Way Thither*. Reprinted, Oxford University Press, 1966.

BUCKLEY, C.B. *An Anecdotal History of Old Times in Singapore 1819-1867*. Reprinted, University of Malaya Press, 1967.

CAMERON, J. *Our Tropical Possessions in Malayan India*. Reprinted, Oxford University Press, 1965.

CHAI HON-CHAN. *The Development of British Malaya 1896-1909*. 2nd ed. Oxford University Press, Kuala Lumpur, 1967.

CHAPMAN, F. SPENCER. *The Jungle is Neutral*. Chatto and Windus, 1954.

CLIFFORD, SIR H. *Bushwacking and other Tales from Malaya*, London, 1929.

CLODD, H.P. *Malaya's First British Pioneer*. Luzac, London, 1948.

COMBER, L. *Chinese Secret Societies in Malaya*. Donald Moore, Singapore, 1959.

COOPE, A.E. *The Voyage of Abdullah*. Oxford University Press, Kuala Lumpur, 1967.

COWAN, C.D. *Nineteenth Century Malaya*. Oxford University Press, London, 1961.

DONNINSON, F.S.V. *British Military Administration in the Far East*, H.M.S.O., 1956.

EMERSON, R. *Malaysia*. University of Malaya Press, 1964.

FAUCONNIER, H. *The Soul of Malaya*. Reprinted, Oxford University Press, 1965.

HYDE, DOUGLAS. *Confrontation in the East*. London, The Bodley Head, 1965.

IRWIN, G. *Nineteenth Century Borneo*. Donald Moore, 1955.

JACKSON, R.N. *Immigration, Labour and the Development of Malaya 1786-1920*. Government Printer, Kuala Lumpur, 1961.

JACKSON, R.N. *Pickering: Protector of Chinese.* Oxford University Press, Kuala Lumpur, 1966.

JONES, F.C. *Japan's New Order in East Asia.* Oxford University Press, London, 1954.

JONES, S.W. *Public Administration in Malaya.* Oxford University Press, London, 1952.

KEPPEL, Capt. (later Admiral) the Hon. (Sir) Henry. *The Expedition to Borneo of H.M.S. Dido for the Suppression of Piracy.* London, 1845.

LIM CHONG-YAH. *Economic Development of Modern Malaya.* Oxford University Press, 1967.

MCLANE, C. *Soviet Strategies in Southeast Asia.* Princeton U. P. 1966.

MCNAIR, F. *Perak and the Malays.* London, 1878.

MILLER, H. *Menace in Malaya.* Harrap, London, 1954.

MILLER, H. *Prince and Premier.* Harrap, London, 1959.

MILLS, L.A. *British Malaya 1824-67.* (ed. C.M. Turnbull). Reprinted, Oxford University Press, Kuala Lumpur, 1966.

PARKINSON, C.N. *British Intervention in Malaya 1867-77.* University of Malaya Press, Singapore, 1960.

PERCIVAL, A.E. *The War in Malaya.* Eyre and Spottiswoode, 1949.

PIRES, TOME. *Suma Oriental, (1512-1515).* 2 vols., Hakluyt Society, London, 1944.

PLUVIER, J. *Confrontations: A study in Indonesian politics.* (Oxford in Asia). Oxford University Press, Kuala Lumpur, 1965.

PURCELL, V. *The Chinese in Malaya.* Oxford University Press, London, 1948.

PYE, L.W. *Guerrilla Communism in Malaya.* Princeton University Press, New Jersey, 1956.

RATNAM, K.J. *Communalism and the Political Process in Malaya.* Oxford University Press, 1965.

RAUF, M.A. *A Brief History of Islam.* Oxford University Press, Kuala Lumpur, 1964.

ROBINSON, J.B. *Transformation in Malaya.* Secker and Warburg, 1953.

ROFF, W.R. *The Origins of Malay Nationalism.* University of Malaya Press, 1967.

RUNCIMAN, S. *The White Rajas.* Cambridge University Press, London, 1960.

RYAN, N.J. *The Cultural Background of the Peoples of Malaya.* Longmans of Malaysia, 1962.

RYAN, N.J. *Malaya Through Four Centuries.* Oxford University Press, London, 1959.

SMITH, T.E. *Population Growth in Malaya.* Oxford University Press, London, 1952.

SWETTENHAM, SIR F. *British Malaya.* Allen and Unwin, London, 1948.

SWETTENHAM, SIR F. *Footprints in Malaya.* Hutchinson, London, 1942.

SWETTENHAM, SIR F. *Malay Sketches.* London, 1895.

SWETTENHAM, SIR F. *The Real Malay.* London, 1899.

TREGONNING, K.G. *History of Modern Sabah, 1881-1963.* University of Malaya Press, Singapore, 1965.

TREGONNING, K.G. (ed.). *Papers on Malayan History.* Singapore, 1962.

WANG GUNGWU, (ed.). *Malaysia, a survey.* Singapore, Donald Moore, 1964.

WURTZBURG, C.E. *Raffles of the Eastern Isles.* Hodder and Stoughton, London, 1954.

ARTICLES

BASSETT, D.K. 'European Influence in the Malay Peninsula, 1511-1786'. *JMBRAS*, Vol. 33, Pt. 3, 1960.

BOGAARS, G. 'Singapore and the Opening of the Suez Canal'. *JMBRAS*, Vol. 28, Pt. 1, 1955.

BROWN, C.C. 'Sejarah Melayu'. *JMBRAS*, Vol. 25, Pts. 1 and 2, 1952.

COWAN, C.D. (ed.). 'Sir Frank Swettenham's Perak Journals 1874-76'. *JMBRAS*, Vol. 24, Pt. 4, 1951.

DE EREDIA. 'Description of Malacca, 1613'. (trans. J. W. Mills), *JMBRAS* Vol. 8, Pt. 1, 1931.

FATIMI, S.Q. 'Islam comes to Malaysia'. *Malaysian Sociological Research Institute, 1963.*

GULLICK, J.M. 'Kuala Lumpur 1880-95'. *JMBRAS*, Vol. 28, Pt. 4, 1955.

HERVEY, D.F.A. 'Achin Piracy'. *JMBRAS*, V(2) 1927.

HILL, A.H. (trans.). 'Hikayat Abdullah'. *JMBRAS*, Vol. 27, Pt. 3, 1954.

HILL, A.H. 'Hikayat Raja2 Pasai'. *JMBRAS*, Vol. 33, Pt. 2, 1960.

LEUPE, P.A. 'Siege and Capture of Malacca from the Portuguese'. *JMBRAS*, Vol. 12, Pt. 1, 1934.

LIGHT, FRANCIS. 'A Brief Account of the Several Countries Surrounding Prince of Wales Island with their Productions'. *JMBRAS*, XVI(1) 1938.

LIGHT, F. 'Letter to Lord Cornwallis'. *JMBRAS*, Vol. 16, Pt. 1, 1938.

MARRISON, G.E. 'The Coming of Islam to the East Indies'. *JMBRAS*, Vol. 24, Pt. 1, 1951.

MIDDLEBROOK, S.M. 'Yap Ah Loy'. *JMBRAS*, Vol. 24, Pt. 2, 1951.

PARKINSON, C.N. 'Tin-Plate, an Outline History'. *Malaya in History*, Vol. 3, No. 2.

SADKA, E. (ed.). 'Journal of Sir Hugh Low, Perak, 1877'. *JMBRAS*, Vol. 27, Pt. 4, 1954.

TARLING, N. 'British Policy in the Malay Peninsula and the Archipelago 1824-1871'. *JMBRAS*, Vol. 30, Pt. 3, 1957.

THIO, E. 'Extension of British Control to Pahang'. *JMBRAS*, Vol. 30, Pt. 1, 1957.

WILKINSON, R.J. 'The Malacca Sultanate'. *JMBRAS*, Vol. 13, Pt. 2, 1935.

WILKINSON, R.J. and WINSTEDT, SIR R.O. 'History of Perak,' *JMBRAS*. Vol. 10, Pt. 3, 1932.

WINSTEDT, SIR R.O. 'History of Johore'. *JMBRAS*. Vol. 10, Pt. 3, 1932.

INDEX

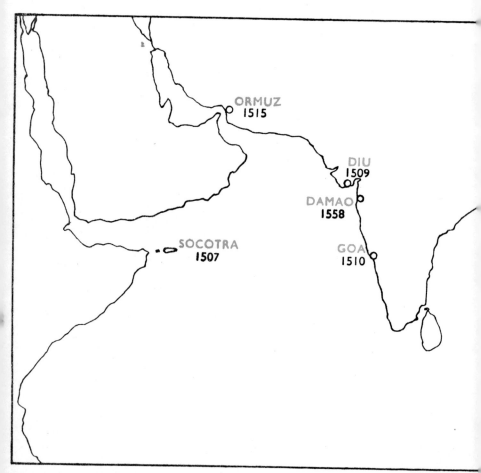

PORTUGUESE SETTLEMENTS IN ASIA